INDIA

PICTORIAL AND DESCRIPTIVE

INDIA

PICTORIAL AND DESCRIPTIVE

WILLIAM HENRY DAVENPORT ADAMS

GYAN

Published by

Gyan Publishing House
5, Ansari Road
Daryaganj, New Delhi-110002
Phone: 011-47034999, 9811692060
E-mail: books@gyanbooks.com

Distribution Network
gyanbooks.com
India, USA, Canada, UK, Australia, France

ISBN: 978-81-212-8800-2 (PB)
First Published, 1888

2nd Impression 2023

Printed at: Gyan Press, Delhi.

INDIA PICTORIAL AND DESCRIPTIVE
Author: William Henry Davenport Adams

INDIA

PICTORIAL AND DESCRIPTIVE.

Grand Alley of the Taj Mahal.

INDIA

PICTORIAL AND DESCRIPTIVE

By the Author of

"THE MEDITERRANEAN ILLUSTRATED"

&c. &c.

SHAH JEHAN'S PALACE IN THE ISLAND OF JUGMUNDER, OODEYPUR.

LONDON

T. NELSON AND SONS, PATERNOSTER ROW

EDINBURGH; AND NEW YORK

1888

PREFACE.

IN the history of the world nothing is more wonderful than the acquisition by England of her Indian Empire, except her retention of it. That, at a distance of some thousands of miles, a population of thirty-five million should control the destinies of a population of two hundred and fifty million is a fact the romantic and extraordinary character of which cannot be wholly explained away.

It must be regarded as exceptional that, until a very recent period, the English public took very little interest in that great Eastern dependency which had been conquered by the most brilliant courage and preserved by the most consummate statesmanship. No doubt it exercised a certain influence on the popular imagination, which was not insensible to the attractions of its "barbaric magnificence" and singular civilization, and could not fail to be dazzled by pictures of gorgeous palaces, prosperous cities, glowing landscapes, and inexhaustible resources. Nor could it fail to be stirred by narratives of successful campaigns, and of glorious victories, in which the heroism of England's soldiers prevailed over vastly superior numbers. Moreover, a large class of English society, which contributed its sons to the military and civil services of India, was necessarily alive to the importance of the transactions by which a company of "merchant adventurers" had gradually extended its rule over the great eastern peninsula. But England as a whole gave little thought to India. Neither in Parliament nor in the country did it command the attention it deserved. Englishmen were proud of it; but, conscious of their ignorance of its necessities as of its responsibilities, committed its destinies, without hesitation, to the hands of a few officials. It was the catastrophe of the Sepoy Mutiny that rudely awakened the national conscience, that reminded us of a truth we had forgotten, and taught us that a great trust cannot be safely neglected. The last twenty years have done a good deal in the way of educating Englishmen, so far as our Eastern Empire is concerned. The more thoughtful have learned something of its capabilities, of its history, of its inhabitants, of the nature of the responsibility that its government devolves upon them. And as their knowledge of it has extended, their interest in it has deepened. This is shown by the constant discussion of the weighty question, Is India a gain to England? To this question it is not easy to furnish an answer which everybody will accept. If we do not take into account the indirect advantages which India confers, by opening up to our young men a variety of careers, by elevating the standard of imperial policy, and by extending our national sympathies beyond the comparatively limited sphere of our home interests, we may find it difficult to demonstrate that any tangible profit results from our possession of India. The theory that commerce follows the flag is probably true; but against the commercial advantages which our occupation of the principal Indian seaports offers must be set the drain on our military strength necessitated by the maintenance of a sufficient army to garrison India, and the extent to which the protection of our communications with it renders us liable to entanglement in Continental quarrels. For our part, we are convinced that both morally and materially the nation is benefited by its Eastern Empire. It is, no doubt, a strain upon us; but the very strain tends to strengthen the fibre of the national character, and to develop all the best qualities of the national manhood. The trust has fallen into our hands—the trust of training the peoples of India to self-government, of raising them to the level of the Western civilization, of securing them in the possession of the blessings of peace, order, and individual freedom; and it is one which we cannot lay down, except at the call of the Indian peoples themselves, or when we have grown too weak to discharge it honestly.

What is really necessary and desirable is, that the recently-awakened popular interest in India should be confirmed and extended by the diffusion of trustworthy information respecting it. We ought to make the public as well acquainted with its affairs as they are with the affairs of the United Kingdom. We ought to accustom them to look upon it as an integral part of the Empire, to regard its inhabitants as their fellow-subjects, and to quicken in them an anxiety to promote the welfare of the masses of its population. The present volume is a contribution towards this great end. It does not, we admit, touch upon delicate points of religion or education; it does not profess to examine into the condition of the natives, or to adjust their relations towards the Imperial Government: it is, in fact, a book of description, and not of criticism; and yet we are willing to hope that its usefulness will be recognized.

CONTENTS.

CHAPTER I.

THE WAY TO INDIA.

Gibraltar—Malta—Alexandria—Suez—Aden 15-19

CHAPTER II.

GENERAL VIEW OF THE INDIAN PENINSULA.

Boundaries—Provinces—Modes of administration—Geographical features—Climate—Mountains—Rivers: The Ganges—The Indus—The Brahmaputra—The Narbada—Minor rivers 20-32

CHAPTER III.

BOMBAY.

Island of Bombay—Appearance from the sea—The Fort, or Kilah—The Parsees' bazaar—A bungalow described—Malabar Hill—Walkeshwar—A sacred spot—The Tower of Silence—The Byculiah quarter—Population of Bombay—Various nationalities—A ramble through its streets—Indian jugglers—The Jain Asylum for Animals—Architectural features of the city—About the Parsees—A Parsee "reception" 33-41

CHAPTER IV.

ELEPHANTA—KENERY.

Island of Elephanta—Its caves—Image of the god Mahadeo—The Sanctuary of the Lingam—Ancient sculptures—Island of Salsette—Cave-temples of Kenery—Buddhist temple 42-45

CHAPTER V.

BARODA.

The Guikwar's capital—The suburbs—The Palace—A regal sowari, or procession—Its gorgeous aspects—Antelope-hunting—The Motibagh 46-49

CHAPTER VI.

PUNA—KARLI—ELLORA.

Puna—Hill of Parvati—Caves of Karli—The finest chaitya in India—A Buddhist "vihara"—Caves of Ellora—A scene of beauty—The Great Cave—Grottoes of Ajunta—The Valley of Caves—An excursion to Golconda—Aurungabad 50-60

CHAPTER VII.

THE NORTH-WEST CAPITAL: ALLAHABAD.

Its central situation—Its English character—The cantonments—Its streets—Confluence of the Ganges and the Jumna—The great Triveni—Bathing pilgrimages—The Indian quarter—An indigo-planter's bungalow and factory—The railroad bridge—Allahabad in the Mutiny—A touching incident 61-65

CHAPTER VIII.

DELHI, THE CITY OF THE MOGUL.

1. General description of Delhi—The Chandnee Chowk, or "Street of Light"—About the houses—About the shops—Trades of the people—The Great Mosque—Its marble domes—Mohammedan rites—View of Delhi from a minaret—The Palace—Court of the Mogul—Grand Hall of Audience—Private Hall of Audience—In the days of old—Ruins of earlier cities.—2. Excursion to the Kootub—The Black Mosque—Humayoon's mausoleum—Mausoleum of Suftur Jung—The Kootub described—Akbar's college—Ruins of the Kootub Mosque—An iron column—An ancient legend—An imperial mausoleum—Ruins of Toghlukabad—The Old Fort—Return to Delhi.—3. A saunter through its streets—Another visit to the Chandnee Chowk—The Kotwali, or town-hall.—4. Historical sketch of Delhi—The Great Mutiny—An alarming telegram—Outbreak in Delhi—A scene of massacre—Preparations to recover the city—Position of the British army—The besiegers besieged—Plan of attack—Storming of Delhi—Death of Nicholson—The city taken—The Royal Family of Delhi—Hodson captures the king—Later history of Delhi—The Prince of Wales's visit 66-86

CHAPTER IX.

FROM DELHI TO PESHAWAR.

1. At Meerut—Description of the town—The "Monkey Tank"—A Moslem tomb.—2. Umballa—The English cantonment.—3. Simla: A mountain sanitarium—Travelling by post-garry—Arrival at Kalka—View of the Himalaya—What is a doolie?—A dâk bungalow—A forest of rhododendrons—The road from Kalka to Simla.—4. In and about Simla—The native town—British Simla—Winter at Simla—The Mall—Something about monkeys—A misadventure—The Himalayan forest—Some lofty trees.—5. Return to Umballa, and visit to Dehra—Mussoorie—Landoor—The Red Hill—Plantations of the Debra Tea Company.—6. At Amritsar—About the Sikhs.—7. Lahore—Descriptive sketch—The Fort—The Great Mosque—Tomb of Runjeet Singh—Mosque of Wuzir

Ali—Tomb and Garden of Jehangir—The Montgomery Hall—Meanmeer.—8. To Jummoo—Wazirabad—Sealkote—The boundary of our Indian Empire—Jummoo—The Grand Trunk Road—The Cabul River—Nowshera—Peshawar 87–101

CHAPTER X.

AT AGRA.

The North-West Provinces—City of Agra—Description of the Taj Mahal—Eulogies by different writers—A palace among tombs—The memorial of an emperor's love—Terraces and gardens—The Imperial Palace—Akbar's Tribunal—The Great Hall, or Armoury—The Somnauth Gates—Bath-room of the Zenana—The Jasmine Bower—Tomb of Akbar—Its inscriptions—Curious narrative of the death of the empress—Futteypur Sikri—Akbar's Summer-Palace—Tomb of Itmad-ood-Doulah—Later history of Agra—The durbar of 1866—The Prince of Wales's visit 102–117

CHAPTER XI.

THE STORY OF CAWNPUR.

Situation of Cawnpur—Its military importance—The English cantonments in 1857—Outbreak of the Mutiny—Sir Hugh Wheeler's excessive confidence in the Sepoys—Nana Sahib—Open revolt—The British besieged—A gallant defence—Nana's device—Terms of surrender agreed upon—The British march to the place of embarkation—A massacre—The Savada House and its captives—A second massacre—The Well of Slaughter—Arrival of Havelock—Cawnpur recovered—The Memorial 118–123

CHAPTER XII.

LUCKNOW.

View of Lucknow—Its origin—The Imperial Palace—The Martinière—Story of Claude Martin—The Kaiser Bagh—Its associations—Court of the kings of Aûdh—The Sepoy Mutiny—Siege of the Residency—Death of Sir Henry Lawrence—Memorable places—Lord Lawrence's durbar—The Hosseinabad Imambara—The Prince of Wales's visit 124–130

CHAPTER XIII.

THE CITY OF TEMPLES.

The holy city of the Hindus—Its name and origin—Its ancient splendour—Temples of Benares—Bathing in the Sacred River—Life in Benares—Street-scenes—A festival day—Shops and shopkeepers—A Hindu tradesman—The temples described—The Golden Temple—Worship of Siva—The Sacred Well—The Mirror of Doorga—The Temple of Ganesa—Great festival of Ganesa—The river—A succession of novel scenes—Scindia's Ghat—A lively picture—Ramnuggur—Hindu ceremonies of sepulture—Cremation—Some other aspects of life in Benares—The Prince of Wales's visit 131–143

CHAPTER XIV.

IN CENTRAL INDIA.

Visit to Dholepur—Its mosque—Sacred Lake of Muchkoondo—Temple of Juggernaut—In the Bundelcund—Duttiah—Its temples—The Golden Mountain—Jhansi—Its Ranee, and her share in the Mutiny—Oorcha—A garden of flowers—Chutterpur—Hindu festival of the Holi 144–151

CHAPTER XV.

AJMIR—JAIPUR—BHURTPUR.

Situation of Ajmir—Its bazaars—Its women—A saint's shrine—A Jain mosque—Kishengurh visited—Jaipur—Founded by Jay Sing II.—The Royal Palace—Jay Sing's Observatory—Ulwur—Its romantic position—Bhurtpur—About the Jâts—Two great sieges of Bhurtpur—The Prince of Wales's visit 152–158

CHAPTER XVI.

OODEYPUR AND THE RAJPUTANA.

From Bombay to Ahmadabad—Ahmadabad described—The Great Mosque of Shah Alum—The "Tomb of the Queens"—The land of the Bheels—Characteristics of the Bheels—Tintool, the residence of a Rajput Thakoor—Khairwara—Oodeypur—The Maharana's palace—Another durbar.. .. 159–167

CHAPTER XVII.

GWALIOR—AN INDIAN FORTRESS.

Situation and history of Gwalior—The old town—The fortress—The King Pâl Palace—The Vihara temple—A Valley of Silence—The "Tirthankars"—About the Jains 168–175

CHAPTER XVIII.

BHOPAL.

The Begum of Bhopal—Her territory—Her capital—A mountain-bordered lake—The Moti Masjid, or Mosque of Pearls—Citadel of Futtehgurh—The Mohammedan New-Year festival—Phases of life at Bhopal—Reception of the Begum—Route to Gwalior and Agra indicated—Nursingurh and its temple—Chopaya-travelling 176–186

CHAPTER XIX.

SANCHI TO PUNNA.

An ancient Buddhist settlement—The Lions' Lât—What is a tôpe?—About the gaur or Indian bison—The Indian forest—The land of the Gonds—Kingdom of Myhere—Govindgurh—A man-ape—Tiger-hunting—Palace of Govindgurh—Kingdom of Rewah—Punna, the "Land of Diamonds"—A diamond-mine described—Two great fortresses 187–199

CHAPTER XX.

MADRAS AND ITS NEIGHBOURHOOD.

Madras from the sea—Difficult of access—Mussulah boats—The catamarans—The English quarter of Madras—About caste—A Deccan village described—Visit to Conjeveram—Indian agriculture—Temple of Siva—Its idols—The arrack-palm—How the juice is obtained—Mahabalipur—Temples of Vishnu—A cave-temple—Its sculptures—Other antiquities—Monolithic temples—A French settlement, Pondicherry—Its inhabitants—Its houses—Tour to Trichinopoli—Its Fort—The Prince of Wales's visit—The Great Temple of Seringham—Sect of the Vishnavites—Tanjore—Its temples—Madura—Tank of the Golden Lotus... 200–210

CHAPTER XXI.

HURDWAR: AND THE GANGES.

The sacred city and the sacred river—The Indian grasses—The plantain—In the jungle—The "Gate of Hari"—Description of the city—The temples—The great Ganges Canal—A bathing-ghat—The great fair of Hurdwar.. 211-216

CHAPTER XXII.

CALCUTTA: THE CITY OF PALACES.

Situation of Calcutta—Its general aspect—Described by M. Grandidier—The English quarter—Native quarter—Native houses—About the Baboos—The burning-ghat—The Temple of Kali—Sanguinary *cultus* of the goddess—The Churuk-Pooja—Animal sacrifices presented—The adjutant-birds—The hackrie, or bullock-cart—Calcutta merchants and shopkeepers—"Piece-goods" merchants—Afghan traders—The Maidan, or Esplanade—The Botanical Garden 217-226

CHAPTER XXIII.

IN THE NEIGHBOURHOOD OF CALCUTTA.

The road to Orissa—Wayside relics—Scenes on the road—At Puri—Temple of Juggernath—The sacred bulls—Within the temple—Monster images of the gods—Juggernath's daily rations—A curious spectacle—The ape-god—A sacred pool—The triumphal car—The Sundarbans—Chandernagar—Ghat of Triveni—Pandooah—Burdwan—Murshidabad—Rajmahal Mountains—Patna.. 227-233

CHAPTER XXIV.

THE ISLAND OF CEYLON.

Dimensions—Physical characteristics—Vegetation—Animal life—Inhabitants—The chief towns—A coffee-farm—Visit to Kandy—Lake of Kandely.. 234-239

CHAPTER XXV.

VEGETABLE LIFE IN INDIA.

Cotton—Opium—Cereals—Fruit trees—Spices—Forest and timber trees—The banian—The bamboo—The deodar—The phulwara—The mhowa 240-249

CHAPTER XXVI.

ANIMAL LIFE IN INDIA.

Its Fauna—Birds—Reptiles.. 250-267

INDEX 269-271

LIST OF ILLUSTRATIONS.

1. GRAND ALLEY OF THE TAJ MAHAL, ... *Frontispiece*
2. GIBRALTAR, ... 16
3. HARBOUR OF VALETTA, MALTA, ... 18
4. SCENERY OF THE HIMALAYA, ... 23
5. MOUNT EVEREST, THE HIMALAYA, ... 24
6. KANCHINJINGA, THE HIMALAYA, ... 25
7. BOATS AND BOATMEN ON THE GANGES (*Full-page*), ... 27
8. CROCODILE OF THE GANGES, ... 29
9. BUNDER-BOAT, BOMBAY, ... 34
10. COTTON-MARKET—MERCHANTS AT BOMBAY, ... 35
11. THE TOWN-HALL—IN THE FORT, BOMBAY, ... 35
12. THE VILLAGE OF WALKESHWAR, BOMBAY, ... 37
13. A PALANQUIN, BOMBAY, ... 38
14. HINDU WOMEN OF BOMBAY IN CEREMONIAL DRESS, ... 41
15. ENTRANCE OF CAVES, ELEPHANTA, ... 43
16. CAVE OF LIONS, ELEPHANTA, ... 44
17. FACADE OF A GROTTO AT KENERY, ... 45
18. THE GUIKWAR IN THE GREAT SOWARI, BARODA (*Full-page*), 47
19. ANTELOPE-HUNTING WITH THE CHEETAH, BARODA (*Full-page*), 51
20. ENTRANCE OF THE GREAT CAVE OF KARLI, ... 53
21. TEMPLE OF KAILAS, ELLORA, ... 54
22. EXTERIOR OF CHAITYA, AJUNTA, ... 55
23. MONUMENT IN ROYAL NECROPOLIS AT GOLCONDA (*Full-page*), 57
24. PILLAR OF ASOKA, ALLAHABAD, ... 62
25. INDIGO-PLANTER'S BUNGALOW, ALLAHABAD, ... 63
26. INDIGO FACTORY, ALLAHABAD, ... 64
27. THE CHANDNEE CHOWK, DELHI (*Full-page*), ... 67
28. THE JUMA MASJID, ... 69
29. FACADE OF THE JUMA MASJID, DELHI (*Full-page*), ... 71
30. PRINCIPAL ENTRANCE OF THE PALACE OF THE MOGULS, DELHI (*Full-page*), ... 75
31. TOWER OF KOOTUB, IN THE PLAIN OF DELHI, ... 79
32. RHODODENDRONS OF THE HIMALAYA, ... 90
33. SIMLA (*Full-page*), ... 91
34. ARGUS PHEASANT, ... 94
35. VICINITY OF LAHORE, NORTHERN INDIA, ... 96
36. KASHMIRIAN BOATMEN (*Full-page*), ... 97
37. AGRA, FROM THE OPPOSITE BANK OF THE JUMNA, ... 102
38. GENERAL VIEW OF THE TAJ MAHAL (*Full-page*), ... 103
39. GATE OF THE GARDENS OF THE TAJ MAHAL, ... 106
40. GRAND ALLEY OF THE TAJ MAHAL (*Full-page*), ... 107
41. ORNAMENTS OF THE GATES OF SOMNAUTH, ... 111
42. AN IMPERIAL DURBAR AT AGRA (*Full-page*), ... 115
43. MEMORIAL AT CAWNPUR, ... 123
44. PAVILION OF LANKA, IN THE KAISER BAGH, ... 125
45. IMAMBARA, LACKNOW (*Full-page*), ... 127
46. THE MADHORAY GHAT AND THE MOSQUE OF AURUNGZEBE, BENARES (*Full-page*), ... 133
47. FEAST OF GANESA (*Full-page*), ... 139
48. PALACE OF BIRSING-DEO (*Full-page*), ... 145
49. MAUSOLEUM OF BIRSING-DEO AT OORCHA, ... 148
50. THE "GOLDEN MOUNTAIN," SEEN FROM VILLAGE (*Full-page*), 149
51. GENERAL VIEW OF BHURTPUR (*Full-page*), ... 155
52. PALACE OF DURGUN SAL, CITADEL OF BHURTPUR, ... 157
53. TRAVELLERS ATTACKED BY BHEELS (*Full-page*), ... 161
54. SAMBHOO SING, MAHARANA OF MEYWAR, ... 164
55. DURBAR OF THE MAHARANA OF OODEYPUR (*Full-page*), ... 165
56. JAIN TEMPLE OF ADINATH, GWALIOR, ... 168
57. THE KING PAL PALACE, GWALIOR (*Full-page*), ... 169
58. VIHARA TEMPLE, IN THE FORTRESS OF GWALIOR, ... 172
59. "TIRTHANKARS," IN THE OURWHAI, GWALIOR (*Full-page*), ... 173
60. HER HIGHNESS SECUNDER, BEGUM OF BHOPAL, ... 176
61. PROCESSION OF THE TAZEEAS (*Full-page*), ... 177
62. HER HIGHNESS SHAH JEHAN, BEGUM OF BHOPAL, ... 179
63. MOOLLAHS OF BHOPAL, ... 180
64. RECEPTION OF A KHILLUT AT COURT OF BHOPAL (*Full-page*), 181
65. MAIL-CART TRAVELLING, ... 184
66. FORDING THE RIVER PARBUTTI (*Full-page*), ... 185
67. INDIAN BISON, ... 188
68. CHOPAYA-TRAVELLING (*Full-page*), ... 189
69. ENTRANCE TO THE PALACE OF GOVINDGURH, ... 192
70. AT THE TABLE OF THE RAIS OF MYHERE (*Full-page*), ... 193
71. COURT OF THE PALACE OF GOVINDGURH, ... 195
72. DANCING-GIRLS AT THE COURT OF REWAH, ... 196
73. HUNTING-PARTY AT GOVINDGURH (*Full-page*), ... 197
74. A DIAMOND-MINE, PUNNA, ... 199

75. TIGER-HUNTING NEAR GOVINDGURH (*Full-page*), ... 201
76. IMAGE OF HANUMAN, THE MONKEY-GOD, ... 205
77. TEMPLE AT SERINGHAM, ... 209
78. BAMBOOS, ... 212
79. CARAVAN ON THE ROAD TO HURDWAR (*Full-page*), ... 215
80. THE PORT OF CALCUTTA, ... 218
81. LOW CASTE BENGALEES, ... 219
82. THE GODDESS KALI, OR DURGA, ... 221
83. WATER-CARRIERS OF CALCUTTA, ... 222
84. THE MAIDAN, CALCUTTA (*Full-page*), ... 223
85. MARWARI MERCHANTS, CALCUTTA, ... 226
86. DIAMOND HARBOUR, AT THE MOUTH OF THE HUGLI, ... 230
87. THE GRAND MOSQUE OF HUGLI (*Full-page*), ... 231
88. BREADFRUIT-TREE OF CEYLON, ... 235
89. BRANCH OF THE CINNAMON-LAUREL, ... 235
90. AN ELEPHANT CORRAL, CEYLON, ... 236
91. THE OPIUM POPPY, ... 241
92. CAPSULE OF THE OPIUM POPPY, ... 241
93. BANANA-TREE, ... 242
94. COCOA-NUT PALMS—A SCENE IN THE VICINITY OF BOMBAY, 243
95. THE BANIAN-TREE, ... 246
96. A THICKET OF BAMBOOS, ... 247
97. CEDRUS DEODARA, ... 248
98. THE INDIAN ELEPHANT, ... 251
99. THE INDIAN RHINOCEROS, ... 252
100. THE ROYAL TIGER, ... 253
101. THE PANTHER, ... 254
102. THE ORYX, ... 255
103. THE ZEBU, ... 256
104. YAKS, ... 256
105. THE PEACOCK, ... 258
106. THE IMPEYAN PHEASANT, ... 259
107. THE RHINOCEROS HORNBILL, ... 261
108. NESTS OF THE GROSBEAK, ... 262
109. ARGALIS, OR ADJUTANTS, ... 263
110. COBRA DI CAPELLA, ... 264
111. SERPENT-CHARMERS, ... 265
112. THE GIANT PHASMA, ... 267

INDIA PICTORIAL AND DESCRIPTIVE.

CHAPTER I.

THE WAY TO INDIA.

GIBRALTAR—MALTA—ALEXANDRIA—SUEZ—ADEN.

THE Indian traveller, bound for "far Cathay," usually embarks at London on board one of the noble steamers of the Peninsular and Oriental Company, and thence proceeds to Gibraltar, Malta, Alexandria, through the Suez Canal, by Aden, to Bombay. But he can also adopt the Marseilles or the Brindisi route, each of which materially shortens the maritime part of his expedition. We shall suppose, however, that he prefers to proceed by steamer direct. After crossing the Bay of Biscay, he approaches the coast of the Iberian Peninsula at Cape Finisterre, and runs along the verdant shores of Portugal, with their picturesque bays, stretches of high cliffs, and jutting headlands, surmounted by lighthouses.

As the voyager draws near the broad estuary of the Tagus, he catches sight of the Rock of Lisbon, a sea-mark of strange and almost savage character; and then, looking up the gleaming river, he sees the spires and roofs of the Portuguese capital. To the south of the Tagus he passes Cape Espartel, easily recognized by its boldness of configuration and the lighthouse on its summit; and strikes across to Cape St. Vincent, where, in 1797, Sir John Jervis and Nelson almost annihilated the Spanish fleet. He enters next the Bay of Cadiz, and loses sight of land until the vessel nears Cape Trafalgar. We need not dwell upon the associations which it recalls to the mind of every Englishman, or tell again the oft-told tale of the victory which so gloriously terminated the career of the greatest "sea-general" the world has ever seen, and finally established the naval supremacy of Great Britain. The voyager, as he gazes on the misty headland, may remember, perhaps, the noble "home thoughts" of Robert Browning, suggested by the very scene which now meets his eye :—

> "Nobly, nobly Cape St. Vincent to the north-west died away;
> Sunset ran, one glorious blood-red, reeking into Cadiz Bay;
> Bluish 'mid the burning water, full in face Trafalgar lay;
> In the dimmest north-east distance dawned Gibraltar grand and gray.
> 'Here, and here, did England help me: how can I help England?'—say,
> Whoso turns as I, this evening, turn to God to praise and pray,
> While Jove's planet rises yonder, silent over Africa."

GIBRALTAR.

At the entrance of the Mediterranean rises the huge Rock of Gibraltar, one of those Pillars of Hercules which, to the early navigators, marked the boundary-line between the Known and the Infinite.

Gibraltar derives its name from the Moorish commander, Tárik, who captured it from the Spaniards in 711; hence, *Jabala'l Tárik*, "The Mountain of Tarik." The Moors kept possession of it until the beginning of the fourteenth century, when it was recovered by the Spaniards. In 1333 the Moors again made themselves masters of it; but in 1462 it finally fell into the hands of the Christians.

In July 1704, the combined fleet of England and Holland laid siege to the fortress. On the 21st, about eighteen hundred English soldiers and marines, under the Prince of Hesse, were

GIBRALTAR.

disembarked, and on the following day the fleet opened up a terrific cannonade, firing fifteen thousand shot in half-a-dozen hours. The sea-defences were carried on the 23rd by a small body of seamen, and next day the town capitulated. Thus, in three days, with a loss of only sixty-three men killed and two hundred and twenty-five wounded, this great military position, "the stronghold where the tyrant comes in vain," passed into the power of Great Britain.

A powerful French and Spanish fleet was despatched to regain it. Fifty line-of-battle ships, besides frigates, carrying twenty-six thousand men, and about four thousand guns, were under the command of Admiral le Comte de Thoulouse. The English fleet, under Sir George Rooke, did not exceed forty-five sail of the line, besides frigates, fire-ships, and small vessels, and carried twenty-three thousand men and three thousand seven hundred guns. Its victory, however, was complete; and, after losing three thousand men, the French were driven back to Toulon, leaving Gibraltar in the hands of England, to whom it was confirmed by the Treaty of Utrecht.

Numerous attempts have been made to wrest it from us; but in vain. The most memorable was in 1779–1783, when it was besieged by an immense French and Spanish armament, and the most vigorous and persistent efforts were undertaken with a view to its recapture. The defence, however, under General Elliot, afterwards Lord Heathfield, was conducted with equal skill and resolution. The huge floating batteries of the enemy were set on fire by red-hot shot. A well-directed cannonade shattered the attacking ships; and reinforcements and supplies arriving, under convoy of a powerful English squadron, the besiegers eventually abandoned their enterprise, after sustaining a heavy loss in killed and wounded. During the prolonged war of 1800 to 1815, it was left unmolested; and as its fortifications have of late years been strengthened and enlarged on the most approved principles of engineering science, we may safely predict that, as long as England holds the command of the sea, it will never be conquered. Our flag will continue to wave from a post which, more than any other, testifies to the strength and resources of the Empire; a post which seems to guard the path to our vast possessions in the East.

We now steer our course towards Malta, keeping tolerably close to the African mainland, "whose shores were empires" in the times of old. Bright and beautiful is the view of Algiers, with its surrounding orchards and gardens, and the blue Atlas Mountains towering against the distant horizon. We pass Cape Faroe, the romantic group of the Seven Capes, Cape Bon, and the island of Pantellaria, with its lava-black sides, and memorials of volcanic convulsion.

MALTA.

We now arrive at Malta, the second of the great fortified posts which guard our communications with India. It lies about two hundred miles from Africa, and sixty miles from Sicily; an arid, rocky mass, seventy miles long, nine miles wide, one hundred and sixty miles in circumference, and attaining at its culminating point an elevation of six hundred feet. It can lay no claim to the possession of beautiful scenery; but its connection with the history of the famous order of the Knights of St. John gives it a perpetual attraction. Nor can the Christian traveller fail to remember that it is probably identified with the *Melita* visited by St. Paul in the course of his voyage to Rome; the *Melita* where he wrought the miracle that filled the minds of the savage islanders with wonder.

The port of Malta is divided by the rocky ridge of Mount Xiberras into two fine harbours. The capital, Valetta, is situated on this ridge; with Marsamusatta, or the quarantine harbour, on the west, and Valetta, or the Great Harbour, on the east. The former is defended by Fort Ricardi; the latter by Fort St. Elmo;—both of them amazingly strong, and armed with the heaviest ordnance. Numerous creeks branch off from the Great Harbour, as they do at Portsmouth, and these are lined with quays, docks, warehouses, the victualling-yard, and the arsenal. All around the town, and along the coast, bristle military works of the most formidable character; so that Malta is as strong as science can make it, but not stronger than our great Mediterranean rendezvous and naval station needs to be.

There is much in Valetta to interest the visitor; and he will constantly come upon places associated with the long rule of the Knights. The Cathedral of St. John is specially worthy of a pilgrimage. It dates from 1580, and its internal decorations testify to the wealth and taste of the old chivalric order. The mosaic marble pavement is relieved with numerous figures of the dead Knights buried beneath, each figure being inlaid in white marble. The palace of the Grand Master is now occupied as the residence of the English Governor. Its armoury contains ten thousand stand of muskets, besides a superb collection of medieval arms and armour, many of which are beautifully emblazoned with gold.

One of the most brilliant episodes in the history of the island was its defence by the Knights against a powerful Turkish armada. It was in this siege that the Grand Master, La Valette, distinguished himself by his chivalrous heroism. The gallant spirit which then animated the Knights gradually decayed, as the Order became less in harmony with modern institutions; and the island was surrendered without a blow to Napoleon Buonaparte, on his

HARBOUR OF VALETTA, MALTA.

expedition to Egypt. It was soon afterwards besieged and captured by a British fleet; and ever since has been jealously held as, in effect, the key of the Mediterranean.

ALEXANDRIA.

From Malta our course lies direct to Alexandria. Before we approach the harbour we catch sight, one by one, of tower, and minaret, and windmill, the lighthouse, Pompey's Pillar, and Cleopatra's Needle, rising high above the level sandy shore. From Lake Mareotis to the Egyptian sea-port, or for a length of about one mile, the dunes or sand-hills of the littoral waste are crowded with windmills, which, as they are about thirty feet in height, with arms twenty feet long, and are provided with eight vanes, all set in different directions and moving with the wind, produce a very singular and striking effect.

On landing in Alexandria, the traveller feels at once that he has crossed the threshold of the Eastern World. The sights and sounds around him are Eastern, though he recognizes the existence of a strong European element. It is true that this element increases yearly; but while the dockyards and arsenals, the steam-engines and steam cranes, the mills and the factories, are all familiar enough to the Western pilgrim, he is conscious of a refreshing air of novelty when he marks the long processions of camels and mules, the groups of turbaned Moslems, eunuchs, and veiled inmates of the harem, the wares exhibited in the shops, and the palms, orange-trees, and bananas, which make up, as it were, the framework of the picture. Here, says a recent writer, comes a file of tall camels, laden with merchandise, stalking with deliberate, solemn step through the bazaars; there rides a stately-looking native gentleman, in all the pomp of ample turban and flowing robes; yonder passes a lady on her donkey, shrouded in black silk *habura* and the immemorial white muslin veil. And if the carriages have a European touch, they are driven and attended by men in Oriental dress; and, even stranger still, preceded by bare-legged Arab runners, who shout to the pedestrian to get out of the way—the shrill cries of these *avant-coureurs* resounding on every side. At the platform of the Alexandria railway-station, as Mr. Hopley reminds us, we may see a similar mixture of East and West, of old and new. "A motley crowd," he says, "of wily Greeks, dusky Arabs, and soft-featured Syrians, ferments before you: men, women, and children in every variety of costume, and no costume; water-sellers, sweetmeat-sellers, bread-sellers persistently pestering everybody; ghostly women in white, visible as human by their flashing dark eyes and naked feet, flitting hither and thither in frantic search for a lost husband or friend. You will see solemn Turks and crafty-looking Jews, and, perhaps, a batch of recruits for the Khedive's army."

The principal objects of interest in or near the city which Alexander the Great founded, which the Ptolemies endowed, and Cleopatra and Julius Cæsar and Antony have dignified with their memories,—the city which founded a new philosophy, and was the scene of the great struggle between Arians and Athanasians,—are, Pompey's Pillar, Cleopatra's Needle, and Lake Mareotis.

The old route from Alexandria to Suez was by railway, canal, and river; and it enabled the traveller to catch a glimpse of Cairo, the "great Alcairo" of Milton, the city of Saladin and the Arabian Nights, which still retains a truly Eastern air. Thence he was at liberty to make a visit to the Pyramids, or the Petrified Forest; and, afterwards, on his way to Suez, he gained an experience of the Desert.

But the enterprise of M. de Lesseps has diverted the stream of travel into a different channel. The steamer, after stopping at Alexandria, continues her eastward journey as far as Port Said,—an artificial harbour, formed by two massive piers,—and enters upon the Suez Canal, passing through it to

SUEZ,

once "a poor walled town," but now a thriving and populous "commercial emporium," where the traders of the East and West meet together, and fleets of steamers and sailing-vessels make a goodly show.

The Gulf of Suez, or northern part of the Red Sea, is about three miles wide at this point. From Suez to Aden the distance is 1308 miles due south-east; and from Aden to Bombay, 1664 miles east by north.

CHAPTER II.

GENERAL VIEW OF THE INDIAN PENINSULA.

BOUNDARIES—PROVINCES—MODES OF ADMINISTRATION GEOGRAPHICAL FEATURES—CLIMATE—MOUNTAINS—RIVERS: THE GANGES—THE INDUS—THE BRAHMAPUTRA—THE NARBADA—MINOR RIVERS.

THE great Indian peninsula, which has been the scene of so many important events in the history of the world, is bounded on the north by the lofty range of the Himalaya Mountains, which, under various names, stretch their huge barrier from the Indus on the west to the Brahmaputra on the east. On the south it is washed by the Bay of Bengal and the Indian Ocean. On the west it is separated by the Suliman range from Afghanistan and Baluchistan. From the mouth of the Indus to its southern extremity, Cape Comorin, the Arabian Sea defines its limits. Thus it assumes the configuration of an irregular triangle, each side of which has a coast-line of about two thousand miles; while its breadth, measured along the 25th parallel of north latitude, may be estimated at sixteen hundred miles.

British India, however, adds to the vast area included within the above boundaries several provinces, such as Pegu and Burmah, on the eastern side of the Bay of Bengal. Roughly speaking, the Empress of India holds rule over a realm that extends from the Himalaya to Cape Comorin, or about 1800 miles; and from Karachí to beyond Mandalay, or about 2300 miles. The area of our Indian Empire covers 1,770,000 square miles, with a land boundary of about 5000 miles.

For the purposes of government, British India is divided into various presidencies and provinces, which are subdivided into certain local governments. There are several native states, moreover, which are under the direct control of the Indian administration; while others, though ruled by native princes, own its absolute supremacy. The Queen is, in fact, the Empress of *all* India, representing the Mogul, and, indeed, extending her sway over a wider domain than was ever ruled from the throne of Delhi or Agra. The following are the chief political and administrative divisions of her empire :—

PRESIDENCIES AND PROVINCES.

1. Assam.
2. Burmah.
3. Bengal.
4. Madras.
5. North-West Provinces, Oudh.
6. Punjab.
7. Bombay and Sind.
8. Central Provinces.
9. Ajmir.
10. Curg and Mysore.
11. Berar.

At home the Indian administration, as settled by the Act of 1858, which terminated the one hundred years' *raj*, or rule, of the East India Company, is vested in a Secretary of State, assisted by a council of fifteen members, chosen from men who have distinguished themselves by their Indian services. The secretary is independent of the council, and has a seat in the British Cabinet. He has an under-secretary, who must be also a member of the legislature; and there are a permanent under-secretary and an assistant-secretary.

The executive government, which has its principal seat at Calcutta, consists of a Governor-General, or Viceroy, who is appointed by the Crown for a term of six years; and of a council of five ordinary members, three of whom are named by the Secretary of State in council from servants of the Crown of not less than ten years' standing, and the other two by the royal warrant. The Commander-in-chief is generally an extraordinary member; and there is also a financial member, who may be described as chancellor of the exchequer for India. The executive council is transformed into a legislative council by the addition of from six to twelve members—half of whom must be non-official, and at least three of whom may be natives of India nominated for two years by the Viceroy.

The Governor of the old presidency of Madras is assisted by a council, consisting of the commander-in-chief and two civilians, and the Governor of Bombay by a similar council and a legislative council of from four to eight members; but their acts are not valid until confirmed by the Viceroy, and they are also subject to the veto of the Crown. Bengal is now administered by the Governor-General of India in Council. It has of late been the wise policy of Great Britain to open up to native talent a share in the administration of the empire; and the various councils, therefore, have each their quota of native members.

The administration of the native states varies in detail according to circumstances; but usually the hereditary prince has a native minister and a council of nobles, under the more or less direct control of a British agent or Resident. The strength of his army is regulated by treaty, and in some cases he retains the power of life and death; but whatever his position, he is distinctly subordinate to the British Crown, and a failure of allegiance would be punished by deposition.

The Indian military force, since the Mutiny, has been completely reorganized, though it is considered to be in urgent need of another reorganization. It is no longer a distinct army, but simply a portion of the regular British army, enlisted for service in India, and usually numbering about 70,000 men of all arms. The auxiliary native force consists of about 120,000 men, with a certain proportion of European officers. The civil and military police, moreover, forms a strong and efficient body.

We now return to the geographical features of the Indian peninsula.

But, first, we may observe that the names *Indus, India,* are derived from the Sanskrit appellation of the great river *Sindhu,* which, in the plural form, applied also to the people who dwelt along its banks. The appellation, with some slight modifications, spread to the adjoining countries. Thus, *Hendu* is the form in the Zend or Old Persian, and *Hoddu* in the Hebrew. The Greeks, after their manner, softened down the word by omitting the aspirate "h"; hence, Ἴνδος, Ἴνδια. The native form is preserved by Pliny, who says, "Indus incolis Sindus appellatus."

The vast area of India necessarily includes a great diversity of surface, and, with its mountains, plains, valleys, rivers, forests, deserts, it presents, as has been said, an epitome of the whole earth. Its mountains are the loftiest, its rivers among the largest, of the world. It comprises the extremes of arctic cold and tropical heat. It exhibits Nature in her most exuberant fertility and in her dreariest barrenness. Its landscapes, at one time cold and stern and uninviting, are at another full of harmony and colour. Its forests are composed of trees which clothe the sides of European uplands, and of palms which overshadow the vales of Polynesian islands. In a word, it is inexhaustible in its variety.

Physically speaking, however, we are assisted in studying its details by the recognition of four principal features,—the northern mountain-mass of the Himalaya and its tributary ranges, the river-basins or valley-plains of the Indus and the Ganges, and the table-land of Central India. To these may be added the southern peninsular region, beyond the Vindhya Mountains, and generally known as the Deccan.

Roughly speaking, India may be defined as an elevated peninsular plateau, bounded by mountain-chains, with a couple of extensive river-basins to the north-west and north, and beyond them a mighty mass of snow-crowned mountains, extending fifteen hundred miles in length, and varying in breadth from fifty to one hundred and twenty miles. Its climate necessarily differs greatly in different regions; but all over India three distinct seasons divide the year between them,—the cool, the hot, and the rainy. The cool season begins in October, and lasts until about the middle of February; the hot, dry season follows, terminating at the beginning of June; then comes the rainy season, which, with a few refreshing breaks, endures until October. Even in the cool season, however, the heat of day, at least in the lowlands, is very considerable, though frosts will occur in the morning. It is this rapidity of change which renders the Indian climate so trying for Europeans, rather than the intense summer-heat. At Calcutta the mean annual temperature is 79°; at Madras, 83°; at Bombay, 84°. Some mitigation of the heat is produced by the monsoons, which blow periodically from the south-west and north-east, prevailing alternately for about half the year; the south-west blowing from the middle of April until the end of September, and the north-east from the end of September until the middle of April. It is the south-west which, rolling across the expanse of ocean in cloud and mist, brings the heavy rains to the Malabar coast and the basin of the Ganges. The north-east is less rainy in character, but its arrival on the Coromandel coast is always attended by heavy showers. Owing to the course and momentum of these winds, the amount of rainfall varies greatly at various points. Thus it does not exceed 20 inches in the year at Delhi, and 27 inches at Allahabad, but it amounts to 64 at Calcutta.

THE MOUNTAINS OF INDIA.

The principal mountains of India, and those which naturally occur to every mind as connected with the grandest aspects of its physical character, are the Himalaya.

The Himalaya (from the Sanskrit *hima*, snow, and *âlaya*, abode—"abode of snow") is the loftiest and grandest mountain-system on the globe. The popular conception of it, as of most mountain-masses, is that of a single stupendous chain of snow-crowned peaks; but it is, in reality, an immense congeries of rugged heights, of the most diverse size and shape, thrown out, as it were, from the Tibetan table-lands, and spreading, with an average breadth of eighty to one hundred miles, from the Indus in the west to the Brahmaputra in the east (long. 73° 23′ to 95° 40′ E.), a distance of nearly fifteen hundred miles. No marvel that in the Hindu mythology it is associated with the celestial residences of the gods!

The slopes of the Himalaya are clothed with abundant vegetation, and up to the very snow-line—which on the south is about fifteen thousand feet high, and on the north eighteen thousand feet—breadths of forest foliage extend.

Three distinct zones or regions may be traced on the southern slope of the Himalaya: the *Tarai*, a grassy, marshy plain, rising slowly from the plains of Hindustan; the *Sal* or *Saul*

SCENERY OF THE HIMALAYA.

Forest; and, above it, the *Dhoons*, an area of detritus, which extends to the foot of the true mountain-peaks.

Above four thousand feet, oaks and rhododendrons largely increase in number; and, along with andromeda, form the great mass of the forest, from six thousand to eight thousand feet. Species of the deciduous trees of the temperate clime are gradually introduced as we rise; and these, again, with the addition of other conifers, predominate in the upper forest-region, or from eight thousand to eleven thousand five hundred feet. The rhododendron flourishes as high as twelve thousand feet; and a few species, though greatly dwarfed and stunted, battle with the elements even at an altitude of fifteen thousand feet. With these are associated the birch, the alder, and the willow; while their shade protects an innumerable host of ranunculaceæ, compositæ, saxifragæ, and primulaceæ. To these succeeds all the varied army of mosses and lichens, until we reach the broad expanse of everlasting snow.

The highest summit of the Himalaya, and probably of the world, is Mount Everest (lat. 27° 59′), 29,002 feet. Kanchinjinga is 28,156 feet; Dhaulagiri, 26,826 feet; and Juwahir, 25,670 feet.

The western boundary of the trans-Indus region is formed by the Suliman Mountains, which reach their greatest altitude in Takht-i-Suliman, or Solomon's Throne, 11,000 feet

MOUNT EVEREST—THE HIMALAYA.

above the sea-level, in N. lat. 31° 35′. The average breadth of this range does not exceed ten to twelve miles.

Hindustan proper is separated from the peninsula of the Deccan by the Vindhya range, which strikes across India between the twenty-second and twenty-fifth parallels of north latitude, and connects the northern extremities of the Western and Eastern Ghats. Their spurs intersect the table-lands of Central India, and shelter deep-wooded valleys, the haunt of the panther, the hyena, and the jackal. This is the great Indian hunting-ground, where the greediest sportsman is sure to find abundance of game, and where the native princes have long been accustomed to indulge their passion for the chase.

Affiliated to the Himalaya, if such an expression may be used, are the Hindu Kush, or Indian Caucasus, extending from the Paropamisan Mountains of Afghanistan to the beautiful valleys of Kashmir ; and, in a different direction, the Bhotan and Assam Himalaya, the lower slopes of which are extensively cultivated as tea-plantations.

Above the rich plains and valleys of Népal and Bhotan, the summits of the Himalaya, at an elevation of twenty-eight thousand feet, whiten with everlasting snows. In Bhotan, however, the range declines with great rapidity—the fall being equal to one thousand feet in a mile. The valleys, says a traveller, are so deep and narrow, and the mountains that hang over them in menacing cliffs are so lofty, that their recesses are shrouded in perpetual gloom, except where the rays of a vertical sun penetrate their depths. Owing to the steepness of the descent, the rivers shoot down with the swiftness of an arrow, filling the caverns with foam and the air with mist. At the very base of this wild region lies the elevated and peaceful valley of Bhotan,

KANCHINJINGA—THE HIMALAYA.

vividly green, and shaded by glorious forests. Another swift descent of one thousand feet, and the great mountains sink into the plain of the Ganges.

RIVERS OF INDIA.

The three great rivers of India are the Ganges, the Brahmaputra, and the Indus, all fed by the perpetual snows and secret waters of the colossal range of the Himalaya.

The Ganges, Gangá, the sacred river, is made up of three separate streams—the Janahir, the Bhagirathi, and the Alaknanda. The second is the one to which pilgrims chiefly resort, and it is esteemed the holiest, many Hindu myths being associated with it. The Alaknanda, however, is the most copious, and its source is the most remote. It wells out from the southern slope of the Kamet peak, near the village of Niti, at an elevation of 25,733 feet above the sea-level. The Bhagirathi rises in a rugged, wild, and romantic glen above Gungutri, forty miles to the westward of the sister-source, issuing from an ice-cave, called "The Cow's Mouth," at the bottom of a glacier, about three hundred feet in perpendicular height. These streams unite at Deoprayag, ten miles below the enchanting groves of Srinuggur, and 1500 feet above the sea; whence in a single channel the combined waters flow on to the holy city of Hurdwar, one of the most famous shrines of Hindu pilgrimage.

Here the Ganges emerges upon the broad plain of Hindustan proper, and takes a south-easterly direction, passing Agra and Allahabad, and receiving the tributary streams of the Jumna and Son, on the right bank; the Ramgunga, the Gumti, the Gogra, the Gunduk, the Cosi, the Mahanada, and the Atri, on the left. It swells to a great breadth after its confluence with the Jumna, frequently measuring three miles across, with a depth of about sixty feet in the wet, diminished to thirty feet in the dry season. Its valley is remarkable for the richness of its soil and the consequent exuberance of its vegetation. On either side spread carefully cultivated fields, yielding immense crops of rice, cotton, sugar, opium, and indigo, while wheat and cereals generally flourish in the northern section. The Ganges is, in fact, the main artery of India, to which it owes its life and vigour. In the rainy season its waters, rising far above their usual level, overspread the country for hundreds of miles, with as fertilizing an influence as that of the Egyptian river; and like it, in retiring, it deposits a layer of the richest mould. Moreover, in conjunction with its tributaries, it provides inner India with facile routes of intercommunication; and its importance has scarcely been affected by the construction of the great lines of railroad. As it is navigable for boats of a large size for nearly fifteen hundred miles, it necessarily constitutes a highway of the utmost value; and hence its banks are studded with populous and prosperous cities, with Farakhabad, Cawnpur, Allahabad, Benares, Patna, Behar, Murshidabad, and Calcutta, which it serves to connect with one another and with the sea.

In the religion of the Hindus the Ganges has long played a conspicuous part. It is preeminently their sacred river, and its goddess is endowed with all the attributes of beneficence. To die on its banks is to die in the assurance of future bliss; to wash in its waters is to be cleansed from the most heinous sins. The odour of sanctity prevails all along its course, from Gungutri and Hurdwar to the island of Sagur, at the mouth of the Hugli, or Hooghly. Its water is esteemed for its supposed medicinal properties; and Brahmans are sworn upon it in the British courts of justice. To such stations as Hurdwar and Benares and Allahabad pilgrims flock in great numbers to perform their ablutions; and to purchase from the priests small phials of its water, to be carried away for use in future ceremonies.

At Sahibgunge, about two hundred miles from the sea, the river forms a delta, the area of which is more than double that of the Nile. This alluvial level measures from eighty to two hundred miles in breadth, and below Calcutta is known as the Sundarbans, a malarious and dreary region, partly covered with wood, and intersected with a complete network of streams and canals, fresh, salt, and brackish, some of which are connected with the deltoid channels of the Brahmaputra. These watercourses teem with fish, and mostly run through tracts of forest and jungle, which are haunted by tigers and other wild beasts, while crocodiles frequent their shallower parts. The latter are often of a very ferocious nature, and will attack men as well as cattle, though their chief sustenance is provided by the dead bodies which come down the river. On the sea-coast eight openings are visible, each of which forms a mouth of the Ganges; but

BOATS AND BOATMEN ON THE GANGES.

navigation is possible only through the Sundarban passage, which opens into the Hooghly, about sixty-five miles below Calcutta, and the Balliaghat, which leads into a shallow lake on the east side of the city. The Hooghly is the sole channel practicable for ships that draw fifteen feet of water.

The valley-plain of the Ganges is, as we have said, abundantly fertile, but, generally speaking, the scenery is neither very striking nor very beautiful. There are occasional landscapes, however, of singular charm, where the deep colouring of tropical vegetation fills in the outlines of a glowing picture. These we shall hereafter describe; and in this place we shall be content to point to the Fakir's Rock, near Sultangunge, in the province of Behar, as the centre of an eminently picturesque scene. Masses of gray granite are here piled upon one another in a succession of terraces, each of which is the site of a temple, the summit being crowned with a

CROCODILE OF THE GANGES.

principal temple, like the crest of a pyramid. A few trees raise their tall trunks here and there, and reflect their shifting shadows in the calm wave beneath. For ages this spot has been an abode of Fakirs, whose supposed sanctity generally extracts a tribute from the passing voyager. In the neighbourhood of Hurdwar, we may add, and from thence to Gangutri, the scenery is of a very impressive character.

Early in the rainy season begins the periodical inundation of the Ganges, the heavy tropical storms filling its channel with a turbid, swelling, rapidly rolling flood, that quickly bursts the accustomed bounds, and extends itself far and wide in one immense lake. The rise, at first slow and gradual, begins about the end of April, and for the first fortnight does not exceed an inch a day. Then, as the area of the river increases, and the highlands send down a larger supply of water, the swell amounts to five inches; and so continues until the river has attained, near Sahibgunge, a height of thirty-two feet above the ordinary level. The Bengal plains, adjacent to the Ganges and the Brahmaputra, are completely covered, over a breadth of about one hundred miles, by the end of July; and the stranger, as he surveys the vast expanse, broken only by the mound-built villages and the tops of the taller trees, is almost inclined to believe that he looks upon a repetition of the Deluge. From point to point the natives convey themselves in quaintly-constructed boats of the lightest kind, and the whole population seems given over to aquatic pursuits. Towards the end of August begins the subsidence of the waters; and the overflow is entirely carried off by the beginning of the following April.

Figures are not very successful in conveying ideas of quantity to the mind; and yet the reader may be assisted to realize the extent of the Gangetic inundation if we tell him that the volume of water poured into the ocean by the sacred river rises from 100,000 cubic feet per second in ordinary months to 500,000 cubic feet per second in the four months of flood—May, June, July, and August. The quantity of mud brought down annually by the current has been computed at 235,521,387 cubic yards; and it discolours the sea to a distance of sixty miles from the coast.

The boundary of the conquests of Alexander the Great was defined by the broad channel of the Indus, the greatest of the Indian rivers, and one of the greatest of the rivers of Asia. Its classical and modern name is obviously derived from the Sanskrit *Sindhu,* and has furnished the designation of the peninsula of which it forms the western limit.

Rising in Tibet, on the north side of the sacred peak of Kailas, near the sources of the Sutlej and the Brahmaputra, and not far distant from those of the Ganges and the Jumna,—at an elevation of 18,000 feet above the sea,—it flows in a north-westerly direction, chiefly through ravines of a rugged and savage aspect, for some five hundred and seventy miles, when its vexed waters escape from the gorges and precipices of the Himalaya, and take a south-west course. This change takes place at Makpon-i-Shagaron; and thence, down to Mittun-Kote, it forms the western boundary of the province of the Punjab, passing the towns of Derbend, Attock, Kalabagh, Bukkur, and Dera-Ghazee-Khan. Opposite Attock it is joined by the river of Cabul, which comes from the west with bright clear waters; and near Mittun-Kote it receives, from the east, the united stream of the "five rivers,"—namely, the Sutlej, the Bais, the Ravi, the Chenab, and the Jelum or Jailum (the ancient *Hydaspes*). At Derbend its maximum breadth is three hundred feet; at Attock, it is crossed by two bridges of boats, one of which is eight hundred and the other five hundred and forty feet in length. The rivers of the Punjab, it should be observed, vary in width according to the season. Thus the Chenab, during the rains, swells into a terribly rapid torrent, fully three miles and a quarter across. Communication between the banks is often impossible, as no boat can live in waves which swirl and roll like those of a storm-tossed sea.

The total length of the Indus is estimated at sixteen hundred and fifty miles; and the annual quantity of water it pours into the sea cannot be less than one hundred and fifty million tons.

Let us now turn our attention to the Brahmaputra—that is, the "son of Brahma"—which, though a river of considerable importance, is less useful to commerce than the Indus or the Ganges, and less famous in history. Nor can it compete in sanctity with either of the foregoing; though it has its god, and, at a place three days' journey from Dacca, pilgrims annually assemble to offer propitiatory sacrifices on the day it begins to rise.

It is formed by the junction, in Upper Assam, of three streams—the Dihong, Dibong, and Lohit. Which of these should be regarded as the head stream is a matter of dispute; but we shall do no wrong if we ascribe that honour to the Dihong, which seems to be a continuation of the Sanpo. The Sanpo is a noble river, with its source on the northern slope of the Himalaya, nearly opposite that of the Ganges on the southern, and at no great distance from that of the Indus. Rolling eastward through the rugged defiles and precipices of Tibet, it passes Lassa, the residence of the Grand Lama, and, curving boldly to the southward, forces its way in a succession of mighty torrents and cataracts through the colossal barrier of the Himalaya, and descends into Upper Assam under the name of the Dihong. Receiving the Dibong and the Lohit, it becomes known as the Brahmaputra, strikes through the centre of Assam in a south-west direction, and enters Bengal at the frontier-town of Goalpara.

There it makes a circuit round the western extremity of the Garo Mountains, and rolls its great volume of waters through Dacca, until it receives the Megna, which, though a comparatively small stream, gives its name to the united channel for the remainder of its course. Broadening into a turbid expanse of four to five miles, it takes a south-easterly course to the Bay of Bengal, swollen by the Issamutti and the Pudda, which is an eastern branch of the Ganges. Here it forms a delta, contiguous to the Gangetic, and spreads its numerous arms over a considerable tract of country. Assuming that the Sanpo is the head stream, the total length of the Brahmaputra will exceed fourteen hundred miles; while the Brahmaputra proper will measure between five hundred and six hundred miles. From the Himalayan snows it receives immense quantities of water; and from the middle of June to the middle of September the plains of Upper Assam are converted into an inland sea, and the only means of communication between the different villages are the elevated causeways, ten to twelve feet high.

At the other chief Indian rivers we can permit ourselves but a glance. The Deccan is watered by the Narbada ("pleasure-giving"), the Tapti, flowing westward; the Mahanadi, the Godavari, the Krishna, flowing eastward. The Narbada is a considerable stream, and fertilizes the provinces of Khandeish, Malwa, and Gujerat. It falls into the Gulf of Cambay.

About ten miles from Jabalpur, or Jubbulpore, the Narbada rolls its waters through the defile known as the Marble Rocks. First, it spreads over a rocky ledge, in a turbid, foamy sheet, about three hundred feet wide, and after a fall of thirty feet enters a chasm not exceeding sixty feet, the glittering cliffs on either side rising from eighty to one hundred and twenty feet high—cliffs of solid marble, being composed of dolomite and magnesian limestone.

"I went up between the Marble Rocks," says a traveller, "in the early morning in a boat, by moonlight, and floated down in sunlight; and as we moved slowly up that romantic chasm, the drip of water from the paddles, and the wash of the stream, only showed how deep the silence was. A tiger had been doing some devastation in the neighbourhood, and one of the boatmen whispered that we might have a chance of seeing it come down to drink at the entrance of the cleft, or moving along the rocks above,—which, of course, made the position more interesting. The marble walls on one side, which sparkled like silver in the moonlight, reflected so white a radiance as almost to illumine the shadow of the opposite cliffs; but the stream itself lay in deeper shadow, with here and there shafts of dazzling light falling upon it; and above, the moonbeams had woven in the air a silvery veil, through which even the largest stars shone only dimly. It did not look at all like a scene on earth, but rather as if we were entering the portals of another world."

South of the Krishna the principal rivers revealed to us by the map are the Pennair, the Palar, and the Kaveri. The first-named waters the Carnatic, and flows into the sea at Gungapatnam, one hundred and eight miles north of Madras. Crossing Mysore and the Carnatic, the Palar falls into the sea at Sadras. Mysore and the Carnatic are largely indebted for their agricultural wealth to the celebrated Kaveri, which rises from several sources in the hills of Curg and Mysore, near the Malabar coast, and falls into the Bay of Bengal by numerous mouths, after a winding course of about four hundred and fifty miles. The Hindus regard it as one of the most beneficent of their deities; and the rising of the waters is an occasion of annual festivity. The anniversary of the marriage of the river-goddess to the god Renganadur is also observed with great pomp and rejoicing.

At one part of its course the Kaveri forms an island called Siva Samudra, and descends in a couple of magnificent cataracts. The great fall of Gangan Chuka occurs in the northern channel, where the water leaps over a precipice of two hundred feet; the southern, that of Bur Chuka, is divided into ten or twelve streams, with a total descent of one hundred feet.

From the nature of the country, India has but few lakes. There are no deep hollows or confined basins within which the waters can accumulate. Of the few which exist, the largest would seem to be the Chilka, which divides Cuttack from the Northern Circars. It lies close to the sea, and apparently has been formed by the influx of the billows over the narrow strip of sand that lies between. Its length is thirty-five miles, and its breadth eight miles. It is fed by a branch of the Mahanadi, and sends its overflow into the sea through a deep, narrow channel. The water is salt, and very shallow. The Pulikat Lake, or Lagoon, has evidently originated in the same manner. Its length is thirty-three miles, its greatest breadth eleven miles. The Kolair Lake, between the Krishna and the Godavari, is nothing more than a reservoir of the waters collected by these rivers during their periodical inundation. There are two small lakes beneath the walls of Ajmir, which we shall hereafter describe; and North Canara contains the Lake of Honore, the waters of which are salt during the dry season, but fresh during the rainy season, when they are swollen by the torrents and springs of the mountains.

CHAPTER III.

BOMBAY.

ISLAND OF BOMBAY—APPEARANCE FROM THE SEA—THE FORT, OR KILAH—THE PARSEES' BAZAAR—A BUNGALOW DESCRIBED—MALABAR HILL—WALKESHWAR—A SACRED SPOT—THE TOWER OF SILENCE—THE BYCULLAH QUARTER—POPULATION OF BOMBAY—VARIOUS NATIONALITIES—A RAMBLE THROUGH ITS STREETS—INDIAN JUGGLERS—THE JAIN ASYLUM FOR ANIMALS—ARCHITECTURAL FEATURES OF THE CITY—ABOUT THE PARSEES—A PARSEE "RECEPTION."

BOMBAY may appropriately be termed the Western Gate of India. It is the chief port of communication with the ruling country, and has been brought into comparatively close connection with it by the construction of the Suez Canal. Gibraltar, Malta, Suez, Aden, Bombay—these are the main landmarks and resting-places on the highway to India. On reaching Bombay, the traveller stands, as it were, on the threshold of our Indian Empire; and certainly nowhere else in all India, not even in Calcutta, does he find such palpable evidence of the reality of British supremacy. Nowhere else has the conquering race made so deep a mark. In truth, to British enterprise and industry it may be said to owe its existence. It is really and truly an Anglo-Indian city.

Bombay proper, be it remembered, is a small island, about eighteen square miles, forming one of a group of islands which may be regarded as the delta of several river streams. These islands, lying close together, constitute, along with the mainland, a noble and spacious bay, capable of accommodating securely all the navies of the world. The convenience of this great natural harbour was appreciated by the earliest races; and hence many cities of importance were successively founded along its shores, and carried on a flourishing commerce with Hindustan and the Deccan. How wealthy and prosperous some of these must have been, we learn from the gigantic ruins of Kenery and Elephanta. And there can be no doubt but that the archipelago we speak of is identical with the *Sesekreienai nesoi* of the geographer Ptolemy.

When the Portuguese first trafficked in the precious products of Cathay, they colonized the largest of the group, the island of Salsette; and it was long after the foundation of Bassein and Tannah that they fortified Bombay—so called from the goddess Bomba, or Mumba Devi, to whom it was consecrated. In 1661 Bombay was ceded to England, as part of the dowry of Catherine of Braganza; and in 1669 the Crown made it over to the East India Company, then in the very infancy of its astonishing career. It soon sprang into commercial importance, but, for a time, was closely rivalled by Surat and Goa; until the conquest of Salsette in 1775, and the gradual extension of British power, threw them out of competition.

To the voyager, Bombay, with its mast-studded harbour, its terraces of square-built, Venetian-windowed houses, its masses of tropical vegetation, and its grand background of azure-tinted mountains, presents a most attractive spectacle. He sees it as a whole, and is deeply impressed by its vast extent and picturesque aspect; and it is not until he has been some days on shore that he finds it to be "a conglomeration of vast districts," at a short distance from one another. In some respects it may be said of Bombay, that distance lends enchantment to the view. At all events, from the sea it exhibits a beauty and even a grandeur which are scarcely confirmed upon closer inspection. The view from the harbour is one of the loveliest of the world's lovely scenes. The traveller gazes upon it with ever-increasing delight. A soft, transparent air rests on the palm-groves which thickly clothe the lower hills. Island after island, each blooming with verdure, is brought into the sparkling, many-coloured panorama; and glittering inlets of sea reach far up into the hearts of mountains which attract by the infinite variety of their outline. Then the waters are crowded with ships from every clime and of every rig: ships at anchor in the bay; ships loading or unloading at the wharves; steamers churning the blue waters into shining foam; and numberless native boats, with large sails of canvas, and covered poop, darting to and fro as if possessed with a supernatural activity. Beyond the ships and masts are seen tiers of white houses embosomed in foliage, and here and there a steeple, indicating the position of Colaba, and the long, far-spreading area of the great city, with its motley population of gold-worshippers and fire-worshippers, gathered from almost all parts of the known world.

BUNDER-BOAT, BOMBAY.

On that side of the island which faces the harbour stands the Fort, or Kilah, the oldest quarter of Bombay. Here are the crowded docks, the vast loaded warehouses, and some cotton-presses, side by side with huge chaotic heaps of the all-important fibre, which will shortly be converted into bales, and despatched to the looms of Manchester. In the centre of the town, and around a large circle, are situated the great commercial houses,—"factories," as they were once called,—the banks, the town-hall, and the Mint. In a word, the Fort is to Bombay what "the City" is to London. During the day it is a scene of incessant toil and bustle; at night it is deserted. "Go to the Fort at seven o'clock in the morning," says a recent writer, "and traverse those long, dark, narrow streets; you will find them abandoned, except by the policemen on duty. But about ten o'clock a change comes o'er the spirit of the dream! At the extremity of the vast esplanade that surrounds it on three sides, appears an army of carriages, conveying masters, *employés*, merchants, and purchasers. All direct their course to the Fort; the streets fill, and in a few minutes the silence gives place to the noise and tumult of a great,

COTTON-MARKET—MERCHANTS AT BOMBAY.

busy town. At four o'clock a fresh change is seen. The population retire from the Fort with greater haste than they used in entering it; the carriages are filled; horsemen ride away; and files of natives, armed with umbrellas, and clad in white, pass along the esplanade. Half an hour later, the streets are again given up to the rats and the policemen."

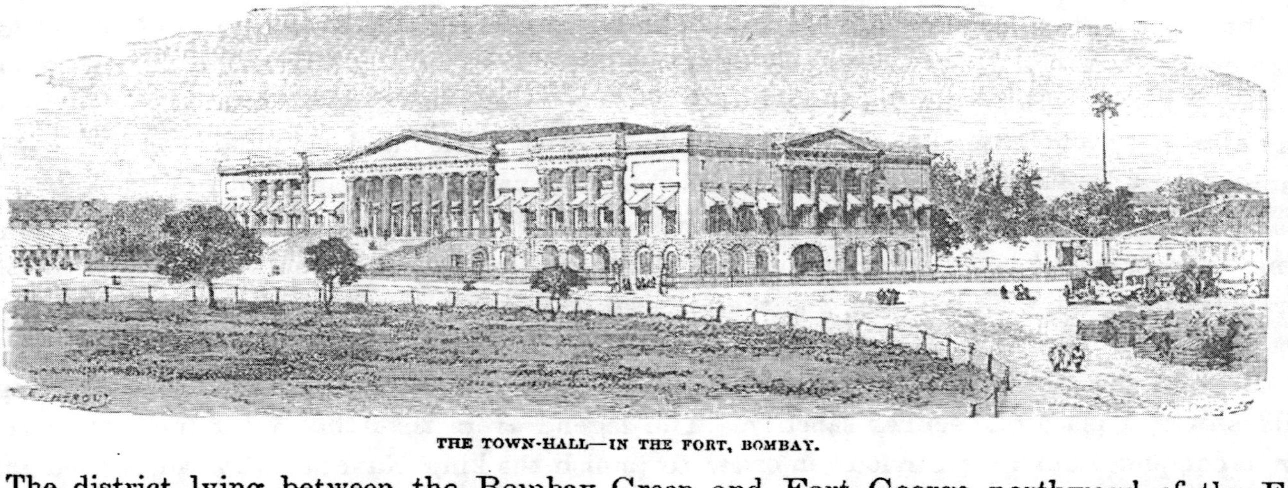

THE TOWN-HALL—IN THE FORT, BOMBAY.

The district lying between the Bombay Green and Fort George, northward of the Fort proper, is called the Parsees' Bazaar, and is almost wholly occupied by the Parsee and Bhorah traders. The long winding street is lined on either side by tall and beautiful houses with wooden balconies, gaily painted, and numerous windows with carved lintels. The ground-floors are laid out as stalls and warerooms.

Colaba, a long narrow promontory separating the harbour from the Back Bay, is one of the European quarters, and, with its gardens and bungalows, is not unlike a London suburb. The barracks are situated on the extreme tongue of the promontory, in a healthy and airy situation, and beyond them rises the tall white tower of the lighthouse.

But here we must pause to describe a bungalow, which still forms the favourite residence of the European, though handsome stone houses are being built in considerable numbers. It is a villa or cottage of one floor only, with wide doors, and an abundance of large windows, provided with Venetian blinds or lattices instead of glass. It is built of brick, but plastered with a fine white lime, called *chunam*, made from sea-shells; and is always surrounded by a wide verandah, where the inmates may recline at ease, enjoying the grateful shade and the cool sea-air. Within, the bungalow consists of clean, neat, spacious apartments, having *chunam* floors covered with matting, and furniture tastefully made of the blackwood from the Malabar coast, together with objects of ornament in sandal-wood or ivory. Over the dining-table and over the couches hang *punkahs*, or movable ventilators, which by their motion diffuse a pleasant coolness. The curtains are of bobbinet, and hung so as to complete the elegant *ensemble* of the fairy-like abode. Nearly every bed in the bungalow is likewise enclosed in bobbinet curtains, without which protection the ubiquitous mosquitoes would assuredly murder rest.

The kitchen and "offices" are in the "compound," or enclosed ground to the side or rear of the house; and here the large staff of native servants, nearly all men, obtain accommodation. Shrubs of much beauty and variety, mingled with feathery palms and acacias, render the compound attractive; and frequently a garden is formed, with soft lawns and beds of flowers. But unless it is plentifully watered by artificial irrigation, its appearance is anything but inviting.

Another of the English quarters is Malabar Hill,—a wooded, undulating ground three miles beyond the city, which slopes gently to the sea-shore. Here the bungalows are arranged in a succession of open sunny terraces, which are shaded by groves of palms and adorned with ferny growths. At certain points huge blocks of granite overhang the road; and among them are interspersed leafy clumps of cocoa and date, palms, aloes, and daturas, with their violaceous bell-like blossoms. Some of the houses are on a very large scale, and excessively rich in their ornaments and "appointments." Shapely pillars support portico and verandah, and broad flights of stone steps lead to terraces enriched with statues, vases, fountains, both of European and Asiatic design. In the gardens are cultivated some of the finest trees of the country,—the gold mohur (properly, *gul mohâ*) acacia, with its clusters of golden flowers; the papayer, with its enormous fruit; the Chinese pine, and the colossal baobab.

Beyond the Governor's House, on the west coast of the promontory, lies the village of Walkeshwar, a place of peculiar sanctity. The legend avers that the god Râma, when on his way to conquer Lunka (or Ceylon), in order to punish the king Ravana, who had carried off his wife Sita, halted here for one night. His brother Lukshman, through the agency of a genie, sent him every night an emblem from Benares, that he might not intermit his devotions to Siva.

On this occasion, however, the emblem did not appear; and Râma, taking a little sand from the sea-shore, fashioned it into an idol. The spot from which the sand was taken became a deep pool; and the village that grew up around the divine idol is to this day known as Walkeshwar, "the Lord of Sand."

THE VILLAGE OF WALKESHWAR, BOMBAY.

The pool of Râma is now situated in the centre of a square, surrounded by temples. It lies some forty feet below the level, and large flights of steps lead down to the water. Here may be seen, almost always, a great crowd of Hindus, male and female, engaged in religious ceremonies—either plunging into, or besprinkling themselves with, the holy water, or absorbed in an ecstasy of devout meditation.

At the highest point of the Malabar Hill rises the Tower of Silence, the Great Dokhma of the Parsees, whither they bring their dead to be devoured by the vultures that crowd the surrounding trees. None but the *Dustoors*, or Priests of the Fire, are permitted to enter the sacred precincts. The body of the departed is left by his kinsmen at the door; the priests carry it within the tower, where it is placed on a grating, which enables the vultures to tear off the flesh, while the bones remain intact. From the grove which encloses and partly conceals the tower a delightful view may be obtained.

Descending the hill in an easterly direction, the traveller reaches the Byculla quarter, extending over a wide, marshy, and unhealthy plain, and inhabited chiefly by Parsees, half-castes, and the scum of the motley population of Bombay. Round the hills of Mazagon, just beyond, clusters the suburb of the Portuguese, the climate of which is injuriously affected by the exhalations rising from a too luxuriant vegetation. Here flourish dense thickets of palm-trees, nîms, and acacias, woven together by festoons of parasitical plants; groups of colossal banian-trees, in the shade of which thrive euphorbias, cactuses, daturas, and tall grasses; and groves of mango-trees, famous for their height and the lusciousness of their fruit. The mango, called in India the "amb," is of an oblong shape, about three or four inches in length, containing, under a thick green rind, a delicious aromatic pulp of an orange yellow, with a large stone in the centre.

Into this Eden, however, the serpent enters; being no less formidable a reptile than the *nâga*, or cobra di capella, the bite of which is death. The luxuriant vegetation nourishes, moreover, a plague of insects. Jackals frequent the thickets, and make night hideous with their melancholy howls; and the animal life of the district also includes the flying-fox, with its black wings extending a couple of feet; the immense bandycoot rat; the strongly-smelling musk-rat; and the sonorous and enormous bull-frog, which constitutes a living negation of a well-known fable of Æsop's.

With this general view of the quarters of the city we must be content. Let us now proceed to mingle with its population, and examine their avocations and customs. The most

A PALANQUIN—BOMBAY.

melancholy-minded of men would surely be stirred into something like animation by the variety of the aspects of life which meet us on every side. The hot, dusty streets seethe with continual currents of heterogeneous crowds, together with the curious conveyances common to the place: carts and waggons, hackneys, with meek-eyed bullocks in front and shouting drivers behind, buggies, cabs, and palanquins, or "palkies." The last-named are not unlike our eighteenth century sedan-chairs; only the poles on which they swing are carried on the shoulders of muscular coolies. The said coolies wear little else than a cloth around their loins. Among well-dressed men the usual garment is a piece of bleached shirting, folded with much grace about the body; the legs being bare from a little below the knee, and the feet cased in coarse red slippers with curved toes, like the peaked shoes of the Plantagenet period. The head is protected by a huge turban, or else by a fantastic and brightly-coloured "puggery." The Parsees are easily distinguished by their characteristic costume. They wear the *angrika*, a kind of surtout of white silk or cotton, with silk *payjamas*, or trousers, and a peculiar high square hat. Much more gorgeous is the attire of the Persian citizens, who figure in velvet and gold, and may be contrasted with the Fakir, who crouches in the thick dust, begging for alms, his naked distorted body and filthy matted hair rendering him an unwholesome and ungrateful object.

As we pass along we are attracted by a group of jugglers,—the Indian jugglers being famous all the world over for their superior dexterity and invention. One of them rapidly beats a tom-tom with his hard, sinewy fingers; another extracts monotonously doleful tones from a curiously-shaped flageolet; while a third is opening his display of "properties," including a cobra and a large rock-snake. The chief juggler, seeing us pause, prepares to astonish us with the celebrated mango-trick. Singing a kind of low chant, he smooths a place in the gravel, and places over it a basket covered with a thin blanket. The said basket is made of open wicker-work, and careful examination convinces the bystander that neither about his person nor in the basket is anything concealed. Sitting down, the juggler, singing and smiling, stretches his naked arms under the basket, lifts it off the ground, and, behold! a green plant about a foot in height. Of course you applaud so remarkable a trick, and the incantation is resumed. A little time is allowed for the plant to grow; the basket is again removed, and the plant is two feet high. Wait a little longer, and you are asked to taste the fruit. You then examine the ground with a stony stare of surprise, but find it perfectly smooth and solid.

Resuming our excursions, we shall next pay a visit to the Jain Asylum for Animals. It is the creed of the Jain that every man is purified of his sins by the gradual passage of his spirit through various forms of animal life, until at length, the process of cleansing being complete, the spotless soul finally enters into *nirvâna* (extinction). Such a creed necessarily implies on the part of its believers a great reverence for animal life, as every animal is simply the embodiment of some suffering human soul.

Architecturally, till of late, little has been done for Bombay. It has its Christian churches, Mohammedan mosques, Hindu temples; its colleges, hospitals, and town-hall. The University buildings, Post-Office, Secretariate, and several other tasteful erections, are quite recent. Some of the private houses, however, are very rich and handsome; and many are fitted up with a profound feeling for the æsthetic. Otherwise, it is an Indian Liverpool or Glasgow, though more finely situated, and rejoicing in a brighter sky and warmer sun. Business is its *primum mobile;* and the commercial transactions of which it is the centre are truly immense. Many of the principal merchants are Parsees; and if their wealth be enormous, it is but fair to own that they dispense it with great liberality. As for their hospitality, it is boundless; and Europeans with respectable credentials are sure of a cordial welcome.

A "nautch party" is a recognized form of receiving friends; and evilly as it sounds in English ears, we are bound to say that the taste of the most fastidious spectator is seldom offended.

The reader may suppose himself to have received an invitation to such an entertainment, and we will accompany him to the house where it is to be held. As we approach, we observe that every window of the two-storied mansion is ablaze with light; while lanterns, like

HINDU WOMEN OF BOMBAY, IN CEREMONIAL DRESS.

fireflies, gleam among the branches of the trees and shrubberies. At the hall door, to which we make our way through a dazzling illumination, we are received by the host, surrounded by a staff of native servants in livery; and, after a few words of courtesy, conducted upstairs to the grand drawing-room, which occupies the entire length of the building, and is lighted by upwards of a hundred lamps of cocoa-nut oil. What a radiance bursts upon us as we enter,—a radiance reflected and intensified by the bright colours and rich sheeny stuffs of the assembled guests, who form a dazzling and romantic circle!

Having taken our places on the seats of honour prepared for us, rose-water, flowers, and betel-nut are successively presented. These preliminaries happily over, a nautch-girl makes her appearance, at the head of a cortége of musicians. Three of the latter squat upon the floor, and proceed to elicit from a tom-tom, a triangle, and a two-stringed banjo, an exceedingly doleful, not to say discordant music, the characteristic of which is that it consists of a single two-barred phrase, continually repeated. The nautch now advances into the centre of the room, and moves her hands and feet, slowly and gently, to the plaintive cadence of the orchestral accompaniment. After a while, she breaks forth into a kind of recitative, which gradually increases in force and spirit, producing a corresponding acceleration of the movements of the feet and hands.

This performance at an end, a second performer steps forward, and goes through very similar evolutions to those of her predecessor. Her dress is of a peculiarly gorgeous description, from which we infer that she enjoys greater distinction in her profession; and her performance is decidedly more dramatic, while the accompanying or explanatory recitative is given with much greater energy. This, however, may be accounted for by the difference of theme. She is narrating a story of love which has not run smoothly; while her companion had simply to moralize on the Divine compassion, as exemplified in the date tree, which drops its fruit to the ground for the benefit of the poor.

At length the two performers advance together, and a kind of duet or dialogue ensues, in which the one solicits the love the other seems reluctant or coy to give. The pantomime is expressive, but it is still accompanied by a droning chant; and as we weary of it, the two nautch-girls are liberally rewarded and bidden to retire. If we have shown no great interest in the performance, the rest of the company have exhibited less, sitting all the time with blank faces, and in complete silence, as if they had no concern whatever in what was going on. This is not to be wondered at, when we reflect that no women are present, and that the nautch is an amusement which does not improve upon repetition.

If we are afterwards introduced to the ladies of the family, we observe that they are splendidly attired in Kashmir shawls, embroidered silks, and a profusion of jewellery. But as conversation is contrary to etiquette, and a silent interview has no particular charms, we are glad when, after a due exchange of salutations, we are at liberty to take our leave.

CHAPTER IV.

ELEPHANTA—KENERY.

ISLAND OF ELEPHANTA—ITS CAVES—IMAGE OF THE GOD MAHADEO—THE SANCTUARY OF THE LINGAM—ANCIENT SCULPTURES—ISLAND OF SALSETTE—CAVE-TEMPLES OF KENERY—BUDDHIST TEMPLE.

ELEPHANTA, of which in one's boyhood one hears so much and dreams so vividly, is an island in Bombay Harbour. To this ancient asylum and sanctuary of the Hindu creed the visitor is now conveyed in a small steamer, which in itself seems to express, as it were, the vast changes of human history and progress since Elephanta was first frequented by priests and devotees. About five hundred yards from the place where we disembark are situated the famous Caves, to which we ascend by means of a long flight of stone steps, constructed at the cost of a Hindu merchant. As we climb the steep, we revel in the glorious vegetation which so profusely surrounds us—in the plumed crests of the palms and the tall pillar-like trunks of the baobabs, in the beautiful blossoms of the creeping plants which hang in festoons from every stalwart bough, and in the balmy airs which steal upon our sense; while the picture is everywhere full of light and colour, with blue sky and blue sea, hazy isles, and long curving shores.

The name of Elephanta was given to the island by the Portuguese, in allusion to a colossal elephant of stone which reared its head near the landing-place, and was formerly represented with an animal on its back, but is now a shapeless mass, in which the hand of the sculptor can with difficulty be recognized.

From the shade of thickets of cocoa palms we emerge upon the threshold of a large cave excavated in the front of a precipice, the height and mass of which have been concealed from us by the exuberant vegetation. Two columns and two pilasters form three great square gateways, through which we peer into the darkness of the temple-cave.

The cavern has been excavated on a cruciform plan; and it has three fronts—one towards the interior, the other two over the lateral passages. The extreme length is one hundred and thirty-two feet; and the roof rests upon twenty-six columns and sixteen pilasters, each from sixteen to eighteen feet in height, of which nearly half are now reduced to ruins.

At the back a basement supports a gigantic bust, representing a divinity with three heads, two of which only are in profile. At one time this was supposed to be Brahma; but it is now correctly identified with the god Mahadeo or Siva, to whom the temple was formerly consecrated. The principal face is calm and benevolent, and, though mutilated, not deficient in expression. A mitre-like diadem, enriched with delicate carvings in imitation of necklaces and trinkets, crowns the forehead.

The sanctuary which enshrines the lingam, or emblem, of Siva, is to the right of Trimoorti; the said lingam being a stone pillar, rounded at the top, which stands upon a square stone, the yoni, having a small trench round it to carry off the water with which it is besprinkled by the faithful. The lingam is Siva, the symbol of Generation; the yoni, the emblem of Reproduction: in other words, they represent the two great principles of Nature.

The walls of the cave are covered with lofty figures in relief. These describe the mythic actions of the god, and his various incarnations: they are executed with spirit rather than with grace. But the trap rock on which they are carved being of a friable character, and the

ENTRANCE OF CAVES—ELEPHANTA.

Portuguese having found here a vent for iconoclastic zeal, they are considerably defaced, and, in many places, cannot be identified. A recent traveller, however, asserts that it is still easy to follow the subjects suggested by the fertile imagination of the ancient sculptor. Siva and his wife Parvati appear in the most diverse attitudes: sometimes sitting together in Kailas, or tenderly embracing each other; sometimes surrounded by all the deities of the Hindu Olympus, who are engaged in paying them homage. The spaces between the pilasters are filled with the details of their marriage, the birth of Ganêsa, the sacrifice of Daksha, and numerous other scenes of Saiva mythology. To describe them would be impossible; enough to say that they throw a flood of light on the customs and manners of the far-distant time in which they were executed.

KENERY.

The island of Salsette, to which reference has been made in a preceding section, lies to the north of Bombay, with which it is connected by a narrow causeway. Its principal town is Tanna, but Ghora Bandar is more picturesque. The objects of attraction to the traveller, however, are its Caves, of which there are several groups; the most important being that of Kenery, on the western slope of the hills. Tanna lies beyond the eastern slope.

Numerous excavations are found on the two declivities of the hill of Kanha. Most of the temples and monasteries date from the beginning of the present era, and are simple square cells, or chambers, hollowed in the rock, to which access is obtained by a gallery or vestibule with or without columns. According to some Oriental scholars who have tried to decipher the fragments of obscure inscriptions engraved on the walls of these sanctuaries, one of the most ancient may probably date as far back as 65 B.C., to receive the precious relic of a tooth of Buddha—

CAVE OF LIONS—ELEPHANTA.

which, two centuries and a half later, was placed in a dagoba by one of the sovereigns of the Andhra dynasty.

The Great Chaitya, or temple, claims our attention. Passing into the vestibule, we find each end occupied by a figure of Buddha, fully twenty feet high. The philosopher is represented in a long floating robe, with his right arm raised, and the hand half-open, apparently in the act of blessing; while the left hand is opened wide, in token of liberality and benevolence. The face is calm and thoughtful; the lobes of the ears droop to the shoulders, and the crisped hair is gathered on the head so as to form a diadem.

The wall separating the vestibule from the body of the temple is pierced by three doorways. Within, the roof is supported by thirty columns, of which eleven on the left and six on the right are enriched with sculptures; the remainder are octagons without either base or capital. The plinth is composed of three courses of stone of gradually diminishing size; they are surrounded by a string of pearls. The base takes the form of a *chatti*—the splendid large-mouthed copper vessel which the Hindus from time immemorial have used for drawing water. At the extremity of the nave, or central aisle—for this vast hall is divided by its rows of columns into three aisles—rises a huge altar, sixteen feet high, representing the dagoba, or reliquary, almost always found in Buddhist temples. Its shape is that of a hemispherical

FACADE OF A GROTTO AT KENERY.

dome, resting on a cylindrical base, and bearing on its summit the pedestal or capital which formerly supported the venerated emblem. Through a great arched window the light falls on this altar with startling effect, the rest of the hall remaining in shadow. In this way the attention of the worshipper was entirely concentrated on the idol to which he addressed his prayers.

CHAPTER V.

BARODA.

THE GUIKWAR'S CAPITAL—THE SUBURBS—THE PALACE—A ROYAL SOWARI, OR PROCESSION—ITS GORGEOUS ASPECTS—ANTELOPE-HUNTING—THE MOTIBAGH.

BARODA is the capital of the territory of one of the most powerful princes in Western India, the Guikwar. It is seated on the river Vishwamitra, an impetuous and irregular stream, which flows in a deep channel, spanned by an old Hindu bridge of two rows of arches, one above the other. Great flights of stairs lead down to the water's edge; and above them rise a thousand bell-towers of temples, together with tombs and kiosks, half-hidden among the clustering foliage.

The suburbs consist of a maze of narrow crowded streets, teeming with a population of one hundred and fifty thousand souls,—a larger population than that of the town itself. The houses are nearly all of timber, and built in the most picturesque varieties of style. At all the cross-ways stand pagodas and idols, surmounted with coloured banners.

Passing through this busy labyrinth, the visitor arrives at a large monumental gateway, flanked by high round towers, the façade of which is painted with huge figures of monsters and divinities, and enters the city. It is crossed by two spacious streets, which, bisecting each other at right angles, divides it into four quarters,—one being occupied by the Guikwar's Palace, while in the other three cluster the houses of the rich and noble. At the point of intersection rises an immense pavilion, a pyramid of wood, with balconies in several stories, supported upon a foundation of lofty stone arches. The stories are all painted of different colours; and the whole is surmounted by a large clock.

In the time of the late Guikwar, deposed by the Indian Government on account of his sensual and cruel tyranny, Baroda glittered, day after day, with splendid spectacles. Amongst these, the most conspicuous for Oriental magnificence would seem to have been the regal sowari, or procession, in which the Guikwar himself appeared in state. It is thus described by M. Rousselet, an eye-witness:—

The road was obstructed by the multitudes who hurried to the festival; and our escort had much difficulty in forcing a way for us by the use of strong language. Crowds covered the approaches to the river, and banners and oriflammes gaily decorated every house. At a little distance a balcony had been fitted up for us with arm-chairs and carpets, overlooking a long street, through which the sowari would pass. The maharajah, a short time before, had purchased one of the most famous diamonds in the world, the "Star of the South," and had resolved to give this new acquisition the honour of a triumphal entry into his capital, and a solemn

THE GUIKWAR IN THE GREAT SOWARI, BARODA.

procession to the chief temple, where it would receive the benediction of the priests. Delighting in such spectacles, all the inhabitants of Baroda had poured out to sēe the procession, and lined the streets awaiting its approach.

The scenes were wonderful in their variety. A magnificent giraffe, saddled, bridled, and splendidly harnessed, was led through the bazaars by the royal servants,—the crowd expressing their admiration in loud shouts which might well have startled the timid creature. The air resounded with a tumultuous din of songs, and shouts, and instrumental music, which swelled into a tempest as the sowari drew near. The march was led by the prince's regular troops, under the command of European officers; then came corps of Arabs, squadrons of Mahratta cavalry, *pendassis*, field-artillery, musketeers, halberdiers, and gunners mounted upon dromedaries; and, lastly, some regiments of the Guikwar's army. Behind them stalked a magnificent elephant, covered with embroidered housings, and carrying the bearer of the royal standard,—a flag of cloth of gold, waving from a staff more than forty feet in length. He was surrounded by picked horsemen, whose duty it is to protect the standard in the stress of battle. They are armed with long lances and broad curved *tulwairs*, or sabres; steel gauntlets cover their hands; and they are richly attired in close-fitting tunics of crimson velvet, with tight breeches, and pointed shoes. Some wear a small steel morion, bound on by the turban, and a Saracenic coat-of-mail; others thick cuirasses of buffalo-hide, richly embroidered. Their lance-heads are of silver, and their shields of transparent rhinoceros-skin adorned with bosses of gold.

A favourite sport with the nobles of Baroda is antelope-hunting. For this purpose cheetahs, or hunting-leopards, are carefully trained. A day being fixed for the chase, and a rendezvous appointed, the animals are conveyed thither in palanquins, each carried by four men. Their eyes are covered with small leather hoods, and notwithstanding the tumult that surrounds them they remain perfectly quiet. A great gathering of huntsmen—some attired in gray or green, others in felt helmets and boots of deer-skin—fill the air with their shouts. On all sides herds of antelopes may be seen, either watching the proceedings with curiosity, or hurrying out of danger. They feel no alarm at the presence of the horsemen, as they are in the daily habit of seeing people in the fields; but some of the more timid are disturbed by the increasing commotion. When the hunting-party have arrived within a sufficient distance, a cheetah is let go, the hood being removed from its eyes. For a moment it is motionless; then it darts arrow-like on the nearest herd, which take to flight at its approach; but, with two or three swift, vigorous bounds, it leaps upon a victim, and brings it to the ground. At full gallop, up come the horsemen, to be in at the death. The cheetah holds the prey with its claws, and plunges its teeth into the creature's neck, until an attendant comes up, replaces the hood, and drags it away from the wished-for banquet. In compensation, it receives a bowlful of the antelope's blood; after which the cheetah is replaced in its palanquin, and the chase resumed.

The public buildings of Baroda are not specially interesting. The Palace is striking only from its immense size. At a short distance from the suburbs stands the elegant summer-palace of the Motibagh, or "Garden of Pearls," which is surrounded by shrubberies and orchards, and adorned with pavilions, statues, and fountains.

CHAPTER VI.

PUNA—KARLI—ELLORA.

PUNA—HILL OF PARVATI—CAVES OF KARLI—THE FINEST CHAITTA IN INDIA—A BUDDHIST "VIHARA"—CAVES OF ELLORA—A SCENE OF BEAUTY—THE GREAT CAVE—GROTTOES OF AJUNTA—THE VALLEY OF CAVES—AN EXCURSION TO GOLCONDA—AURUNGABAD.

PUNA, the capital of the Deccan (seventy miles from Bombay), is situated, with its gardens and picturesque native houses, on the banks of the Muta (Mula), in the centre of a vast and almost treeless plain, which stretches far away to the blue mountains of Sattara. The English cantonments stand apart from the town, in a broad open parade-ground, close to the barracks. The town itself is divided into seven quarters, each named after one of the days of the week. Some of the streets are wide and well-built, but most of them are little better than narrow winding lanes. Here, as in other Hindu cities, the houses of the more opulent natives are covered with painted devices of gods, elephants, and tigers. The temples are small, but their bell-towers and turrets produce a pleasing effect. Indeed, the general aspect is not unlike that of a medieval European city, with its combination of gables, high peaked roofs, and towers, and its massive palaces, battlemented, and with loopholed windows.

Westward of Puna rises the hill of Parvati, covered with temples, and crowned with the sanctuary of Parvati herself, containing, among other treasures, a massive silver statue of Siva, holding on his knees the golden and jewelled images of Parvati and Ganesa.

From Puna to Lanowli we travel by rail. At Lanowli we engage a bullock-garry to convey us to the Caves of Karli, which, though less known, are not less remarkable than the Caves of Elephanta.

The garry is one of the most primitive of vehicles. As it was in the days of the Veda, so is it now. Reform has not meddled with it, and the hand of change has passed it by. It is neither more nor less than a square wooden box, mounted on wheels, but without springs, and drawn by a couple of bullocks. As an easy vehicle, it cannot be commended; but it is certainly safe.

At last we reach Khandala, where we take our rest in a dâk bungalow, erected by the British Government for the convenience and accommodation of travellers. Similar asylums are placed at intervals along all the great roads which have not been rendered obsolete by railways. The Great Indian Peninsula line now traverses this part of the country, and here completes its ascent of the Ghats—a stupendous engineering work, which Europe itself cannot surpass. The total height surmounted is one thousand eight hundred and thirty feet on a line of fifteen miles, and with a mean incline of one in forty-eight. Eight viaducts, of from thirty to fifty arches, and from fifty to one hundred and forty feet in height, have been constructed, and

ANTELOPE-HUNTING WITH THE CHEETAH, BARODA.

(See page 49.)

twenty-two tunnels, of a total length of about one mile and three-quarters. The various embankments contain upwards of six millions of cubic feet; and the entire work, which occupied seven years, cost upwards of £800,000.

The Karli Caves are situated on the west side of a low hill, a few miles east from Khandala. The principal excavation is considered the finest chaitya in India, and was unquestionably worked and elaborated when the Buddhist style had reached its climax of purity. The façade is singularly imposing. In a recess on each side of the entrance elephants in bold relief front the spectators with huge heads and trunks, and seem to uphold on their mighty backs the whole mass of sculptured rock above. Not less imposing is the vast interior. The central aisle has fifteen

ENTRANCE OF THE GREAT CAVE OF KARLI.

pillars, twenty-five feet high, on each side, separating it from the lateral aisles. At the end, within a seven-columned apse, rises the dome-shaped dagoba, on which the light falls dazzlingly from the great open window in front. The total length of this subterranean temple is one hundred and twenty-six feet, while the breadth is forty-five feet, and the height forty-five feet.

Around the Great Cave are the various cells and apartments of a vihara, or monastery, all hewn out of the solid rock. They are arranged in three stories, and the ascent is not altogether convenient. The uppermost is a hall, with an open balcony supported by stone pillars, from which is obtained a view so extensive and romantic that one might be tempted to turn anchorite in order always to enjoy it. Cells branch off on either hand, and the walls are enriched with the carved figures of halo-crowned saints.

Returning to Puna, we next arrange for a visit to the Caves of Ellora and Ajunta.

Our road takes us through a somewhat bare country to Ahmednuggur, a busy and populous town; and thence to Aurungabad, which was a favourite residence of the Emperor Aurungzebe, and owes to him its ramparts and round towers, its mosques with their shapely minarets, and its palaces embowered in bloom and leaf. The Hindu temples and the Tomb of Rabia Daurani, erected in imitation of the Taj of Agra, but inferior to it in beauty, are worth examination.

About twelve miles to the north, an isolated conical mass of granite, one hundred and eighty feet high, is crowned with the celebrated fortress of Dowlatabad, the "Abode of Fortune," formerly the capital of the rulers of the Deccan.

Proceeding across a hilly country, we debouch upon a plain, enriched with venerable trees which overshadow the ruins of Mohammedan tombs and mausoleums. At its further extremity lies the village of Rauzah, or "Paradise," where, in the Mohammedan cemetery, stands the tomb of Aurungzebe. At the foot of a curved wall of rock on the south-west side of Rauzah we come to the village of Ellora; and here, in the face of the hill, are the well-known Caves. They are between thirty and forty in number, including four temples, or chaityas, and some Buddhist viharas, or monasteries; besides a few Jain caves, which combine the characteristics of both.

TEMPLE OF KAILAS, ELLORA.

The whole mass of rock at Ellora is excavated into temples of wonderful grandeur, suggesting the lofty conceptions of the architects, as well as the extraordinary resources which they must have had at their command. It is evident, too, that they were not without a profound sense of natural beauty; for the scenery around is of a beautiful and picturesque character, where the charm is heightened by the deep shadows of luxuriant foliage and the music of falling waters. The broken crags are shrouded thick in brushwood; dark gorge and glen, sheltering venerable but stalwart trees, penetrate into the mountain. An impression of awe has been produced upon the mind before the visitor reaches the chief wonder of this place of wonders—the temple of Kaïlas—which the skill and industry of man has sculptured out of a single rock in all the perfection of its swelling pinnacles and tapering obelisks. In the centre of a spacious court rises a great pagoda to an elevation of one hundred feet. Ascending by a twofold flight of giant steps to a handsome portico, we pass into a noble hall, supported by sixteen columns, and opening upon an area on which are five chapels. The court itself, which is overhung by graceful balconies, measures upwards of three hundred and seventy feet in length by a hundred and fifty in breadth, and is shut in between ramparts of rock of varying elevation. At the back of the temple are placed colossal lions and elephants, in such a manner that they seem to uphold the entire structure, as Atlas sustains the world. The portico is connected by light bridges of stone with a graceful pavilion in front, which stands between two shapely obelisks. The whole is a miracle of symmetry, grace, and grandeur, and overpowers us with the thought of the continuous labour that, inspired by devotion and directed by genius, accomplished this truly colossal work.

About fifty miles from Ellora lie the grottoes of Ajunta, which may fitly be described in this connection. Their latest visitor, M. Rousselet, says of them :—

The valley of caves is nearly four miles from the town, and is gained by a picturesque path winding through a narrow defile, hemmed in between the mountains, and abounding with full-grown forest-trees; among which we recognize the banian, the peepul, and the nîm—the giants of the Indian forest. Monkeys leap from bough to bough, and parrots disport themselves over the banks of the torrent. The gorge contracts rapidly until it reaches the beautiful

EXTERIOR OF CHAITYA, AJUNTA.

waterfall of the Satkound, which tumbles headlong from a height of three hundred feet. It then diverges suddenly to the right; and in the high perpendicular wall that faces it are found the caves. For nearly six hundred yards the mountain-side is pierced with doors and verandahs, which at a distance, owing to their great elevation, seem little better than pigeon-holes, but are really of enormous dimensions. Considered archæologically, India can furnish no other group of Buddhist caves equally complete and beautiful. They surpass anything to be seen at Ellora or in the Concan; and, in truth, they are not *caverns*, but subterraneous palaces, of admirable proportions, of exquisite workmanship, and richly adorned with paintings which still retain much of their original vividness of colour. Every column has its wreaths of flowers, its masks, and its graceful geometrical designs; every ceiling is enriched with rosework, where the figures of men and women and animals are fantastically blended with the outlines of cunning arabesques; while every panelled wall lives with living scenes of the manners and customs of a remote age. Here a group of princes and nobles bend in adoration before the sacred emblems; there a multitude of believers are gathered with ears intent round a Buddhist missionary. Here a splendid procession winds its way to the temple—the king on horseback surrounded by his warriors, and elephants carrying the sacred relics in costly caskets; there contending armies meet in the shock of battle, and soldiers from massive battlements hurl their weapons full upon an attacking foe. Other and softer scenes—those of the court and the harem, the convent and the school—are portrayed with similar vigour and fidelity; and so perfect an exposition of the life of a people is nowhere else to be found, perhaps, except in the tombs and temples of Egypt. But the reader must understand that all does not belong to the same period: on the contrary, while the most ancient excavations may date from a hundred years before Christ, the most recent will not be under thirteen hundred years old.

From Ajunta a visit may be paid to Golconda, the fortress of the Deccan—"a regular eagle's nest, perched on the summit of a steep and rocky hill." It is within the walls of this almost inaccessible stronghold that the Nizam keeps his treasures; a fact which, in M. Rousselet's opinion, has given rise to the proverbial employment of "Golconda" as a synonym for boundless wealth. We are more inclined, however, to ascribe the origin of the allusion to the diamond-mines which lie some miles to the east of the fortress. From these mines have been obtained many of the most precious jewels that flash in the crowns and coronets of the rulers of the world; but lately they have declined in productiveness, and their present value is comparatively insignificant.

The necropolis at Golconda—which is now a ruined and deserted city—contains some superb monuments: conspicuous among them the domed mausoleum of Mohammed Shah, with a dome larger than that of St. Peter's at Rome. This magnificent pile is quadrangular in shape, surrounded by an open colonnade, and adorned with sculptured work of the finest execution.

Another route to Ellora is from Haidarabad to Madras, taking Aurungabad and Dowlatabad, a fortress of considerable strength, on the way. The former city is of sufficient importance to justify us in devoting a page or two to its description.

Aurungabad, on the route to Ellora, was formerly called *Kirki.* It is reputed to have been founded by Malik Ambar in the early part of the seventeenth century; but it was not until Aurungzebe made it his place of residence, in 1650, that it attained to any degree of fame or opulence. In honour of the emperor it received its present name, which means "Thronetown." At one time its population exceeded one hundred thousand, but now does not do more than reach half that number. It stands on the left bank of the Dûdhna, a tributary of the Godavari; and is surrounded by a wall rather lower than the ramparts of most Indian towns, but strengthened at intervals by round towers.

The plain in which it is situated is eighteen hundred feet above the sea, swept by cool and pleasant airs, fertile, and relieved by much picturesque scenery, and bounded by low green hills at a considerable distance. Woods abound, and grassy coverts; and these afford a retreat for tigers and jackals, wild hogs and deer, peacocks, partridges, and quails—so that for the English sports-

MONUMENT IN THE ROYAL NECROPOLIS AT GOLCONDA.

man Aurungabad affords a convenient and attractive centre. The traveller as he approaches the city cannot fail to be charmed by its appearance. It rises from the plain "like an exhalation"—a fairy vision of terraced houses, bright and shining, of large white domes glittering in the sun, and shapely minarets soaring above masses of glossy foliage. It seems a perfect realization of the dreams that all of us form in the days when our fancy is fed by books of Oriental travel and Oriental fable; but the charm vanishes as the traveller penetrates into the streets, and finds that decay has set its seal on the most conspicuous monuments. Yet the city is still famous for its manufacture of rich gold and silver brocades and sheeny silks: its thoroughfares are broad, and many of them busy; and its public buildings are mostly of superior architectural pretensions.

The principal "objects of interest," to use a guide-book phrase, are the Imperial Palace, Rabia Duarani's Mausoleum, and the Juma (or Jama') Masjid.

The Palace stands on the south bank of the river, and is now a ruin. It must at one time have been of considerable dimensions, though never equal in splendour to the magnificent piles erected by Akbar and Shah Jehan. It is not the less to be regretted that here, as elsewhere, so few remains of Aurungzebe's works are extant.

On the other side of the river, beyond the city wall, is the Tomb of Rabia Daurani, erected in 1645, after the model of the beautiful Taj at Agra; that is, the general arrangement of the body of the building is the same, but the details are different; and the general degradation of style is truly remarkable, when it is remembered that the Taj was built by Aurungzebe's father. Something may be allowed, says Mr. Fergusson, for its being a provincial building; and, moreover, it cost only £90,000—a small sum compared with Shah Jehan's outlay on the Taj. But, with all this, it is not easy to understand how anything so tasteless, though so rich, could be erected by the immediate successor of the sovereign who built the beautiful tomb to which it has been unworthily compared. As the Taj was a memorial to Shah Jehan's favourite sultana, so the tomb we are speaking of was raised in honour of Aurungzebe's first wife. The enclosed space around it, covering about thirty acres, is laid out in blooming gardens. The approach is through a gateway with doors of embossed brass, which open upon a noble paved avenue, having a basin of water with thirteen glittering fountains in the centre, and lined by orange, lime, peach, apple, and pomegranate trees. When these are in blossom, the scene is one of great beauty, and the air seems burdened with fragrance.

The tomb stands upon a terraced platform, and forms a square of seventy-two feet. It is built of white marble for five feet from the base, and thence upwards of stone faced with glittering chunam. The marble portion is pierced with three windows, the carving of which is as exquisite as the most delicate lacework, so that it is a perpetual wonder to the spectator how even the most ingenious chisel could carve a material like marble into such airy filagree. The great dome which crowns the building is also of marble. It rises out of a ring of four minarets and two smaller domes, while a tall and graceful minaret springs arrow-like from each angle of the platform.

In the centre of the building is the sepulchre, to which the visitor descends by four-and-twenty steps. Its summit reaches to a level with the terrace. Round it runs an elegant octagonal screen of marble trellis-work. This is loaded with delicate carving, though each face of the octagon, while measuring nine feet in length and height, is only four inches thick. The entire vault is faced with white marble; and this part of the building is certainly as pure in design as it is marvellous in execution.

A few feet above the tomb, the interior of the building is encircled by a gallery, running on a level with the three windows previously described. It is wholly built of marble.

The tomb of the whilom sultana, now but "a handful of dust," is covered with a rich gold-fringed pall of scarlet velvet, fastened by eight marble studs.

The marble used in the construction of this monument was brought from the quarries of Lahore, which, according to the rate of locomotion in Aurungzebe's reign, was distant a four months' journey. Tavernier, the French traveller, describes in his quaint and graphic narrative how he encountered a caravan of three hundred carts conveying large marble blocks from Lahore to Aurungabad (1645).

The minarets which spring from the angles of the platform are seventy-two feet high; and their summit, which commands a wide and varied prospect, instinct with all the glow of Oriental colouring, is reached by a spiral stone staircase of one hundred and twenty-two steps. At the top is a balcony thirty-one feet in circumference. Each minaret measures sixteen feet in diameter at its base.

To the left of the Mausoleum, between it and the gardens, and raised upon a terrace, stands a handsome pavilion, open on one side, twenty-two feet high, and twelve feet long by fifty-four feet broad. The floor, somewhat dilapidated now, was originally a mosaic of white and black marble. The entrance is by a Saracenic arch, which is enriched with much fine carving of the usual pattern. To this pavilion is given the name of the *Jama' Khanah*, or Assembly-room of the Priests. Near a grove of "murmurous limes" is another and smaller pavilion, whither Aurungzebe was accustomed to retire, with his wife Rabia and a learned Moollah, for purposes of study and devotion.

CHAPTER VII.

THE NORTH-WEST CAPITAL: ALLAHABAD.

ITS CENTRAL SITUATION—ITS ENGLISH CHARACTER—THE CANTONMENTS—ITS STREETS—CONFLUENCE OF THE GANGES AND THE JUMNA—THE GREAT TRIVENI—BATHING PILGRIMAGES—THE INDIAN QUARTER—AN INDIGO-PLANTER'S BUNGALOW AND FACTORY—THE RAILROAD BRIDGE—ALLAHABAD IN THE MUTINY—A TOUCHING INCIDENT.

AT the confluence of the Ganges and the Jumna, about eighty miles north of Benares, and four hundred and ninety-eight miles north-west of Calcutta, stands Allahabad, the capital of the North-West Provinces, and the residence of the Lieutenant-Governor, who rules over a territory equal in area to the whole of what was once known as Hindustan. The Government House is a double-storied white building, with spacious verandahs and Italian balconies; a smooth, well-kept lawn in front, and a grove of green and fragrant trees in the rear. Close at hand lies the Park, or Public Garden, pleasantly diversified by excellent carriage-drives, beds blooming with gorgeous flowers, and shining orange-groves. In the centre is an elevated circular parterre of Eastern roses, oleanders, and heliotropes, which runs riot with a wealth of colour; while a small paddock or enclosure is stocked with graceful antelopes.

"Take a glance over the surrounding country from this pleasant stand-point," says Mr. Wheeler, "and you will see how like an English landscape the scene is. There are visible two sharp spires of churches rising above the trees east and west; a majestic stone building, the nucleus of a college, to be called after the ex-Lieutenant-Governor, Sir William Muir. On a piece of hard ground yonder, in front of the Public Library and Museum, bands of laughing boys are playing with kites and peg-tops."

The *English* aspect of Allahabad struck M. Rousselet. The "cantonments" of Allahabad, he says, are a town in every sense of the word, and contain at the present day the largest assemblage of Europeans out of the three Presidential cities. The houses are separated from each other by extensive gardens, as in the suburbs of southern London; the streets are lined with trees, and broad as highroads; the squares as large as esplanades. Allahabad, he adds, is now the model of a European city.

It is difficult to understand why the British Government still fix the capital of the Empire at malarious Calcutta, when Allahabad offers so many superior facilities. Situated at the confluence of the Ganges and the Jumna, it commands the passage of both these great river-highways; while, being at an almost equal distance from Calcutta, Madras, Bombay, and Lahore, it is necessarily the centre to which all the great Indian railways converge. Its climate is warm, but healthy; and the surrounding country wants nothing but scientific cultivation to make it the Garden of India.

Across a plain of white sand the traveller proceeds to visit the junction-point of the two rivers, which there widen into a broad, gleaming lake, that disappears on the horizon between glittering banks crowned with palms. This plain has always been reverenced for its sanctity by the Hindus, who regard as sacred the confluence of all rivers, but more particularly the confluence of the Ganges and the Jumna. Here they place the great Triveni, the centre of three sacred streams; the third being a mystic river, the Saraswati, which falls from heaven. In their united waters lies the power of cleansing even the most terrible sins. The moral leper, bathing in them, is henceforth pure as snow. And it is no marvel that the pioneers of the Aryan race, when first they looked upon the two great rivers flowing through a rich and sunny country to mingle in one channel their abundant waters, should have been moved by a feeling of awe and veneration, that found expression afterwards in traditional observances. Descending from the mountains of Afghanistan or the wastes of the Punjab, they seemed to have discovered at last the Earthly Paradise; and there they erected one of their earliest cities, Prayaga, which retained its splendour when, many centuries later, it was visited by the Chinese traveller, Hiouen Thsang (A.D. 640). After alluding to its palaces, temples, and topes, he writes:—"To the eastward of it two rivers meet together; and beyond this junction spreads a plateau of from fourteen to fifteen leagues in circumference, the ground of which is even and smooth. From remote antiquity down to our own days, kings and great personages, endowed with humanity and affection, resort to this spot to distribute their alms and benefits. For this reason it is called the great Plain of Almsgiving."

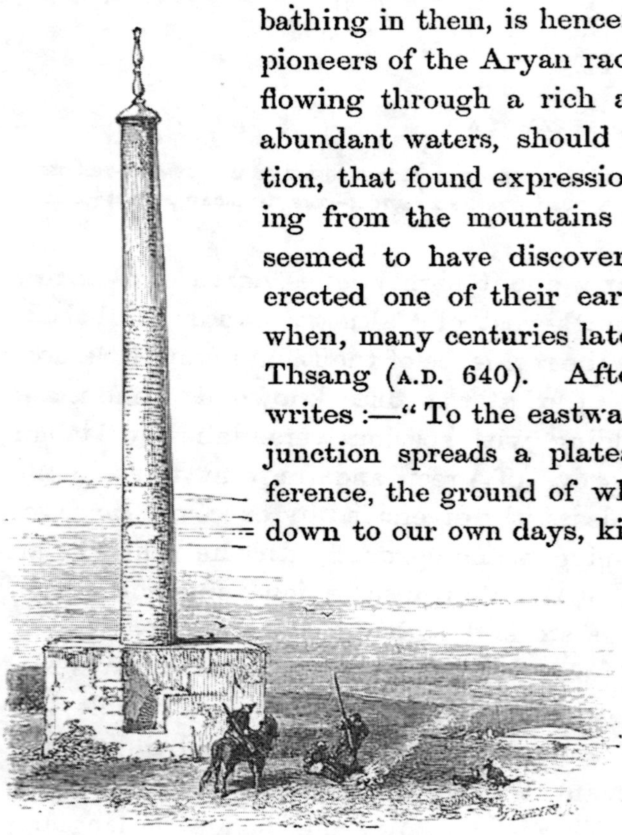

PILLAR OF ASOKA, ALLAHABAD.

The bathing pilgrimages to the confluent waters of the Ganges and the Jumna are falling into desuetude, but crowds may still be seen, especially on great festivals, along the banks of both rivers. A Brahman, enthroned beneath the shade of a far-spreading parasol, receives the pious pilgrim, and guides him through the various processes of purification. Whether man or woman, the votary must throw off all clothing, except a light scarf, which is girt about the loins. Entering the water until immersed to his waist, he begins cutting off locks of hair, which are committed to the stream with all due caution; for each hair thus offered secures the remission of a sin. Thereafter the Brahman who acts as officiating priest takes up a position in front of the hydropathic devotees, and plunges into the water once or twice, and throws a handful towards each of the cardinal points; in all these operations being faithfully imitated by the pilgrims—the imitation being so exact and punctual as to produce the effect of dolls set in simultaneous motion by invisible machinery.

To the west of the plain, and near the confluence, stands the stately fort erected by Akbar in the sixteenth century. Here, too, may be seen a lât or pillar of Asoka, dating from about B.C. 250, and resembling that which towers above the palace of Feroze at Delhi; a fine cylindrical monolith, forty-two feet seven inches in height, tapering slightly towards the summit, and crowned with a delicate honeysuckle moulding.

The Indian quarter of Allahabad is meanly built, with close narrow streets, and pervaded by a disagreeable odour of garlic and ghee. Yet to a European it is full of interest. He observes with pleasure the tall, slender, dusky-skinned Hindus, in their white linen garments; the women, some of whom are comely enough, wearing a long, full-plaited skirt, and a narrow piece of cloth round the upper part of the body, which leaves the bosom bare. He notes the different trades and avocations of the people: the pawnbroker in his store, appraising some silver ornament; the lapidary in his *atelier*, cutting gems with bore and wheel. A peep into a manufactory of lac bracelets is not to be despised; and toy-shops, guitar-shops, sweetmeat-shops, all have their attractions. Or he pauses, if he has an hour to spare, to witness some such scene as this:—A weaver with five shillings' worth of gold presents himself before a working jeweller, and pays him a penny (thirty-two anna) to make it into a nose-ring. The jeweller sets to work and beats the pea into a bar, and shapes the bar into a ring, while the weaver sits by and watches that none of the gold be purloined.

INDIGO-PLANTER'S BUNGALOW—ALLAHABAD.

Our next visit shall be made, in company with M. Rousselet, to an indigo-planter's bungalow and factory. The bungalow, which faces the Ganges, is a large but low brick-walled house, the immense pyramidal roof of which is thickly covered with maize thatching. The simplicity of the exterior contrasts strongly with the elegance and comfort of the interior, which contains four handsome bedrooms, each with its own verandah and bath-room, opening out of a large quadrangular and luxuriously furnished sitting-room. A kitchen-garden, planted with European vegetables, surrounds the house, and separates it from the buildings of the factory.

As for the indigo manufacture:—It is the young shoots, and not the flowers, that supply the material used for dyeing. The gathering of these shoots is a very delicate operation. As soon as they are properly mature, it is essential they should at once be removed; and each cutting must be executed with rapidity, and during the night, for the sun would wither the branches, and deprive them of their properties. A great many hands, therefore, are required; these are distributed through the fields at midnight; and in the morning the produce of their labours is deposited in stone troughs which have been previously filled with water. Then the sun has an important part to play. Under the influence of its beams the substances undergo a kind of fermentation; the water becomes variously tinted, the tints rapidly merging into a uniform blue. After a period of about forty-eight hours the liquid is drawn off from the smallest troughs; its colour is then a bluish-black, and it emits a slight ammoniacal odour. After undergoing a second evaporation, it is drawn off into metal vats, heated by steam, in which, when the evaporation has ceased, a deposit of pure indigo is formed.

Allahabad is about the western limit of indigo-culture, which spreads eastward over vast districts, and supplies the staple trade of Tirhoot, Upper Behar, and Bengal.

INDIGO-FACTORY—ALLAHABAD.

The railroad at Allahabad crosses the Jumna on an iron bridge of admirable workmanship, supported by sixteen massive piers; and then, turning eastward, follows the right bank of the Ganges. To the south of the buttressed table-land of the Rewah, which is visible from the line, lies Mirzapur, with its manufactures of carpets and hangings; and at Chunar, twenty-one miles further, a formidable stronghold is perched on the summit of an isolated rock, one of the sides of which is a precipice of nearly one hundred and fifty feet. Here may be seen the ruins of a Hindu palace, gloomy and massive. In the centre of one of the courts, beneath the shade of a banian-tree, lies a slab of black marble, consecrating what the Hindus regard as the sacredest spot in the whole world. Tradition reports that for nine hours of each day the eternal and invisible god, whose awful symbol, Ôm, may not be spoken aloud—the Zeus of the Hindu pantheon, ruler of both gods and men—is wont to seat himself upon it. The court is without idol or sculpture, but contains a solitary mystic symbol—a circle enclosed within a triangle, the signification of which has been forgotten by the Hindus.

In the Great Mutiny of 1857 Allahabad played an important part. The possession of its Fort would have been of immense value to the rebel Sepoys, and have enabled them to command the passage of both the Ganges and the Jumna. When the news of the outbreak at Meerut reached the officer in command, he gathered the Europeans of Allahabad, with their wives and children, within the walls of the Fort, and put arms in the hands of all who were able to use them. Its occupants, however, were too few to defend it successfully, nor was it provided for a siege. Happily, on the 7th of June fifty gallant fellows of Neil's famous regiment, the "Madras Lambs," arrived, after a night-march of eighty miles, at the Benares end of the bridge of boats, and in the evening were smuggled into the Fort. On the 9th another detachment was sent forward by the indefatigable Neil. On the 11th he himself appeared, having pushed on with incredible speed under a burning sun, and, though nearly prostrated by his sufferings, drove the mutineers out of their positions around the Fort, and secured Allahabad for the British.

On the 18th of June cholera broke out in Allahabad, and carried off forty out of a hundred Fusiliers. Reinforcements, however, rapidly arrived from Calcutta, and on the 30th Neil was able to despatch a small relieving force towards Cawnpur. Next day Havelock came up. By the 7th of July he had started for the city of the massacre, and on the 15th he was followed by Neil.

A touching incident is related in connection with the Allahabad outbreak. When the moulvee, who had placed himself at the head of the rebels, took to flight, he left behind him a number of native Christians who had been his prisoners. One of them was a cadet named Cheek, who died the same evening, his body covered with wounds and sores, and his mind wandering. Nundinath, a native Christian and a fellow-prisoner, related that when the moulvee endeavoured by threats and cajolery to make him abjure Christianity, this brave lad would call out to him, "Never let go the faith!" And, thus encouraged, Nundinath remained true to the religion of the Cross.

On the 7th of March 1876 Allahabad was visited by the Prince of Wales, who held there a Chapter of the Order of the Star of India.

CHAPTER VIII.

DELHI, THE CITY OF THE MOGUL.

1. GENERAL DESCRIPTION OF DELHI—THE CHANDNEE CHOWK, OR "STREET OF LIGHT"—ABOUT THE HOUSES—ABOUT THE SHOPS—TRADES OF THE PEOPLE—THE GREAT MOSQUE—ITS MARBLE DOMES—MOHAMMEDAN RITES—VIEW OF DELHI FROM A MINARET—THE PALACE—COURT OF THE MOGUL—GRAND HALL OF AUDIENCE—PRIVATE HALL OF AUDIENCE—IN THE DAYS OF OLD—RUINS OF EARLIER CITIES.—2. EXCURSION TO THE KOOTUB—THE BLACK MOSQUE—HUMAYOON'S MAUSOLEUM—MAUSOLEUM OF SUFTUR JUNG—THE KOOTUB DESCRIBED—AKBAR'S COLLEGE—RUINS OF THE KOOTUB MOSQUE—AN IRON COLUMN—AN ANCIENT LEGEND—AN IMPERIAL MAUSOLEUM—RUINS OF TOGHLUKABAD—THE OLD FORT—RETURN TO DELHI.—3. A SAUNTER THROUGH ITS STREETS—ANOTHER VISIT TO THE CHANDNEE CHOWK—THE KOTWALI, OR TOWN-HALL.—4. HISTORICAL SKETCH OF DELHI—THE GREAT MUTINY—AN ALARMING TELEGRAM—OUTBREAK IN DELHI—A SCENE OF MASSACRE—PREPARATIONS TO RECOVER THE CITY—POSITION OF THE BRITISH ARMY—THE BESIEGERS BESIEGED—PLAN OF ATTACK—STORMING OF DELHI—DEATH OF NICHOLSON—THE CITY TAKEN—THE ROYAL FAMILY OF DELHI—HODSON CAPTURES THE KING—LATER HISTORY OF DELHI—THE PRINCE OF WALES'S VISIT.

DELHI, the capital of India during the brief supremacy of Mohammedanism, is situated on the bank of the river Jamna or Jumna. Called in native language Shahjehanabad, it was founded by Shah Jehan in 1631. Former Delhis there had been, but each had been destroyed, or had silently decayed with the dynasty to which it owed its rise; so that now an area of four and twenty miles round the modern city is covered with their ruins. Delhi itself is about seven miles in circumference; it is surrounded by formidable walls, the strength of which was proved by British guns in 1857. At a distance the traveller sees a host of glittering domes and cupolas rising above these fortifications, with the spires of the Juma Masjid glittering in the centre of the picture. As he draws near, he makes his way through the remains of enormous forts, huge tombs with colossal gateways, and marble mosques, contrasting strangely with the piles of red sandstone in their immediate vicinity. At length he arrives on the marge of the Jumna, which waters the sandy plain with numerous winding rills; and here the washermen and washerwomen are plying their useful trade, chattering loudly and volubly the while. Opposite stands the fort or citadel, with its embattled walls of red granite, towering full forty feet in height; and above the famous Kashmir Gate swells the white dome of the Christian church.

Crossing the bridge of boats, he enters Delhi, and finds himself involved in a maze of streets filled with all the bustle and picturesque confusion of an Eastern crowd. By degrees he notes that though many of the streets are tortuous, and others squalid, yet as a whole the city has a prosperous and even imposing aspect. The Hindu element is scarcely noticeable; but while Afghans and Sikhs, with their stalwart forms and bright costumes, are numerous, the general character of the crowd is Mohammedan, and the atmosphere, as it were, suggestive rather of Turkey than of Hindustan.

The principal thoroughfare is the Chandnee Chowk, or "Street of Light," which leads direct from the Lahore Gate to the ancient Palace, and measures about ninety feet in width, and a mile

THE CHANDNEE CHOWK, DELHI.

in length. A row of trees runs down the centre, and casts a pleasant shade; while on either side is an uninterrupted succession of verandah-girt houses and well-filled shops.

THE JUMA MASJID.

The buildings, however, are generally of small dimensions, while overloaded with terraces and balconies. Some of them exhibit faint traces of the gilding which adorned them in the days of Mogul splendour, others are covered with sculptured ornaments in more or less complete preservation. The walls and doorways are generally illuminated with painted symbols and figures, chiefly of a religious significance. Among them figures the sacred and favoured peacock, with glittering tail outspread, and in an attitude of prudent watchfulness. Elephants, standing on nothing, or else perched on terrestrial spheres "a world too small" for their colossal bulk, are of frequent occurrence. Brahma may also be seen, sitting cross-legged on a lotus-leaf, or ascending to heaven with uplifted arms; or some demon, sufficiently hideous in aspect, and depicted as terrifying out of their senses a group of unbelievers. It must be remembered that these designs are intended for something more than mere ornament; like the horse-shoes formerly affixed to cottage-doors in England, they are talismans to ward off the approach of evil.

The shops of the Chandnee Chowk are abundantly stocked with wares which would enchant a European lady, and artistic products that would rouse the cupidity of a European virtuoso. They literally coruscate with their show of gold and silver embroidery, beads and bangles, sheeny silken stuffs, delicate lace-work, fantastic toys, gorgeous head-dresses, and still more gorgeous marriage-caskets. The jewellers do not make much display, but if you express a desire to purchase they will quickly unfold the most bewildering variety of filagree ornaments in gold and silver, gold studs exquisitely wrought, links and jewelled breast-pins, bracelets, rings, necklaces, and ivory paintings, not less wonderful for complexity of design than brilliancy of colouring. In some of the thoroughfares which branch off in many directions from the Chandnee Chowk, the various pursuits of the people may be studied at the visitor's leisure. Men-milliners, dyers, toy-makers, pipe-makers, and the rest, may be seen, seated in tailor-fashion generally, busy at work in their respective shops. It is remarkable with what success the dyers and calico-printers carry on their avocations in narrow recesses that seem scarcely to afford elbow-room. One end of the tiny cell constitutes the print-shop, the other the dye-work. The process of dyeing is simple: the cloth is dipped in pots of clay or brass containing a supply of the requisite liquids. That of printing is not less devoid of mystery—the patterns being carved on little blocks of wood, and the printing-table being a board supported on the crossed legs of the operator. Yet, rude as is this apparatus, the printed stuffs of India are excellent in design and colouring, though the superior cheapness of British manufactures is rapidly driving them out of the market.

As at Agra men speak of the Fort and the Taj, so at Delhi they speak of the Great Mosque and the Palace. These are the crowning glories and special attractions of the city. Dr. Macleod speaks of them as both unquestionably worthy of the capital of the once great Mohammedan Empire of the East. Mr. Grant Duff, on the other hand, does not consider either equal to the Jasmine Bower or the Pearl Mosque of Agra, though built on a larger scale. Yet the Great Mosque is a pile which commands and deserves admiration. It may lack the simplicity of the Taj, and its oneness of design, but it is infinitely more imposing. If it has less beauty, it exhibits more grandeur.

The rocky eminence on which it stands was scarped and levelled on the summit, so as to supply a great natural platform—an open square of fourteen hundred yards. This quadrangle is enclosed by an immense outer wall of red sandstone arches, at each corner of which is built up a tower, with a marble dome resting on shapely red pillars. The entrances are three in number; the most magnificent facing Mecca-wards, or to the east, and each being approached by a noble flight of stairs. Through the gateways you pass into an open court, surrounded on three sides by airy arched colonnades of red sandstone, interrupted at intervals by seated pavilions. In the centre sparkles a marble fountain for ceremonial ablutions. The fourth side of the square is occupied by the Mosque, with its front towards the east. It measures in length about two hundred and sixty-six feet. A fine effect is produced by its richness and vividness of colour; for while the sandstone is of a deep red, this is relieved by white marble ornament, and verses from the Koran in huge letters of black marble. The three domes on the summit are of pure white marble, fluted with black; while the tall minarets, one hundred and thirty feet high, are variegated with red and white alternately, and enriched with three projecting galleries of marble white as sea-foam. Every little turret, moreover, is crowned with a marble dome resting upon red pillars. To complete the picture thus faintly outlined, we must add the marble roofs and walls seen within a soft subdued light, the cornice extending along the whole building, and divided into compartments two and a half feet broad; and the whole culminating in the gilded pinnacles which crown the whitely-shining domes, and flash like arrows of gold against the clear blue sky.

The cost of this mosque to Shah Jehan is placed at £120,000; equal, probably, to ten times that amount at the present value of money. Like all other mosques—and it is said there are forty in Delhi—it is open at all hours and seasons, and you seldom enter it without finding some worshippers at their devotions. They take off their shoes, lay down their bundles, go

FACADE OF THE JUMA MASJID, DELHI.

through the necessary ablutions at the central fountain, utter their few words of prayer, and then resume their ordinary occupations. It is incumbent upon every faithful Mohammedan to pray five times a day—at dawn, at noon, in the afternoon, at sunset, and at nightfall. Before praying, if he cannot bathe he cleanses his hands, feet, and face; using earth or sand, should not water be obtainable. Then he bows to the ground, laying his forehead in the dust. His prayer is accompanied by numerous changes of posture; and when he is pressed for time, these will occur as often as eight or ten times in a minute. Now with hands extended he stands erect, repeating the ninety-nine attributes of God; next, lying prone upon the earth, he covers his mouth with his hands; then his hands are laid palm to palm; again they are raised heavenward, while his body is bent to earth or curved backwards, but always facing Mecca.

If the visitor ascend one of the tall minarets of which we have spoken, he will obtain a magnificent view of the city and its neighbourhood. Immediately below expands the ample court; on one side, without, is an open space; and beyond that again, about a quarter of a mile off, rise the Titanic sandstone walls of the Mogul's Palace. From this central spot streets radiate to the outskirts of the busy city, while these are defined by the embattled ramparts which the Jumna washes on the east. Green trees and slender minarets lend an air of brightness and fancifulness to the city itself, contrasting with the world of ruins which spreads over the surrounding plain, where you may trace some memorial or other of each successive emperor of the great Pathan dynasty. And away to the north runs the low, long rocky ridge where the British camp was pitched in the Great Mutiny of 1857,—that camp which, for the time, held the fortunes of our Indian Empire within its narrow bounds.

But we must now proceed to

THE PALACE—

a vast citadel, with red sandstone ramparts, occupying almost the entire eastern quarter of the city. Its massive and elaborately-constructed walls, ornamented with raised bands and indented battlements, rise abruptly from a deep moat, which our English engineers have masked to some extent by earthworks.

It is impossible to gaze upon this stronghold of the great Moguls, which at one time ranked among the wonders of the world, and glittered with scenes of the most dazzling Oriental magnificence, without emotion. It recalls to the memory those marvellous pictures which light up the narratives of Bernier and Tavernier; it assists the spectator in realizing the pomps and ceremonies which occupied so largely the great Mohammedan Court. It has been justly remarked that Tavernier, a jeweller by trade, was less likely than another to be dazzled by "barbaric splendour;" and yet his descriptions read as if borrowed from a fairy tale. Crowds of courtiers and soldiers in gorgeous attire; the tumult of palanquins; horses with nodding plumes; elephants with howdahs of ivory and gold; slaves carrying richly-embroidered parasols;—such was the sight which met the eye of the stranger as he approached the gate of the Imperial Palace, the very walls of which were almost concealed beneath the silken folds of the khanats of embroidered fabric and the long state banners. But scarcely had he penetrated into the enclosure when all the joys of fairy-land seemed to throng around him. Marble-paved courts, musical with fountains, and groves of orange and other spreading trees, were surrounded by palaces which shone like structures of polished ivory, and exhibited within their deep arcades the gleam of gold and silver and precious stones.

The Palace measures three thousand feet in length by eighteen hundred feet in breadth, and in its great open court fully ten thousand horsemen can be mustered. At the outbreak of the Mutiny it contained a population of five thousand persons, including three thousand members of the blood royal.

The entrance gateway is almost ponderously massive. Within is a second gate, which admits into the inner court; and here, on one side, rises the Palace proper, consisting of the Great Hall of Audience, two hundred and eight feet long and seventy-six feet broad. It is built wholly of white marble, the roof resting upon colonnades of shapely marble pillars. Here, two centuries and a half ago, an English ambassador was first admitted to the sublime presence of the Mogul. Here once stood the celebrated Peacock Throne, the precious stones of which, glittering with rainbow tints, testified to the unsurpassed grandeur of him who took his seat upon it, to give audience and dispense justice. It disappeared, with many other costly things, when the city was sacked by Nadir Shah in 1739. The Great Hall is empty now.

Most beautiful, says a traveller, is the Private Hall of Audience—all marble, with inlaid precious stones of every hue grouped by cunning artists; most beautiful the Court of the Harem—all marble also, with exquisite balconies, looking down into once beautiful gardens on the banks of the Jumna; most beautiful, too, are those marble halls which once were baths, the perfection of luxury; and not less beautiful that small marble mosque beside them. But all their glory has passed away; all the pomp and circumstance of that absolute and irresponsible dynasty, whose kings were as gods upon the earth! What a commentary on the instability of human pride is afforded by the silent and lonely halls of the Palace of the Moguls! The famous inscription in Persian, "If there be a paradise on earth, it is this," still remains, and seems justified by the pure and graceful beauty of this imperial pavilion.

To obtain an idea of this hall as it was in its former days of splendour, we must refer to the pages of Tavernier. The ceiling, he tells us, was encased in a tissue of gold and silver of admirable workmanship, which he, as a jeweller, valued at the enormous sum of twenty millions of francs. Heavy silken draperies, confined by chains of gold, made a framework to the arcades spanning the circumference of the hall; and finally, in the centre stood the wonder of wonders, that Throne of Peacocks to which we have already alluded. This throne, of massive gold, measured six feet in length and four feet in width, forming a kind of estrade, the back of which, covered with delicate enamelling, spread itself out in the form of a peacock's tail; and a dais in solid gold, bordered with a long, thick fringe of fine pearls, and resting upon twelve golden columns, covered the rear of the throne, the front of which was canopied by two colossal velvet parasols, embroidered with pearls, and their gold handles inlaid with diamonds. This masterpiece of the goldsmith's art was executed by one Austin of Bordeaux, a French jeweller attached to the court of Shah Jehan, and is estimated to have cost one hundred and fifty millions of francs.

The Moti Masjid, or Mosque of Pearls, served the purpose of an oratory or a private chapel; and though perfect in itself, is on too small a scale to compete with the Pearl Mosque of Agra.

PRINCIPAL ENTRANCE OF THE PALACE OF THE MOGULS, DELHI.

THE KOOTUB.

Leaving the modern city, the city of Shah Jehan, we must now conduct the reader through the ruins of earlier Delhis which are scattered over the plain for many miles.

We pass out of the historical Kashmir Gate, and make our way to a rising ground about a mile to the right, where among heaps of granite glisten the little white tombstones and crosses which mark the resting-places of gallant English soldiers, slain during the famous siege. Thence the road traverses a dreary region; "mausoleums and temples, mosques, palaces, and columns in every stage of decay, from still handsome marble halls down to blackened heaps of stones, lay scattered over ten miles of a soil chiefly composed of rock and sand,—except where, in an occasional green spot, some miserable crop feebly essayed to struggle into the light, and deepened, if that were possible, the melancholy aspect of the scene."

Among the objects which here attract the traveller's attention is the Tomb of Humayoon. It was this brilliant warrior who, issuing from Persia in 1554, spread his conquest far over India, and founded the mighty dynasty which attained its climax of glory under Aurungzebe and Shah Jehan. His mausoleum is a stately pile of rose-coloured sandstone and white marble, crowned by a dome of finest proportions, and rising in the middle of a vast terrace, which is itself in the centre of a flowery garden, surrounded by graceful red sandstone kiosks.

Not far distant is the Kala Masjid, or Black Mosque, an excellent specimen of Afghan architecture. This long, narrow edifice is surmounted by three massive but shapely domes, and presents a noble façade perforated by five pointed arches of different heights. The body of the building, of red sandstone, is relieved by bands and roses of delicately-sculptured white marble; but the interior is almost without ornament.

Near this mosque stands a handsome stone pavilion, formerly used as a library by the emperors of the Pathan dynasty. Here perished Humayoon,—who, after a long exile, had regained the patrimonial throne,—by falling from the top of a ladder, on which he had mounted to reach a book from the upper shelves.

Humayoon's mausoleum constitutes the centre of a great cemetery, which extends all over the plain, from the Jumna to the western hills. Tombs of every description are found here in labyrinthine confusion, from the modest slab to the lofty edifice, dome-crowned, and shining with curiously-made bricks enamelled in the brightest and softest tints. The principal group gathers round the little village of Arab-ka-serai, and includes a fine mausoleum of the Pathan period (the fifteenth century) covered with graceful arabesques.

Proceeding eastward, we reach at last the mausoleum of Suftur Jung, which faces the road leading from Delhi to the Kootub. Though comparatively modern, it is one of the noblest monuments of Indian architecture; and worthily closes the unequalled series of memorials which here indicate all the transitions and developments of Indian art from the third century before our era. The white marble dome, remarkable for its purity of design, raises its golden pinnacle a hundred feet above the ground, and over-canopies the glorious hall which enshrines the state cenotaph of Suftur Jung. In a crypt beneath lie the ashes of this once powerful statesman, under a simple mound of earth; for, as the inscription at the head reminds us, "however great and pompous man may be in the presence of his fellow-men, he is little and low in the presence of God;"—a sentiment which the Moguls and their ministers would have done well to remember, and act upon, in their lifetime.

But we must now hasten to inspect the Kootub, a stupendous minaret, two hundred and forty feet in height, which towers in solitary grandeur above the plain. It is built up of

TOWER OF KOOTUB, IN THE PLAIN OF DELHI.

dark red sandstone, profusely carved, and covered with inscriptions in gigantic Kufic or old Arabic letters. The effect produced by this architectural colossus is very great, and far surpasses the impression which is derived from gazing on the loftiest cathedral towers or monuments of Europe. This effect is due not so much to its great height as to its absolute isolation and the simplicity of its outlines; while it is assisted by the skill of the architect, who has given the tower the form of an elongated cone, and divided it into four stories, diminishing in height as they ascend from the ground. The diameter of the base is about forty-six feet; of the summit-platform, ten feet. The ornamentation is profuse, very striking, and yet simple. Each story, alternately enriched with perpendicular, round, or angular flutings, is surrounded by a broad belt of flowers and arabesques, and supports a massive balcony, adorned with fine sculptures, which stand out in bold relief from the tower.

When the Moslem commander, Kootub-ood-deen-Eibeg, captured the capital of the Rajput emperor, Pirthi-Râj, he resolved to raise in the very centre of the conquered city, as a memorial of his success, a column which should symbolize the triumph of Islam over Brahmanism. The foundation was laid in the year 1200, but the undertaking was not completed until twenty years later, during the reign of his successor. Two of the upper stories were shattered by lightning in 1340, and reconstructed in 1368 by Feroze III. These are cased with marble.

Round this lofty tower cluster hundreds of Hindu pillars, each different in design; and at a short distance beyond rises one great domed building, remarkable for the beauty of its carving, which Akbar erected as a college where his wise men might assemble for purposes of debate and counsel. Being open on all sides, it serves as a great gateway, as a kind of portal to the colossal minaret and the carved Hindu pillars. Its four sides are alike; deep red sandstone inlaid with white marble, and from base to summit chiselled with rich tracery in bold yet delicate outlines. The entrance on either side is by a flight of steps beneath a tall archway, ornamented with a delicately-cut dog-tooth pattern, very like that of the Norman sculptors. The eye passes from the intensely warm depth of "maroon and claret-coloured shadow" of the interior to the intense sapphire blue of the sky seen through the opposite arch. Over every inch of the interior is prodigally scattered the same abundance of carving in endless variety of geometrical patterns, standing out in bold relief, and characterized by the greatest refinement of execution.

Returning to the ruins of the Kootub Mosque—the first erected in India—we observe in the centre of the outer court an iron column, which is certainly one of the wonders of the place. Yet it is nothing more than a smooth and solid iron cylinder, twenty-two feet in height. But then it is sunk in the earth to a corresponding depth, so that its total length is forty-four feet. And if it be remembered that this huge iron shaft was moulded in the fourth century, when the manufacture of iron was imperfectly understood, or, at least, the improved processes on which science now prides itself were unknown, we think the reader will be of opinion that it is as remarkable an achievement of human skill as even the Kootub Minar.

It bears a short inscription, purporting that it was erected by King Chandra, worshipper of Vishnu, in the year 307, to commemorate his victory over the Bâlhikas. But the popular legend will have it, that one Anung Pâl, having conquered all Northern India, was advised by a learned Brahman whom he favoured to order the manufacture of a long iron nail, which he might bury deep in the earth, so as to pierce the head of the serpent Sêshnaga, and perpetuate his dynasty for ever. The world, be it said, rested on the head of the said serpent. The nail was duly cast, and sunk into the earth at a spot indicated by the Brahman. But in the course of years, the wise counsellor having left the king's court, Anung Pâl began to have his doubts of the efficacy of the plan which he had suggested, and caused the nail to be drawn up. What was his alarm, what the terror of his people, to find its extremity tinged with blood! With all haste they replaced the nail; but, of course, the serpent had had the wit to remove to another spot, and further efforts to clench the nail proved useless. "O rajah!" exclaimed the Brahman, who returned at this critical conjuncture, "as nothing in the world could give this column the stability it has lost through thy impious curiosity, so in like manner can nothing avert from thy dynasty its approaching ruin!" And, not long afterwards, the empire of the Touars was overthrown by the conquering Chohans.

Close beside the mosque stands the mausoleum of the Emperor Altamsh, the most ancient monument of the kind erected by the Mohammedans in India. It dates from 1235. The domed roof has disappeared, but enough remains of the marble walls to delight the spectator with the exquisite beauty of their carving.

Before returning to modern Delhi, we shall visit two of the ruined cities which lie within the circuit of its ample plain.

On the bank of the Jumna is situated Toghlukabad, the capital of Shah Toghluk; who, like most of the Indian emperors, seems to have been smitten with a mania for building, and removed his court and people hither. Its walls, reared on a ridge of rock, enclose a kind of table-land or platform about five miles in circumference. Their solidity is astonishing; they are built up of blocks of bluish granite, and strengthened by huge round towers rising up from the very base of the hill.

These walls, like all the structures they were designed to defend, exhibit a Titanic gloom and grandeur, characteristic of an emperor whom history immortalizes as at once a stern and melancholy tyrant, and a man of unusual culture and refinement.

The mausoleum enshrines the cenotaphs of Toghluk, his wife, and his successor Mohammed. The latter seems to have been one of the cruellest tyrants who ever sat on the throne of Delhi. He was succeeded by his nephew, Feroze, who, lamenting his deeds of violence, hastened to seek out all whom he had plundered or ill-treated; and having amply compensated them for their sufferings, made each of them sign a document expressing his forgiveness of their late oppressor.

Through masses of shapeless ruins and fragments of masonry the visitor may next betake himself to the solid granite gateway, relieved by courses of red sandstone, which indicates the boundary of the city erected in 1415 by the Emperor Daulat Khân Lodi, close to the site of the ruined and desolated Ferozebad. In its turn this capital vanished, with all its wealth and grandeur; but the citadel is still extant, crowning a little eminence which formerly marked the centre of the city. It is now known as Purana Kila, or the Old Fort. Within the vast enceinte of this fortalice are several ancient edifices—such as the Kala Masjid, or Black Mosque, to which we have already adverted. We have now completed the circuit of the plain, and returned to the point from which we originally started.

A SAUNTER THROUGH DELHI.

We have briefly alluded to some of the aspects of modern Delhi; but it will probably amuse and edify the reader if we dwell upon them at greater length, and ask him to accompany us in a saunter through the city. We shall avail ourselves, in our wanderings, of the information afforded by a recent traveller.

Let us begin, then, with a visit to the great thoroughfare already spoken of, the Chandnee Chowk, or Regent Street of Delhi.

It traverses the city in a tolerably straight line from the gate of the Imperial Palace to the

Lahore Gate, and is inhabited by the principal tradesmen. The shops, square cells or recesses of almost uniform size, are stored with products rich and rare: brilliant lacquer-work from Sind, beautifully wrought arms from the Punjab, soft silken shawls from Kashmir, airy gauzes from Berhampur, and wondrously carved caskets from Shekawattee. The bankers come next, in a long row, as in our own dreary Lombard Street; the shoemakers, their stalls covered with elegant Turkish slippers and silk-embroidered prow-shaped shoes; the hatters, with turbans suitable for every caste, and light caps for decent citizens, and golden toques for the Mirzas of the Imperial family; goldsmiths, who exhibit jewelled and metallic work surpassing in delicacy anything manufactured in Paris or Vienna; and pastrycooks and sweetmeat-vendors, all busily preparing their dainties under the watchful eyes of their patrons.

Though shorn of much of its ancient grandeur, Delhi remains the capital and chief city of native India, and excels all other cities in importance—except, perhaps, Lahore. It is the principal money-mart in Southern Asia; and its bankers spread their dealings over Arabia, Afghanistan, Turkestan, and Tibet. Hence the crowds which circulate through the streets of Delhi at all hours of the day are of a motley character. The Hindu and the Mussulman jostle the Afghan and the Balûch; and representatives of all the races inhabiting the valleys of the Punjab and the lower slopes of the Himalaya enliven the scene by the variety and picturesqueness of their costume.

In the Chandnee Chowk may be seen the Kôtwali, or native town-hall, in front of which were executed the rebel Sepoys, after our soldiers had recovered the city in 1857.

Passing the Kôtwali, we enter another broad airy street, which cuts the Chandnee Chowk at right angles, and runs on to the Kashmir Gate. This gate remains in the condition to which it was reduced during the great siege; the ruined casemates and shot-splintered stones are eloquent though mute memorials of that remarkable episode. The walls surrounding the city date from the reign of Shah Jehan; they are constructed of granite, occupy a circuit of seven miles, and are pierced with twelve gates.

A road leads from the Kashmir Gate to the English civil and military cantonments, situated about a mile and a half to the north.

Returning to the city, we visit the narrow, crooked, and crowded bazaars which cluster round the Chandnee Chowk; but the only object of interest that attracts our attention is the Kala Masjid, at a short distance from the Turcoman Gate. It should be noted that this is the only edifice of earlier date than the reign of Shah Jehan which at the present day is found within the walls of the city.

HISTORICAL SKETCH OF DELHI.

There are few cities in the world of higher antiquity, or of more romantic and stirring associations, than Delhi. It seems to gather up in itself all the glories and splendour of that land of far Cathay, the echoes of which reached even to Western Christendom, drew the daring intellect of Columbus across the ocean, and impelled Vasco de Gama to face the wild waters of the Cape of Storms; echoes which long lingered in the legends and poetry of Europe. Not Rome, not Athens, not even Jerusalem can date back its history to so remote a period; but then neither Rome, nor Athens, nor Jerusalem has undergone so many surprising vicissitudes. And what, perhaps, best deserves attention, is the fact that it was not founded by the offspring of the soil, but by aliens and invaders. It was never held by a native dynasty, but was possessed and disputed by the successive conquerors whom the riches of India had attracted to its capital; and thus originated, perhaps, the fanciful belief that it is the Indian palladium, and that the destinies of India are indissolubly mingled with those of Delhi. The English supremacy was never fully acknowledged until our standard waved triumphant from its towers.

According to the earliest Indian traditions, three cities—Madhanti, Hastinapoora, and Indraprastha—succeeded each other on the site now occupied by modern Delhi. The last of these, Indraprastha, the name of which is still bestowed upon their sacred capital by orthodox Hindus, was founded, according to their imaginative chronology, 3101 years B.C. It is more certain that in the great epic of the Mahâbhârata occurs the name of the hero Yudishthira as reigning over Indraprastha in the fifteenth century before our era.

Centuries elapse, and in 57 B.C. we read of Delhi as founded on the venerable ruins of Indraprastha by King Dilvu. This was abandoned on the fall of the dynasty connected with its splendour; but another city arose in 736 at the bidding of Anung Pâl, and became the capital of the Touar empire. His successors deserted Delhi for Canouj. But it was restored in 1060 by Anung Pâl II.; and successively destroyed and rebuilt by Vijala Dêva in 1152, and the Sultan Kootub in 1193.

After becoming the capital of the great Mohammedan Empire in India, Delhi migrated, in obedience to the fancy of different dynasties, to new sites, but always kept within the bounds of the plain washed by the Jumna. As we have seen, these numerous migrations are commemorated by monuments of the greatest interest as well as by piles of shapeless ruins. Modern Delhi, however, founded by Shah Jehan in 1631, has hitherto been characterized by greater stability.

So far as the English reader is concerned, the historical interest of Delhi centres in its connection with the Great Mutiny.

On the 16th of May 1857 the following telegram was flashed from Delhi to the Governor-General at Calcutta, and to every British cantonment in India:—"The Sepoys have come in from Meerut, and are burning everything! Mr. Todd is dead, and, we hear, several Europeans. We must shut up!" The brave man who sent this opportune warning was immediately cut down, with his hand on the signalling apparatus. "The Sepoys have come in from Meerut!" Yes; but they should never have been allowed to come in. Had those in command been gifted with ordinary resolution or presence of mind, the European troops at Meerut could easily have prevented the escape of the mutineers, who had broken out before their leaders were ready, or at least could have intercepted their march upon Delhi. As it was, there can be no doubt that they rode away from Meerut in the belief that the avenging swords of the British were close behind them. They thought themselves hopelessly lost, and trembled every moment lest they should hear the noise of the pursuing dragoons. But hour after hour passed, and as there was no sound of pursuit, their spirits revived; and soon the waters of the Jumna sparkled before them in the morning sun, and the great "City of Refuge" rose upon their view. Under the king's palace they clamoured for admittance. Their arrival, however, was earlier than the king had expected, and, fearing the outbreak would be speedily quelled, he gave them no encouragement. The mutineers rode on: they found the Calcutta Gate closed; but, making their way along the river-bank, they reached the Raj Ghat Gate, which the Mohammedans of the Tauba Bazaar threw open to them, and poured into the city.

"Then," says Kaye, "there ensued a scene of confusion which it is difficult to describe. Cutting down every European they could find, and setting fire to their houses, they doubled back towards the Calcutta Gate, where they learned that Commissioner Fraser, Douglas of the Palace Guard, and other leading Englishmen, would be found. As they rode on, with the cry of "Deen! deen!" they were followed by an excited Mohammedan rabble. The citizens closed their shops in amazement and terror, and from one end of Delhi to the other, as the news ran along the streets, there was sore bewilderment and perplexity, and everybody looked for the coming of the pursuing Englishmen, and feared that they would inflict a terrible retribution upon the city that had harboured the guilty fugitives. But no English regiments were coming to the rescue. And these maddened native troopers, with such vile followers as they could gather up in the streets of Delhi, were now masters of the city. They knew that throughout all the Sepoy regiments in cantonments there was not a man who would pull a trigger, or draw a sword, or light a port-fire in defence of his English officer. Without a fear, therefore, they rushed on, scenting the English blood, eager for the larger game, and ever proclaiming as they went glory to the Padishah and death to the Feringhees."

Before sunset, all Europeans, with the exception of those who had stealthily made their escape along the city ditch, and the ladies and children who had sought refuge in the Flagstaff Tower, were massacred; and not only the Europeans, but all the Christian natives,—all known to be in any way connected with the English. The very walls of the palace were stained with blood. Some who had found a temporary concealment were discovered on the following day, dragged from their hiding-places, and slain. The Sepoys in the cantonments joined the mutineers, and cut down their officers with relentless ferocity. Happily, under shelter of the night the fugitives in the Round Tower effected their escape; and then, by the evening of the 16th of May, every vestige of English power had passed away from Delhi.

The Anglo-Indian Government, as soon as it grasped the extent of the peril, and learned that the mutiny was spreading in every direction, resolved at once upon the recapture of Delhi. Lord Canning, the governor-general, immediately recognized it as his first duty to wrest the imperial city, the palladium of empire, from the hands of the insurgents. He knew that its fall had invested with national importance a movement which might otherwise have been treated as a local outbreak; had, in a word, converted a mutiny into a revolution. To recover Delhi, therefore, was to restore the British supremacy.

Troops were hurried up from every point that could be spared; and as early as the 5th of June, an advanced guard, under Sir Henry Barnard, despatched from Umballa, was within ten miles of Delhi. It was soon joined by another small detachment, under Brigadier Wilson; and on the 8th the battle of Budlee-ka-Serai was won, and the English bayonets flashed from the summit of the rocky ridge that overlooks the Delhi plain.

Sir John (afterwards Lord) Lawrence, who then governed in the Punjab, and was as inexhaustible in resource as he was prompt in action, forwarded to the camp before Delhi every man that could be spared; and, what was more, sent thither some of his ablest and most trusted lieutenants,—a Nicholson, a Taylor, a Baird Smith, and a Neville Chamberlain. Nicholson, a born soldier, a knight without fear and without reproach, after winning the victory of Nujuffghur, joined the besieging army in August, and reinforced it with his enthusiasm and military genius.

In September the siege-train arrived, and by the seventh of that month the heavy guns opened fire. Then, indeed, the siege really *began:* day by day the batteries were pushed nearer; a ceaseless storm of shot and shell descended on the doomed city; and on the 14th it was resolved to carry Delhi by assault.

For this purpose several columns were told off, each being directed against a different point of attack. Nicholson's was ordered to storm the breach near the Kashmir Bastion; Brigadier Jones's, the Water Bastion; Colonel Campbell's, the Kashmir Gate; and Major Reid's, the Lahore Gate; while a fifth column, under Brigadier Longfield, was held in reserve.

Nicholson's column advanced in splendid style, and, in spite of a fierce fire, and showers of stones and bricks from the crumbling walls, gained the ramparts, carried the breach near the Kashmir Bastion, and took up their position at the Main Guard. The second column in like manner went forward at a rush, and planted their flag on the Cabul Gate. By this time Nicholson's eager spirit was chafing at the non-arrival of the fourth column; and as he was annoyed by the ceaseless musketry from the Lahore Gate, he determined to take it with such volunteers as he could get together. The enterprise was hazardous; for the way from the Cabul to the Lahore Gate lay through a narrow lane swept by artillery, and commanded by houses which the enemy had occupied with riflemen. As Sir John Kaye remarks, nothing so disheartens, or at least discourages, the British soldier, as the thought of street-fighting. The rush of cavalry he will withstand undismayed. With steadfast brow he will march straight up to the blazing batteries of the enemy, or enter the breaches in their walls as if engaged in a schoolboys' game. But street-fighting he does not understand. What masked batteries may have been erected, or what batteries suddenly thrown up, he does not know; and every house seems to him full of hostile rifles, every window an embrasure at which may sit concealed a skilful marksman. It was so in this daring march through the narrow streets of Delhi. The men fell fast, and their officers were stricken down by the unseen foe. There was a pause of indecision, of doubt. The British soldier was in a trap—and he likes fair fighting. Nicholson, who had the keen eye of a great commander, saw it all. He drew himself up at once to his full height, waved his sword above his head, and called on his men to follow him. "To some, at least, of the defenders of Delhi, that face and figure must have been familiar. Others saw a man of commanding presence, whose position at the head of the column, and whose gestures of command, indicated that he was a great chief. His lofty stature rendered him so conspicuous, that, if he had been a private soldier, some rifleman at a window or on a house-top would have taken deadly aim at him, and he would have sent one more hated Feringhee to his account. But it was not a single life that he took; it was the life of a whole army."

Nicholson was shot through the body. That it was a mortal wound, he knew at once; but he desired to remain on the scene of action until Delhi was once more in British hands. This, however, could not be, and he was carefully and tenderly removed, with the hearts of his men going out after him, to the hospital on the ridge. There this peerless soldier and great general died on the 23rd of September, like "a noble oak riven asunder by a thunderbolt."

We need not follow the further fortunes of the assault. Delhi was taken; not without severe loss,—for, of Europeans, eight officers were killed, and one hundred and sixty-two rank and file; and of the loyal native troops, one hundred and three were killed. Delhi was taken;

but the conquering force was so small that its commander doubted whether he could retain his conquest. His officers convinced him that retreat was impossible; that the only safety lay in going forward. On the 17th the great magazine fell into British hands; and it was seen after a while that the natives were thoroughly cowed, and, notwithstanding their numbers, had laid aside all thought of resistance. During the night of the 18th the Lahore Bastion was captured; and on the 20th the Lahore Gate. Then arose the cry, "To the Palace—the Palace!" The British warriors felt that their victory would be incomplete until the Union Jack floated from the pinnacles of the Home of the Moguls. A rush was made, and in a few minutes the Palace was taken, its inmates being cut down where they stood. The general at once established there his headquarters, and Delhi was won.

But where were the Royal Family of Delhi? It fell to the lot of Hodson of Hodson's Horse, a partizan leader of the most brilliant courage, but a man in whom, unfortunately, the daring of the tiger was unsubdued by any feelings of human compassion, to crown the British triumph by the capture of the descendants of Timour. Through the treachery of Mirza Elahee Buksh, he ascertained that they were secreted in Humayoon's Tomb, but that they were contemplating an escape. From the general he obtained reluctant permission to take a party of his own men, and bring in, without insult or injury, the last of the Mogul emperors. Flushed with pride, he rode off at the head of fifty of his troopers, and speedily found his way to the asylum of the fallen monarch.

It was necessary to act with wariness. So Hodson concealed his men in some ruined buildings near the gateway of the Tomb, and sent on his emissaries to demand the surrender of the royal fugitives. Two weary hours of suspense passed away before they brought back the answer that the king would surrender to Major Hodson, if he personally assured him that his life would be spared. Hodson gave the required promise, and received the royal sword; observing that if any attempt at rescue were made, he would shoot his prisoner like a dog. Along five miles of road, and through a silent, wondering, but sullen crowd, he and his captive then took their way; and entering the city, passed up the Chandnee Chowk Street, where Hodson was relieved of his dangerous charge by the civil authorities.

Hodson's work was not yet done. Having heard that some of the king's sons and near relatives were hiding in Humayoon's Tomb, he once more galloped thither, and sternly summoned them to come forth. They prayed for a guarantee that their lives would be spared; but Hodson would make no promise. So at length, after a wearisome delay, the princes appeared in covered bullock-carts, made one last despairing and useless appeal to Hodson's compassion, and moved towards Delhi with a guard of troopers on either side.

Then Hodson, with his few remaining horsemen, galloped into the precincts of the Tomb, and called upon the Mohammedans assembled there, numbering at least six thousand, to throw down their arms. With a single rush they might have swept clean over him and his little company; but there was something in the stern, calm, masterful aspect of the "white man" which struck them with a great fear, and almost without a murmur they submitted. Their arms, horses, and carriages were placed in the centre of the square, and their discomfiture was complete.

In the later history of Delhi it will be sufficient for us to glance at a single event—the visit of the Prince of Wales. He arrived in the city early on the morning of Tuesday, January

11th, 1876. Passing through streets lined with soldiers and crowded with natives, he saw, as he rode along, his banner floating from the Palace of the Moguls, and by way of the Lahore Gate proceeded to the royal camp, which had been pitched about a mile and a half beyond.

"The road to the camp," says an English correspondent, "was enveloped in clouds of sand and dust, the accumulation of the dry season loosed and stirred up by the traffic and the wind, and so blinding that we fancied that, even if we did reach the saluting-point, we should never be able to see the movements. The roadways, moreover, were dreadfully uneven, notwithstanding a covering of rice straw which had been laid down in the deeper furrows, and horses were plunging madly and traces were being snapped in every direction. But if the route had its perils, it was most diversified, and the sights we witnessed were so wonderful that recollections of the Derby Day sank into insignificance beside them. More than eighty elephants, each having bells and trappings, and howdahs crowded with English children, passed us, making the ground quake and horses bolt as they pounded rapidly along. Then there were troops of tiny ponies, struggling on with hundreds of the uncomfortable *garries* or carriages of the country behind them, looking like a long line of tea-caddies on wheels. Here and there springless bamboo gigs dashed by, across dykes and over banks and hillocks, the drivers heedless of danger; but the strangest objects of all, in the chaos of moving animals and vehicles, were immense chariots pulled by teams of camels."

The prince arrived on the ground escorted by a squadron of the 10th Hussars, and accompanied by the then commander-in-chief, Lord Napier of Magdala. The Maharajah Scindia was also in attendance, dressed in a coat of black velvet embroidered thickly with gold, and mounted on a spirited Arab. The troops marched past in four divisions, commanding general admiration by their fine appearance and the accuracy of their movements. Afterwards they were put through various manœuvres; and the prince having presented new colours to the 11th Bengal Infantry, the review terminated.

In the evening Lord Napier of Magdala and the officers of the Delhi garrison gave a ball—such is the strange irony of Fate!—in the Palace of the Moguls; and the Prince of Wales danced in the great hall in which the last King of Delhi had been tried by a tribunal of English officers.

On the following morning began a series of elaborate military manœuvres: the army being divided into two nearly equal bodies, one of which, under Major-Generals Hardinge and Stewart, assumed the offensive, and represented an enemy marching upon the capital; while the other, under Sir Charles Reid and Major-General Macdonell, undertook its defence. The operations extended over three days.

On Monday the 17th the European and native cavalry paraded before the prince. Then followed a series of sports, the chief of which were designed to test the skill of certain regiments in sword-exercises and tent-pegging.

Afterwards the prince visited the Tomb of Humayoon and the stately column of the Kootub Minar. He also inspected every place of interest associated with the events of the Great Mutiny, including the breach in the walls near the Kashmir Gate through which the heroic Nicholson led his soldiers.*

* Lord Lytton, as Viceroy of India, held a grand durbar at Delhi on January 1, 1877, to celebrate the Queen's assumption of the title of Empress of India. The festivities lasted a week. Seventy native princes attended; and a review of 15,000 of our choicest troops took place.

CHAPTER IX.

FROM DELHI TO PESHAWAR.

1. AT MEERUT—DESCRIPTION OF THE TOWN—"THE MONKEY TANK"—A MOSLEM TOMB.—2. UMBALLA—THE ENGLISH CANTONMENT.—3. SIMLA: A MOUNTAIN SANITARIUM—TRAVELLING BY POST GARRY—ARRIVAL AT KALKA—VIEW OF THE HIMALAYA—WHAT IS A DOOLIE?—A DAK BUNGALOW—A FOREST OF RHODODENDRONS—THE ROAD FROM KALKA TO SIMLA.—4. IN AND ABOUT SIMLA—THE NATIVE TOWN—BRITISH SIMLA—WINTER AT SIMLA—THE MALL—SOMETHING ABOUT MONKEYS—A MISADVENTURE—THE HIMALAYAN FOREST—SOME LOFTY TREES.—5. RETURN TO UMBALLA, AND VISIT TO DEHRA—MUSSOORIE—LANDOOR—THE RED HILL—PLANTATIONS OF THE DEHRA TEA COMPANY.—6. AT AMRITSAR—ABOUT THE SIKHS.—7. LAHORE—DESCRIPTIVE SKETCH—THE FORT—THE GREAT MOSQUE—TOMB OF RUNJEET SINGH—MOSQUE OF WUZIR ALI—TOMB AND GARDEN OF JEHANGIR—THE MONTGOMERY HALL—MEANMEER.—8. TO JUMMOO—WAZIRABAD—SEALKOTE—THE BOUNDARY OF OUR INDIAN EMPIRE—JUMMOO—THE GRAND TRUNK ROAD—THE CABUL RIVER—NOWSHERA—PESHAWAR.

MEERUT.

THE traveller's first station after leaving Delhi for Peshawar is Meerut, a large and important town, situated in the centre of the barren plain of the Upper Doâb, and unhappily famous in Indian history as the scene of the outbreak of the Great Mutiny. It has no monuments or palaces to attract the eye; and is, in truth, nothing more nor less than a strong military centre. It was originally selected as an advantageous post for the encampment of a European force which might overawe Delhi, only forty miles distant; for, in accordance with treaty arrangements, no British troops could be quartered in the imperial city itself, or in its immediate neighbourhood. There are four principal quarters, in which the infantry, native cavalry, hussars, and artillery are respectively stationed; and as these are plentifully studded with bungalows, each in its own bit of garden, with white or green verandahs and painted thatch roof, the general effect is not displeasing. In front spreads a broad open common, the Maidân, which is used as an exercise-ground, and as the arena for the display of the pomp and circumstance of grand reviews. The town possesses also a very large Anglican church; close beside which, extending over five acres, is the English cemetery, where sleep the sons of England, slain mostly by the terrible climate, a greater foe to our power than the jealousy of race or religion. In one corner, we are told, a line of several hundred tombs, lying in file three deep, marks the graves of the Cameronians, decimated by fever. Another row, a vast number of the Buffs who died of cholera. The men of each regiment are interred together; the infantry in one body, the cavalry in another, the artillery beyond. Civilians keep aloof in death, it is said, as in life. Many are the little ones who repose in the children's quarter. "Here, in one tomb, sleep two hot-headed boys, who fought a duel to decide a dancing question, and both fell mortally wounded. Beyond lies the once beautiful cause of their quarrel, she having fevered and died of grief."

The "objects of interest" in and around Meerut are easily summed up. A large artificial basin is known as "The Monkey Tank," from the number of sacred apes and monkeys which resort to the adjacent temples for their food. The natives, more poetically than truthfully, entitle it Sooruj Koond, "The Mirror of the Sun;" and it is held in reverence by both Mohammedan and Hindu.

Then there is a splendid Moslem tomb, which is a kind of family mausoleum, consisting of several white marble tombs supported on an elevated platform of red sandstone. Each is canopied by a dome, brightly inlaid with green and blue encaustic tiles, and resting on arches and pillars of red sandstone. And at Sirdhana is the spacious Roman Cathedral erected by the celebrated Begum Sombre, who began her career as a nautch-girl, and ended it as an independent sovereign.

UMBALLA.

By the Sind, Lahore, and Punjab Railway, passing Mozuffernugger and Saharunpur, the traveller proceeds to Umballa.

Saharunpur is celebrated for its gardens, which supply all India with seeds and plants. Here may be seen examples of the old Persian Well, in which the water is drawn from a great depth by an endless chain of red earthen jars, fastened between two ropes, and passing over a clumsy wheel; the said wheel being in connection with a driving-wheel, which is kept in motion by bullocks.

The country on the whole is fertile, and good crops are obtained through constant irrigation. Beyond the broad open plain rises a considerable range of hills; these are the low spurs of the Himalaya, and the snow-clad peaks of that mighty mountain-mass are just visible through a screen of fleecy clouds.

The English cantonment is a city of villas, each standing embowered among orange-trees, and pomegranate-shrubs, and tall bauhinias, with their clusters of large white blossoms. It has a handsome and spacious church, military hospitals, and the usual official buildings.

SIMLA: A MOUNTAIN SANITARIUM.

Abandoning the comforts of railway-travelling, the stranger who desires to visit Simla, the great Indian sanitarium, entrusts himself to the conveyance known as the post garry. The garry is simply a long box upon wheels, hung high, so as to keep it out of the water when it is necessary to ford a stream. On each side a sliding door serves instead of a window; there is no glass, and consequently no protection against the clouds of dust which are constantly pouring in. Level with the door is a long cushion, on which the traveller reclines full length, or else squats like a Hindu, or sits cross-legged like a Mohammedan. In a well beneath the carriage is stowed away his baggage; and he arranges his dressing materials, food, books, and other *impedimenta*, on the shelves or in the pockets which are provided plentifully inside.

The garry, it will be seen, is not so bad in itself, though it has not all the luxuries of a Pullman car; but it is rendered uncomfortable by the wretchedness of the animals attached to it. "At each stage," writes one who has suffered, "they seem to grow worse and worse, so that to start them on a fresh run is work for a dozen men, and never done under half an hour. On a tolerably good road you are only allowed one horse; should a second be necessary, he is harnessed outside the shafts as an outrigger, and simply runs alongside. At every halt you are sure of some trouble before you are again under way; constantly the poor beasts that await you are galled and exhausted by their last run. Should they chance to be fresh, they are brought out biting, screaming, plunging, kicking, rearing; held by main force of a dozen coolies and syces. Once harnessed, nothing will induce them to move. Vainly all their attendants seize the wheels, and turn them so as to force on the garry. The stubborn brutes either turn right round or throw themselves down. A rope is now tied to their fore-legs, another to their heads, the wheels are turned by strong arms, and thus they are dragged along for perhaps a mile, accompanied by an ant-like swarm of all but naked coolies, screaming, howling, yelling, shoving, beating; alternately pouring forth maledictions and persuasions, terms of endearment and of opprobrium, with amazing volubility."

In course of time, however, the traveller reaches Kalka, a beautiful village at the foot of the Himalaya, and in the midst of a profusion of flowering shrubs, plantains, and date-palms. The view of the mountains from this point is not what the traveller has pictured in his imagination. They are of comparatively moderate elevation, with red sandstone cliffs, projecting their thickly wooded spurs into a country thickly covered with tropical vegetation. But still, in the far distance, a noble line of peaks, with their huge glaciers illuminated by the sun, shows that as yet we have gained but the lowest terrace of that gigantic accumulation of mountains, which raises its snow-laden crests from 20,000 to 29,000 feet above the level of the sea.

From Kalka to Simla the distance is about fifty-six miles, and it is generally accomplished in four days. No wheeled vehicle is used; but the traveller has the choice of either a *jampan,* a *doolie,* or a *dandie* (unless he prefer to ride). A jampan is a wooden arm-chair, slung between double shafts, and sheltered by a light roof of oil-skin. The coolies behind support the poles on their shoulders, and those in front bear them on their arms, so that the seat maintains a horizontal position. The doolie, also carried by four men, may be described as a long curtained box, with a narrow bed inside. It is slung so low that its inmate gets all the dust from the road, while he sees but little of the scenery. Of the dandie there are two varieties: in the one you sit sideways, on a bit of carpet slung on a bamboo; in the other you are seated just as in a chair, and look straight before you.

At night you halt at a dâk bungalow, or Government post-house, where, on payment of one rupee, you may remain for four-and-twenty hours, at the expiry of which you are required to "move on." The larger bungalows are arranged for six or eight sets of travellers; a room being provided for each, containing a table, two or three chairs, and a *charpoy,* or bedstead. The bungalow has a regular staff of Government servants; and the *khansaman,* or head-man, will supply you with provisions, being chiefly chickens and chupatties (or scones).

The road from Kalka winds upwards through a forest of cactuses and wild barberries, and then enters upon a flowery tract, where the white clematis blooms in all its glory, and stars its leafy tangles with snowy blossoms each about three inches in diameter. Near Simla it passes through a complete forest of rhododendrons,—rhododendron *trees,* all ablaze with gorgeous flowers, which contrast vividly against deep blue ranges of distant hills and the still blue sky overhead. The road is a difficult and a steep one; but the traveller is borne easily along by the coolies, who are Paharis, or hill-men, and strong, muscular fellows, capable of enduring great fatigue. It must be confessed, however, that strength is not in every case associated with physical perfection. Some are short and thick-set, with features of the Mongol type: the flattened nose, high cheek-bones, and small obliquely-set eyes, and the wide mouth opening above a chin covered with thin irregular patches of beard. Looking upon them, we become conscious that we have approached the borders of India proper, and are near Tibet; Tibet, where, it is true, the Hindu rules, but the inhabitants of which are of the same blood as the people who dwell on the tablelands of Ladakh, and extend into the very heart of China.

RHODODENDRONS OF THE HIMALAYA.
1. *Rhododendron Pendulum.*—2. *Rhododendron Dalhousie.* 3. *Rhododendron Nivaie.*

IN AND ABOUT SIMLA.

The native town of Simla is little more than a circular mass of small wooden houses, gathered around the Anglican church. British Simla is a wide space of hill-side, where, under the forest-trees and on the verdurous slopes, are situated the graceful dwellings and bungalows of the Anglo-Indian officials, who resort thither, for health's sake, when the burning summer has taken possession of the plains. As a summer station and sanitarium, it was first adopted by Lord Amherst in 1827. It is now the "hill-capital" of India, and the recognized summer-quarters of the Indian Government.

The visitor to Simla, travelling thither with his imagination full of visions of the Himalayan peaks, is at first disappointed. He sees around him clusters of hills of comparatively moderate elevation, all clothed with the deodar pine, but presenting no features of grandeur or beauty. But by degrees he learns to distinguish, on the far horizon, at a distance of one hundred miles, a long white narrow line, deeply indented, which stretches across the landscape as if to divide it into two parts. *That* is the Snowy Range; the Himalaya, or "Abode of Snow." In time he is able to recognize each colossal peak, and to gather up an accurate conception of the mighty mass to which they belong; a mountain-mass of fifteen hundred miles in length, and of such tremendous breadth that a journey across it occupies tedious weeks; a mountain-mass bristling with forests, and loaded with colossal glaciers, and raising its principal summits twenty thousand feet higher than Simla, though Simla is 7400 feet above the sea.

After a few days' residence, moreover, the visitor is ready to acknowledge that the summer-capital has attractions of its own. He may not care for the Mall, a broad drive round the hill of Jacko, made by Lord Combermere, which is the great rendezvous of the Anglo-Indian society of Simla; he may care less for the deep valley of Annandale, another favourite rendezvous, which affords excuse for numerous picnic-parties; and the waterfalls will have little charm for any one who has seen those of Wales or the Scottish Highlands. But he will find a pleasure in wandering into the recesses of the ancient forest, where he will come upon some little rough stone temples, rudely carved, and roofed with cedar-wood, and dedicated to one of the hill-men's forest-gods; or will meet with sylvan glades of romantic beauty, overhung by gigantic deodars, trees of from twenty-five to thirty feet in girth, and one hundred and fifty to two hundred feet in

SIMLA.

height. Haply he may light upon specimens of the luminous plants which are found in the neighbourhood of Simla; such as the *jyotismati*, or *Anthisteria ananthera*, and the *Dictamnus Fraxitella*. The light of the latter is due to a volatile oil, which sometimes evaporates in such large quantities that, on igniting it with a match, the plant will be wrapped in a transient flame, without suffering any injury.

The monkeys which people Simla will also amuse and interest the visitor. Both the common brown monkey and the large gray, with a fringe of white hair round his forehead, abound. They sit among the great scarlet flowers of the rhododendrons and stare at the passer-by; they leap from tree to tree, swing from the pendent branches, and take flying bounds across the road; they clamber along the roofs of the houses, and sometimes penetrate into the interior, where they disarrange the domestic economy by their mischievous tricks. Lady Barker amusingly describes the *contretemps* that befell her on the occasion of her first dinner-party at Simla. She desired, of course, to distinguish herself, and had daintily arranged her table with newly-imported china figures and ornamental dishes from Europe, which greatly "set off" the show of sweetmeats, flowers, and fruits. When dressing-time came, she instructed her servants to remain in the room until her return; but the temptation of a quiet smoke proved too much for them, and they stole away, forgetting the open window, and the great tree outside, where certain curious spectators sat deeply interested in the proceedings. Who shall describe the hostess's dismay, when, coming down to receive her guests, and taking a passing glance at the dinner-table to see that all was ready, she found a busy company of monkeys enjoying themselves to their hearts' content, chattering and grinning, their cheeks and arms crammed with the choicest viands, and the table a scene of wreck and desolation, of linen soiled, china and glass broken, and flowers pulled to pieces.

A few hundred feet above the Simla hills the traveller finds himself in the real Himalayan forest, and looks down vistas of dark columnar firs, and over the waves of a sea of foliage, out of which, like island-pinnacles, rise here and there some groups of splendid pines, their tall tapering spires seeming to point, like spectral fingers, to the gleaming snowy heights beyond and above.

The general effect of the forest, says Miss Gordon Cumming, is a dark evergreen; yet occasionally the traveller passes beneath high twining arches of transparent golden green, where the light glints rosily through emerald leaves and shining blossoms, staining the sward with glowing hues, like those that fall from an old cathedral window. From that calm solitude comes the soft, murmurous cooing of the wood-dove; while little gray squirrels frisk among the branches, one moment in the shadow, the next in the warm sunshine.

Of the infinite variety of foliage around, the greater part is nearly akin to that of Great Britain. As in other mountain-regions, the different species grow in distinct belts at different elevations. Thus: on the very high levels, at about 13,000 feet, flourish the common birch, gooseberries, and wild strawberries of delicious flavour. A little lower down grows the moza, or edible pine;* a tree with silvery bark, and with cones full of long-shaped nuts, savoury and succulent, which fall out when the cone is half-baked. At about 9000 feet the stately "trees of God," the deodars, thrive on the hard rocky soil, and bear witness to centuries of storm and

* *Pinus Gerardianus.*

sunshine. On the lower levels these decrease in size. At the same height wild apricot trees, swathed with mistletoe, abound; also mulberry and walnut. At about 8000 feet are found sycamore, rhododendron, oak, yew, holly, horse-chestnut, and various conifers. Three thousand feet lower blooms a tropical vegetation, among which the bright oleander, flowery acacias, large cactuses, and plantains may be recognized.

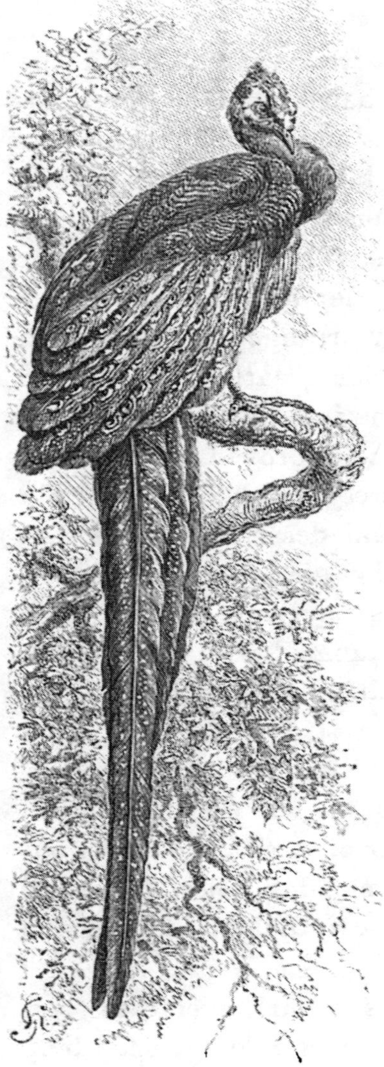

ARGUS PHEASANT.

The *morinda excelsa*, which resembles a spruce fir with very short branches, grows with a perfectly straight trunk to the height of one hundred and twenty feet, and is sometimes twenty feet in girth at the base, is one of the commonest conifers.

Next comes the *rye*, a weeping pine, with branches and needles much longer and more pensile than those of the former. The *cheel* pine is like the Scotch fir. The *kolin* is another common pine, but grows on the lower levels.

Of the Himalayan oak three varieties are found. One of these, the kharso, flourishes at a very considerable elevation, and frequently clothes the eastern side of a hill, while the pine enriches the western.

We can but glance at the animal life. Bears are numerous and dangerous. High in the air float the great eagles and kites; with lammergeiers, and bearded vultures whose wings measure ten feet from tip to tip, and keen-eyed falcons which dart through the clouds like an arrow.

Pheasants, of course, abound; among them the beautiful argus or horned pheasant; the kallidge or black pheasant; the cheer or snow pheasant; and the minaul. The last named is of resplendent plumage; "a dazzling mass of iridescent metallic green, blue, bronze. gold, purple, and crimson, changing in every light, and glossy as satin, with a beautiful crest of drooping feathers." There are also several varieties of snipe, partridges, and woodcock.*

DEHRA.

But we must return to Umballa, in order to prosecute our explorations in a different direction.

Between the Siwalik range and the outer Himalaya lies the district of Dehra; and here,

* In the neighbourhood of Simla there is quite a collection of sanitaria, which are passed, or seen, by the visitor to that more famous place. The first of these, and usually the first stopping-place for the night of those who go by the old bridle-road from Kalka, is Kussowli, famous for its Himalayan beer, which is not unlike the ordinary beer of Munich. It is more rainy than Simla, more windy, rather warmer, and not so high, and is chiefly occupied as a depôt for the convalescents of European regiments. Close to it rises the barren hill of Sonawar, where there is the (Sir Henry) Lawrence Asylum, for boys and girls of European or mixed parentage; between four hundred and five hundred being usually supported and educated there at the expense of Government. Two other sanitaria, Dagshai (Dugshaie) and Sabathu (Subathoo), are also military depôts; the latter having large barracks, and houses with fine gardens and orchards. The British soldier improves greatly in strength and appearance on these heights; but it is said he does not appreciate the advantages of being placed upon them. He does not like having to do so much for himself as falls to his lot when he is sent to the mountains.—WILSON, "Abode of Snow," p. 43.

close upon the summit of the Himalayan spurs, are situated the sanitaria of Landoor and Mussoorie; the former being the military, the latter the civil division of the same hills.

The road lies through the Monan Pass, at the head of which we obtain our first glimpse of the beautiful Dehra valley; a fertile region, with a profusion of tropical vegetation, large-leaved plantains, and large clumps of graceful bamboo; rich crops of all kinds, and picturesque villages dotted here and there. The valley is about sixty miles long and fourteen wide. On its further side rise the Himalaya, with the white bungalows of Mussoorie scattered at an elevation of five thousand feet; and one thousand feet higher, the military sanitarium of Landoor. In the centre of the valley is the town of Dehra,—each house, like the cottages of an English village, embowered in bloom and verdure. A long avenue of graceful bamboos leads through the town; and among the surrounding foliage lie several Hindu temples.

It is a steep ascent to Mussoorie; but the view which it commands fully repays the traveller for any fatigue he may have experienced. Across the Dehra Doon, it extends to the low range of the Siwalik hills; and beyond that again, to the plains which shimmer below in the hot sunshine. Here and there fine threads of silver indicate the course of the great Indian rivers, the Jumna and the Ganges, and their tributaries. All around swell grassy hills, carpeted with flowers and ferny growth, and relieved by clumps of Indian oak and tangled thickets of dahlias; a blaze of colour—purple, maroon, orange, lilac, scarlet, white, and yellow. And everywhere we feel, so to speak, the awful presence of the Himalaya, which, in the distance, raise their gigantic peaks, snow-crowned, into the ethereal blue of a cloudless sky.

Near Landoor is Lallteeba, the Red Hill; and from the summit of the Red Hill may be obtained a glorious panoramic picture of the grandest mountain-chain in the world.

In the western part of the valley are situated the plantations of the Dehra Tea Company. Here the traveller learns the distinction between the Chinese plant and its taller relative, which grows wild in Assam. The variety cultivated at Dehra is a hybrid between these two. Here, too, he learns that Flowery Pekoe is the very finest kind of black tea; deriving its name from the soft down of the young unexpanded leaf which may be seen upon it. Orange Pekoe is much the same, but owes its name to the colour of the unexpanded leaf when dried. He learns, finally, that all black tea, from Orange Pekoe down through Pekoe and Souchong to Bohea (which last is made of the largest and oldest leaves), and all green tea, from young Hyson down to Hyson-skin, are plucked and prepared together. The sorting is an after-process, done partly by sieve and partly by hand.

AMRITSAR.

Our course now takes us on to Amritsar. At Saharunpur, famous for its Botanical Garden, we join the railway, and are rapidly carried across the Sutlej. Then we pass the broad channel of the Beas, and speedily reach our destination.

Amritsar—that is, Amrita Saras, the Fountain of Immortality—is the sacred city of the Sikhs, and the great commercial emporium of this part of India.

The word *Sikh* is a corruption of the Sanskrit word *Śishya*. It means, literally, "a disciple;" and though now borne as a national designation by the people of the Upper Punjab, was originally applied to a religious sect founded in the fifteenth century by Nânak, a high-class Hindu. This enthusiast was so successful in his teaching, that when he died, in 1539, his followers already numbered one hundred thousand; constituting a formidable body on account of their military enthusiasm, which was intensified by their religious ardour.

It seems to have been the desire of Nânak to found an eclectic creed, which, sweeping away caste distinctions, and combining the best features of both Mohammedanism and Brahmanism, might embrace all India in its comprehensive bonds. He gave himself out as a *guru*, or spiritual guide, and recorded his teaching in the sacred pages of the *Âdigranth*, which ever lies open before his successor, the great *guru*, in the Golden Temple of Amritsar.

The Sikh allows no idols, and repudiates the idea of uncleanness which the Moslem and the Hindu attach to certain meats. He abhors tobacco, but does not object to alcoholic stimulants. He is known to his co-religionists by a mark burned in on the left shoulder; and as he is thus purified with fire during life, he considers it needless to burn the body after death. He is a worshipper of one God, vowed to a life of morality, and above and before all things a soldier.

According to a recent traveller, Amritsar is a busy, well-ordered, and extremely picturesque place. Here and there, above the verdure of its gardens, rise the towers of the old nobles, but most of the houses have only two stories. Some of those recently built are remarkable for their architectural merit, and the beauty of their wood-carving. The bazaars are filled with interesting wares; and fine specimens of Kashmir and Rampur shawls load the stalls of the shawl-merchants.

From Amritsar we proceed by rail to Lahore.

LAHORE.

The poet Moore, in his romance of "Lalla Rookh," represents his heroine and her attendants as reaching, in due course, "the splendid city of Lahore, whose mausoleums and shrines, magnificent and numerous, where Death appeared to share equal honours with Heaven," had a powerful influence on her imagination. "The rajahs and omras in her train, who had kept at a certain distance during the journey, and never encamped nearer the princess than was strictly necessary for her safeguard, here rode in splendid cavalcade through the city, and distributed the most costly presents to the crowd. Engines were worked in all the squares, which cast forth showers of confectionery among the people; while the artisans, in chariots adorned with tinsel and flying streamers, exhibited badges of their respective trades through streets brilliant with life and pageantry. The palaces, and domes, and gilded minarets of Lahore, made the city altogether like a place of enchantment."

Not less charming than Moore imagined, or Milton, when he chronicled it in his stately verse, is the prosperous and populous capital of Northern India. It has no minarets of gold, it is true, but it has domes of coloured porcelain. It has no bannered chariots, but it has gorgeously-caparisoned elephants. And for monuments, it can point to its Great Mosque, the Tombs of Runjeet Singh and Guru Govind, the Mosque of Wuzir Ali, and the Gardens and Tomb of Jehangir.

There is also the Fort; which, however, lacks military importance, having been much injured both by Sikhs and Britons. But it contains some beautiful architectural "bits," and commands a noble view of the city, and of the dusty plain which spreads around it. At one time the Ravi flowed under its walls, when in appearance it must have closely resembled the forts of Agra and Allahabad. The exterior is largely ornamented with a coating of what Mr. Grant Duff aptly calls "porcelain plaster;" the secret of making which is said to be lost. It produces just the same effect as the *azulejos* of the Alhambra; and is so admirable a decoration, that one could wish the process might be rediscovered. The exterior sculpture of the Fort belongs to the age of Jehangir, and testifies to his catholicity of taste. Numerous figures of animals contemned by the true Mussulman feeling are introduced, as well as Mithraic emblems, and even, it is said, the European devil.

The Great Mosque was built by Aurungzebe out of the spoils of the confiscated lands of his brother Dara. It is a spacious and stately quadrangular pile, with swelling domes and slender minarets. In the court grows a banian-tree of immense size.

The Tomb of Runjeet Singh, the "Lion of the Punjab," has little architectural merit, and, like that of Guru Govind, the tenth supreme pontiff of the Sikhs, is chiefly noticeable as a historical landmark. Around the old Lion are interred the remains of some of his wives, who were burned to death on his funeral pyre, according to a custom which happily no longer obtains in British India.

The Mosque of Wuzir Ali is decorated with very fine specimens of the Kaslic work, or coloured porcelain, to which allusion has already been made. The Tomb and Garden of Jehangir lie to the west of the city, beyond the Ravi, and must have been very beautiful before they were despoiled by later rulers. Their general style is that of the Taj. The tomb of Jehangir's able and charming wife, Noor Jehan, has suffered even more grievously than that of her husband.

Not to be forgotten among the attractions of Lahore are the Gardens of Shah Jehan, the Shalimar, or "House of Joy." The poet represents the bridal festivities of Lalla Rookh and the supposed Feramorz, the disguised monarch of Bokhara, as being celebrated in the imperial palace here. On the occasion of the Prince of Wales's visit to Lahore, a splendid *fête* was given in these gardens, when the trees sparkled with Chinese lanterns, and the fountains flung into the air their illuminated columns.

The Montgomery Hall is a handsome European building, erected as a testimony of respect for Sir Robert Montgomery, the second Lieutenant-Governor of the Punjab, by those over whom he had ruled. It contains several good portraits of the heroes of North-Western India; and commands from its windows a fine view of the shining reaches of the Ravi,—the traditional limit of the Indian conquests of Alexander the Great.

Near the city is Meanmeer, the military cantonment of the Lahore division. It is worth notice that its church was designed and built by Lord Napier of Magdala, when in command of the division.

TO JUMMOO.

From Lahore we may make an excursion to Jummoo, the capital of "flowery Kashmir."

Alighting at Wazirabad, we transfer ourselves to a dâk garry, a kind of box on four wheels, supplied with a comfortable elastic bed, and drawn by two country-bred horses, in charge of three men. Along a half-formed road, where boggy places are simply covered with reeds and straw,—through miles of boulders and shattered stones,—down deep ravines echoing with the clash and clang of tumultuous waters,—we make our way, at the rate of six miles an hour. The journey is not wanting in objects of interest. Here a clump of tall trees is perched on the summit of a lofty crag; there the tiger-grass, or Sikunder's grass, as the natives call it, springs almost above our heads; here a lammergeier pursues its lofty flight through the clear luminous air; there the music of the hoopooes echoes from a leafy grove. Or now we come upon two or three wild-looking mountaineers, returning to their home among the hills; or a slow-moving train of camels, carrying the picks and shovels and other *impedimenta* of a surveying-party; or a jolting bullock-cart, the occupants of which are shaded from the sun by a red cashmere awning fringed with yellow.

At Sealkote we plunge into the midst of an English military cantonment, situated about eighty miles from the snow-crowned peaks of the Himalaya, but basking in the heat of an almost tropical sun. In hot weather, at this station, the thermometer often stands for weeks at 98° in the bungalows, and 105° in the barracks.

From this point, at dawn, when wreaths of rosy mist curl up the rugged sides of the mountains, the traveller surveys with awe and wonder that tremendous chain of peaks and crags which forms the barrier of the Empire, and seems to confront him with a stern *ne plus ultra*. Towards the north-east the uninterrupted lofty rampart stretches, without cleft or gateway, from the Khybar Pass to the great fortress of Cabul.

Below the snow-line, a belt of giant trees stretches down to the lower hills, where, in the impenetrable jungle, the tiger and the cobra di capella find a home. Lower still, the sloping pastures are enamelled with verdure, and watered by rills from the far-off glaciers, which shine like threads of silver, as they trace their devious course through masses of roses and rhododendrons beaming with gorgeous colours.

The capital of Kashmir is situated on the Towi, a tributary of the Chenab. It is a place of considerable trade, communication with the riverine districts being maintained by water. The Kashmir boatmen are a strong and hardy race, and manage their clumsy craft with much dexterity. Mr. Wilson speaks in almost rapturous terms of the scenery of Kashmir. Here, he says, at a height of nearly six thousand feet, in a temperate climate, with abundance of moisture, and yet protected by lofty mountains from the fierce continuous rains of the Indian south-west monsoon, is to be found the finest amphitheatre in the world. A flat oval valley—as such he describes it—about sixty miles long and from forty broad, is surrounded by magnificent mountains, which, during the greater part of the year, are covered more than half-way down with snow. Further, it is intersected with watercourses, has ample lakes, and is covered with the richest vegetation, including gigantic trees profuse in foliage. And out of this great central valley rise numerous long mountain-valleys, of the most picturesque character; with, above these, dense forests of pine, green grassy slopes, beds of snow, and huge glaciers. The general effect is well portrayed in Moore's familiar lines:—

> "Whose head in wintry grandeur towers,
> And whitens with eternal sleet:
> While summer, in a vale of flowers,
> Is sleeping rosy at his feet."

KASHMIRIAN BOATMEN.

WAZIRABAD TO ATTOCK AND PESHAWAR.

Returning to Wazirabad (or Wuzeerabad), we propose to resume our journey westward. The usual route crosses a bridge of boats; but the railway is now carried across the Chenab by a bridge of remarkably solid construction, completed in 1876. The Chenab, the ancient Acesines, is thirty feet deep at this point, even in the dryest season; in the rains it swells into a mighty torrent, some three and a quarter miles in width, and terrible in its rapidity. Communication between the banks is often impossible, no Indian boat being able to live in its rolling flood.

Journeying along the Grand Trunk Road, which is bordered by long lines of babool, and studded at intervals with comfortable dâk bungalows, we cross the Jhilam, the classic Hydaspes, and approach the boundaries of Kashmir. Then we reach Rawul Pindee, the centre of a military division, and a post of much importance.

Seventeen miles further, and we pass a massive but by no means handsome monument to the memory of the gallant Nicholson. The road traverses a desolate and treeless landscape, until it passes near the site of ancient Taxila, and crosses a bright and picturesque little stream. We enter thereafter a green and fertile country, where long lines of fruit-trees enliven the level fields; and through pleasant scenery, with a lofty chain of mountains on the horizon, we push forward to the famous Indus (or Sindhu, "flood"), one of the remarkable rivers of the world.

At Attock the river is crossed by a bridge of boats in the neighbourhood of an old Mohammedan fort. Opposite the town rises a lofty hill, which geographers identify with the Aornos of Alexander the Great.

Up the western bank of the Indus we proceed to the mouth of the Cabul river, and then strike to the southward, passing Nowshera, where an English garrison is stationed, and in due time arrive at Peshawar. This marks the extreme limit of English territory to the south-west, and lies close to the formidable Afghan frontier. At no great distance, on a clear day, may be seen the mouth of the Khybar Pass.

CHAPTER X.

AT AGRA.

THE NORTH-WEST PROVINCES—CITY OF AGRA—DESCRIPTION OF THE TAJ MAHAL—EULOGIES BY DIFFERENT WRITERS—A PALACE AMONG TOMBS—THE MEMORIAL OF AN EMPEROR'S LOVE—TERRACES AND GARDENS—THE IMPERIAL PALACE—AKBAR'S TRIBUNAL—THE GREAT HALL, OR ARMOURY—THE SOMNAUTH GATES—BATH-ROOM OF THE ZENANA—THE JASMINE BOWER—TOMB OF AKBAR—ITS INSCRIPTIONS—CURIOUS NARRATIVE OF THE DEATH OF THE EMPRESS—FUTTEYPUR SIKRI—AKBAR'S SUMMER PALACE—TOMB OF ITMAD-OOD-DOULAH—LATER HISTORY OF AGRA—THE DURBAR OF 1866—THE PRINCE OF WALES'S VISIT.

AGRA, it may be necessary to inform the reader, is the capital of that portion of our Indian Empire which was formerly known as the North-West Provinces.

These provinces form a fertile, populous, and well-cultivated region, irrigated by numerous canals, which flow into, or are connected with, the great broad waters of the Ganges and the Jumna. Notwithstanding their general aspect of peace and prosperity, they are covered, however, for miles round Agra, with the shattered memorials of a former age, that tell of the havoc and desolation wrought by successive conquerors.

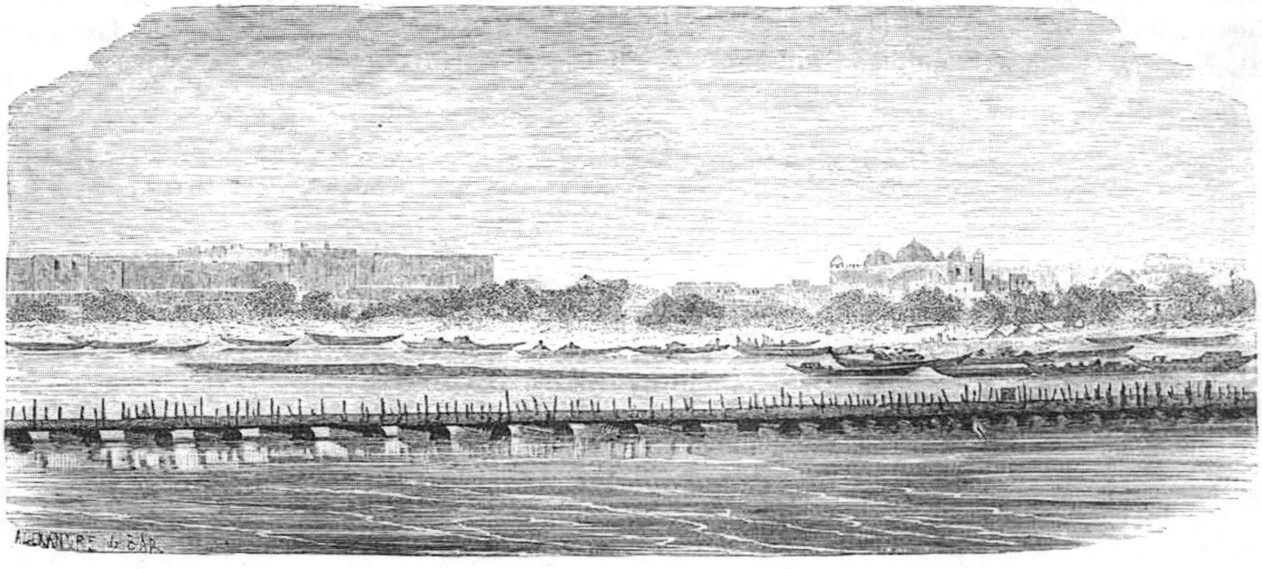

AGRA, FROM THE OPPOSITE BANK OF THE JUMNA.

To the traveller approaching the ancient seat of the Mogul Empire from the opposite bank of the Jumna, Agra presents a fair and picturesque prospect. In the foreground rolls the copious river, with all its burden of life and motion; the strange native craft, unloading at its quays, or slowly making way against the steady current; the hot banks of sand heaped up with

GENERAL VIEW OF THE TAJ MAHAL.

bales of cotton; and the dusky groups of washers, male and female, beating their various-tinted garments on the smooth stones at the edge of the stream. Immediately beyond rise the high embattled walls, with the massive gateway, of its celebrated fort; while above it soar the many domes of the Pearl Mosque, shining white and pure in the soft, transparent, luminous air.

The city itself, however, is far from realizing those dreams of Oriental splendour which, somehow or other, everybody cherishes in connection with Hindustan. Its magnificent imperial structures are completely isolated from the habitations of the common people; while the Government House, the military cantonments, and the handsome villas of the British residents, are placed at some distance from the walls. Hence it comes to pass that Agra itself, the ancient Akbarabad, or city of Akbar,—the city of the *Shish Mehal* or Palace of Glass, of the wondrous *Taj*, and the *Moti Masjid* or Pearl Mosque,—is a maze of close and narrow lanes, surmounted by a few spires, and relieved by a few open spaces of waste ground. The principal street, however, is somewhat better, being paved with stone, and enriched here and there with traces of its former splendour. The better class of houses, moreover, are provided with terraced roofs and balconies, from which inquisitive female eyes can safely scrutinize the whirl and eddy of life below.

It is not our object in these pages to treat of the manufactures or industrial resources of India, but an occasional allusion to the chief occupations of its people may be permitted. At Agra the inhabitants are largely occupied in dyeing cotton cloths; the favourite colours being purple and yellow. The process takes place in the open shop, where the necessary copper vessels are sunken in the floor,—the spaces between being utilized for storing goods and transacting business. Strange to say, the stuffs prepared in this seemingly primitive fashion are not less resplendent in hue than those "dipped by steam-revolving apparatus in the great vats of British manufactories," and are not exported to the marts of London, Manchester, and Glasgow.

At Agra, however, the objects of interest which principally concern the reader and ourselves are the Fort, Sikandra, the tomb of Itmad-ood-Doulah, and the Taj. We shall begin with the last, as being pre-eminent in beauty.

THE TAJ MAHAL.

Travellers in speaking of it run riot in superlatives. A recent writer (Miss Gordon Cumming) describes it in almost poetical language as a cluster of pearly, snow-white domes nestling round one grand central dome, like a gigantic pearl; these all crowning a building of purest, highly-polished marble, so perfect in its proportions, so lovely in its design, so restful to the eye, and so simple yet so complex in its simplicity, that it resembles rather the marble embodiment of a fairy dream than any work of human hands. Its four sides are exactly alike; hence it follows that its perfection of form never varies, whatever the spectator's point of view. Standing apart from the city, or any other building, it is all alone in its transcendent loveliness, with a rich Eastern garden blooming beside it, and with the warm red sandstone walls of the inclosure washed by the blue waters of the sacred Jumna.

Even so sober a writer as Mr. Grant Duff pronounces it the one building which in all the earth equals, or perhaps surpasses, the Parthenon of Athens. He asserts that, often as it has been lauded in glowing panegyrics, none of them have done it justice; and we may wait other two centuries and a half for a worthy description, unless Mr. Ruskin could be induced to visit it and write of it, as he has done of the Campanile at Florence. Men who can really describe such things in fitting language, come only at long intervals.

From a busy Glasgow merchant it would be unwise to expect anything but a frigid estimate. He begins by likening the Taj to a handsome ivory toy, expanded by a strong magnifying influence into palatial dimensions. But before long its beauty has its usual effect, and he tells of the high-walled garden, with its flowers and fountains; of the palace, so reared on an elevation over the country beyond as to have no other background than the sky; of the deep green foliage of the cypress-trees, exquisitely mingling with and partially concealing its pure white magnificence; of its central dome, glistening with a flood of sunshine, while on each side two graceful minarets taper towards the pale azure sky. For him, as for others, the Taj has had a charm that could not be evaded, a magic that could not be ignored.

GATE OF THE GARDENS OF THE TAJ MAHAL.

A wall of red sandstone, about sixty feet high, encloses the entire area, a space of nearly forty acres, and separates it from the river. This wall is finely carved with large groups and clusters of flowers, inlaid with pure white marble, and adorned with beautifully wrought niches, in which the green parrots take up their abode. Above it rises a great quadrangle of pearly marble, nine hundred feet square and forty feet high. On either side of this lofty platform is planted a small mosque of red sandstone, adorned with slabs of black and white marble, and crested with three shapely white marble domes. One of these is for use; the other, not being properly placed with respect to Mecca, is intended only to satisfy the eye.

GRAND ALLEY OF THE TAJ MAHAL.

A second marble terrace or platform rises from the first, and each corner of it bears a tall and graceful minaret, about one hundred and fifty feet high, also of marble, and crowned with a dome. And out of the group of minarets, which seem so many pillars of steadfast light—like that which led the Israelites through the gloom of the wilderness—springs up the Taj itself, a great dome two hundred feet high, resembling in colour an Alpine peak of snow, and of the most exquisite finish and symmetry. It is an inspiration to stand beneath one of the great dark cypresses, the boughs of which are festooned with the glorious lilac-tinted leaves of the beautiful bougainvillea, while numbers of emerald-plumaged parrots flutter among the foliage, and to gaze on the wondrous edifice which commemorates an emperor's love and sorrow.

Yes, an emperor's love and sorrow; for the Taj is but a tomb—a tomb among palaces, and a palace among tombs—raised by the great Mogul emperor Shah Jehan, in memory of his beloved Mumtáz-i-Mahal, or Arjumund Banoo, known also as Taj Mahal, "the crown of Empires." After a happy married life of twenty years, she died, in 1631, giving birth to a daughter. Her imperial husband mourned for her with a profound sorrow. It seemed as if nothing again could give him pleasure; for

> "Of slaves he had many, of wives but one.
> There is but one God for the soul, he said,
> And but one moon for the sun."

But at length the idea occurred to him of erecting a monument in her honour, which should testify to all ages how great had been his devotion. For this purpose he summoned to Agra the finest workers of every nation; and what the Eastern imagination conceived, Italian art reduced to place and proportion. It is on record that for upwards of twenty-two years twenty thousand men were employed on the building, and about £3,000,000 sterling expended; which, of course, takes no account of compulsory labour, or of the tribute furnished by conquered nations. The red sandstone used was found near at hand, in the Metab Hills; the marble was brought all the way from Jeypur or Ajmeer.

When we approach the Taj, we come first to a grand gateway, which in any European city would take rank as an object of first-rate importance. It is built of red sandstone, and inlaid with black and white marble, having central arches of extraordinary elevation. Thence we pass into a garden about a quarter of a mile long and the same in breadth, blooming with roses and the loveliest flowers, and traversed by a long avenue of spreading cypresses and a row of shining fountains, which conduct the eye to the foot of the palace-tomb. The ear filled with music of falling waters, interrupted occasionally by the shrill cries of the green parrots, we advance to the Taj, and, by a low portal, "beneath an arch which seems to reach to heaven," we pass into the interior. This is everywhere lined with mosaic work of the most beautiful execution, but of the conventional Mohammedan patterns; for the reader will remember that the Koran prohibits the Mohammedan artist from attempting the likeness of anything in heaven or on earth. Flowers there are, however, which have evidently grown by the wayside or in the shady hollow of a vale.

Beautiful to see, is this splendid memorial of an emperor's sorrow, in the golden radiance of an Indian summer noon; but if you would view it aright, you must, as Scott says of the ruined abbey of Melrose, visit it by pale moonlight. In the warm sunshine it is defined against the clear blue sky with too much sharpness, like a fantastically-wrought iceberg. But in the moonlight it assumes a softer aspect, as if a mantle of freshly-fallen snow lay upon swelling dome and marble pavement and glittering minaret; the whole aspiring above the dense, dark cypress-foliage like a vision of purity. The spectator holds his breath while he gazes, for it seems to be a dream, an exhalation; a something too lovely for earth, which, having been suddenly revealed to the eye, will as suddenly pass away into "thin air."

THE FORT.

It is, perhaps, to its Fort, as much as to its Taj, that Agra owes its fame among Indian cities. It was built by Akbar, who was unquestionably one of the strongest and greatest of the later rulers of Hindustan. A mass of dark red sandstone, with frowning battlements, its appearance is very formidable; but the military eye quickly discovers that in these days of scientific warfare it could not long hold out against an enemy. Within its high red walls stand the Imperial Palace, and other lovely buildings, all of white marble, reared by Akbar's successors. Among these the foremost place must be allowed to the celebrated Moti Masjid, or "Pearl Mosque," which induced Bishop Heber to characterize the vast pile as a fortress built by giants and finished by jewellers.* Its dimensions are considerable: externally it measures 235 feet from east to west, by 190 feet from north to south, while the courtyard is 155 feet square.

Its mass, as Fergusson observes, is also considerable; for the whole is raised on an artificial terrace, which enables it to stand well out from the surrounding buildings of the Fort. Its beauty resides in its courtyard, which, from the pavement to the summit of the loftiest dome, is wholly composed of white marble. The western part, or Mosque proper, is of the same costly material inside and out; and, with the exception of an inscription from the Koran, charactered in black marble and inlaid as a frieze, all its ornament lies in the lines of its own graceful architecture. According to Mr. Fergusson, it is less ornamental than any other building of the same pretensions; and in this respect it contrasts singularly with the later Moorish buildings in Spain and elsewhere, which, like the Alhambra, depend almost entirely for their effect on the profuseness of the decorative work with which they are overlaid.

Seven open passages, each a rich marble arcade with arched roof, lead into the interior. Here, in the principal hall or chamber, which is adapted for six hundred worshippers, by means of as many spaces or stations marked out on the marble floor, the European visitor will generally discover a few natives, with face as usual towards the sacred *kibla*, rapidly muttering their devotional monologues, and at momentary pauses bending their heads until they touch the stone.

In the Imperial Palace we are shown the once famous "Halls of Marvel," where the eye is gratified and refreshed by the purity of the cool white marble walls. Akbar's Tribunal, where he sat to administer justice, is not unworthy of India's mightiest lord. There, beneath its

* There is, however, an unnecessary exaggeration in Bishop Heber's language, when he says,—"This spotless sanctuary, showing such a pure spirit of adoration, made me, a Christian, feel humbled, when I considered that no architect of our religion had ever been able to produce anything equal to this temple of Allah!" The bishop had surely forgotten the glorious cathedrals of Europe, which are certainly not inferior in artistic beauty.

marble canopy, wrought all over with clusters of blossom in jasper, cornelian, and other precious gems, stands his throne. Observe, too, the panelled walls, with their floral decorations carved in marble; and the airy roof, extending in a series of graceful arches.

In Akbar's time the meanest peasant was free to seek his emperor's presence, when he sat in judgment. One would have thought that the cares of his wide-reaching empire would have left him no leisure for these innumerable personal interviews; but it is on record that he was not less diligent in business than wise in counsel. He appears to have been a proficient in the art of economizing time. Certainly, he lengthened his days, as Moore sportively advises, by stealing a few hours from the night. He was as sparing in his sleep as in his diet; and his ministers were bound to be always ready for his sudden summons.

The Great Hall is now used as an armoury, and contains a choice collection of things both rich and rare. The objects which will most attract the English visitor's eye are those Gates of Somnauth which, some years ago, became widely famous in connection with a rhetorical proclamation by the Earl of Ellenborough. They were said to be of sandal-wood; measuring twelve feet high, richly carved and inlaid, and adorned with shields of gleaming metal; and they formerly guarded the entrance to a great Hindu temple at Somnauth. Thence they were carried off by the Afghan conqueror, Sultan Mahmoud, in A.D. 1025, who, well knowing how they were venerated by the Hindus, removed them to Ghazni. After his death they were converted into the portals of his tomb, so as to witness to the power of the Mohammedans and their abhorrence of idolatry. Nine centuries and upwards passed, and a British army entered Ghazni in triumph, whereupon it occurred to Lord Ellenborough that their removal to Agra would be a significant illustration of the supremacy of the British, and would demonstrate how completely they had succeeded to the power formerly enjoyed by the Moslems. This may have been true; but as the act excited great discontent among the Mohammedans, it was not the less a political mistake.

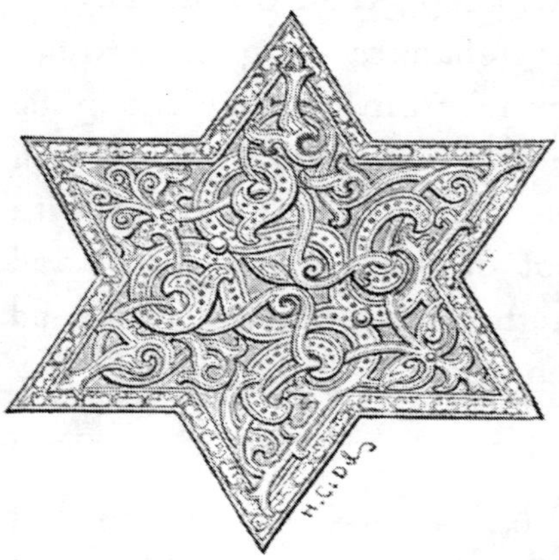

ORNAMENTS OF THE GATES OF SOMNAUTH.

ORNAMENTS OF THE GATES OF SOMNAUTH.

Not long ago a careful examination was made of these historic gates, and it was then discovered that the carving was all purely Mohammedan, and free from the slightest trace of Hindu sentiment or Hindu feeling; also, that the gates were not wrought in sandal-wood, but in deodar pine. Hence it has been conjectured that the original gates were destroyed by fire, and that imitations, made of the timber most easily procurable, were set up in front of Mahmoud's tomb.

Returning to the Palace, we enter a succession of halls, and courts, and gardens, where the trellises are festooned with glowing flowers, and the fragrance of innumerable roses tempers the freshness of the leaping fountains.

Well worth careful study is the bath-room of the Zenana, or women's quarter. Small convex mirrors cover every inch of its walls and ceiling; so that when lighted torches are introduced, the whole place sparkles like a jewelled grotto, such as one reads of in the "Arabian Nights." The spacious marble baths in which the beauties of the harem "sleeked their dusky limbs" were fed by rills of water, which overflowed in a number of tiny cascades, and shone reflected in the gleaming roof. But fairer even than this fair scene are the Zenana pavilions, which, like so many birds' nests, overhung the great river-wall of sandstone; pavilions, all of marble, all daintily ornamented with elaborate carving, all displaying a really exquisite purity of design.

Beautiful indeed is the Jasmine Bower, the fairy chamber reserved for the favourite sultana; and beautiful are all those richly-wrought apartments in which the Emperor Shah Jehan spent in captivity the last seven years of his life. His chief pleasure during this melancholy period centred in the erection of the *Moti Masjid;* and his last sight on earth must have been that "divine and glorious" structure, which to all time will keep green his memory.

The common tradition states that Shah Jehan's lovely daughter Jehanara suggested to her father the idea of the erection of this mosque, in order to divert his mind from gloomy thoughts. With noble self-devotion she voluntarily shared his imprisonment, and by her wit and affection did much to cheer it. She lies buried at Delhi in a white marble sarcophagus, carved with flowers and encrusted with gems, while in the centre blooms a spot of fresh green turf; and an inscription records that, by her own desire, only flowers and grass, things frail and evanescent, mark the last resting-place of the "perishable pilgrim Jehanara."

TOMB OF AKBAR.

At Sikandra, seven miles from Agra, is situated the tomb of Akbar, erected by his son. It stands in a noble square of garden-ground, approached by magnificent gateways, which now exhibit signs of decay; and is built of dark red sandstone, in four huge terraces, each smaller than the one beneath it. At the four corners of every terrace a domed pavilion is planted. In the characteristic Oriental style, it is inlaid with marble and many-coloured encaustic tiles, which preserve their brilliancy in a remarkable manner. The topmost story, high in air, forms a court of white marble, enclosing the cenotaph of the mighty emperor, with nothing above it but the silent sapphire sky. It is inscribed, in Persian characters, with the ninety-nine attributes of God. But the actual tomb lies far below; just in the same position, says Mr. Grant Duff, as that occupied by the dead monarch in the tumulus of Alyattes—or, we may add, as that of the Egyptian king in the so-called Pyramid of Cheops.

The distinctive feature of Agra, that characteristic which contrasts it with all other Indian cities, is very clearly brought out by Dr. Macleod. We all, as he remarks, have visions of the Great Mogul,—a designation, by the way, which historians rightly reject as unwarranted by fact, but which will nevertheless remain, like many a fruit of fairy tale, or of prosaic fibbing,—visions of pearls, gold, and diamonds, of power and of cruelty, and of all that a young reader of the "Arabian Nights" could desire, had he only the powerful magic charm to minister to his pleasures. But nowhere else do we obtain so vivid, so true an idea of Mohammedan architecture.

In Agra the traveller is, as it were, in a new world, which is Oriental, but certainly not Hindu; "a splendid exotic, flowering in beauty and brilliancy beside the dark and ugly form of Siva." And nowhere is this Orientalism so conspicuous, this beauty and brilliancy are nowhere so plainly visible, as in the Taj, which is truly the gem of India, and the very culmination and perfection of Mohammedan art. Were we to recognize it as symbolical, we might conclude that the life and worship of Islam were perfect purity; for it is pure as alabaster, simple in its forms, and void of every ornament except radiant gems blended with the snowy marble, like flowers of spring blooming in the chinks and fissures of the quarries of Carrara.

FUTTEYPUR SIKRI.

About twenty-four miles from Agra, among the Bhurtpore Hills, lies Futteypur Sikri, which may here be mentioned in connection with the imperial Akbar.

It presents an imposing mass of walls, towers, and palaces of red sandstone, crowning an abrupt and elevated precipice. These, of old, composed the summer-palace of Akbar—his "regal Windsor;" but were abandoned in deference to the will of a half-crazy anchorite, whose reputed sanctity had originally drawn the emperor to the spot.

Among other objects of interest in Agra, may be named the Tomb of Itmad-ood-Doulah. "Here it was," says Mr. Grant Duff, "that my attention was first drawn to the distinction between the tombs of men and women in this part of the world." Upon those of the former is carved a writing-case, on those of the latter a slate, to indicate their respective relations as active and passive, as doers and recipients.

Itmad-ood-Doulah is a corruption of the official title, Akmat-ood-doulah, or treasurer of the empire; a post formerly held by Khwajah Ghaias, father-in-law of the Emperor Jehangir. On his death, in 1610, this mausoleum was erected for the reception of his remains by the imperial order. It is situated in the midst of a beautiful garden, which is surrounded by walls and palaces. Its actual size is not great, for it is only twenty feet high and fifty feet long; but its terraced roof is crowned by four turrets and a pavilion, raising the total height to forty feet. Architecturally, it combines the features of the Hindu and Mogul styles. It is built of white marble, but every inch of space is covered with mosaics, and this prodigality of ornamentation perplexes the spectator.

From this splendid mausoleum, the banks of the Jumna bloom with gardens, which surround the tombs or palaces of the nobles of Akbar's Court. Among these we may indicate the Rambaugh, containing large pavilions, which the municipality of Agra has furnished for the reception of travellers; and the remarkable ruined mausoleum known as Chini-ka-Rozah, or "the Tomb of China." This noble domed structure, built of bricks, is overlaid with enamelled designs and arabesques. Their richness and grace are undeniable.

Of late years Agra, the imperial city of Akbar, has been distinguished by some remarkable events.

Here, in 1866, was held a grand durbar, by Sir John (now Lord) Lawrence, then Governor-General of India, who summoned thither, as vassals or allies of the Queen of England, the great chiefs and feudatories from Cape Comorin to the Himalaya.

The governor-general entered Agra in state on the 11th of November. On the 13th, an hour after sunrise, in accordance with Indian custom, he sent a deputation of officials to wait upon the Maharajahs of Gwalior, Jeypur, and Joudpur, and the Begum of Bhopal, the only chiefs entitled to such a mark of distinction. At ten o'clock he held a grand levee. At one the Indian princes began their visits to the viceroy, occupying the rest of that day and the next. Afterwards he returned these visits; so that for several days the streets of Agra blazed with gorgeous costumes.

Scindia, one of the most powerful of the Indian chiefs, who remained faithful to our rule throughout the dark days of the Mutiny, had formed the idea of giving an entertainment at the Taj, which the municipality of Agra had placed at his disposal. It proved to be a realization of one's dreams of Fairyland. The visitor, on entering the first court, passed between two lines of Scindia's grenadiers, and then entered the garden under the lofty monumental archway, which shone with a thousand lamps. But who shall describe that garden? It seemed like a dream—a vision;—the fountains throwing up showers of many-coloured spray, the trees covered with fruits and flowers, and the sounds of exquisite music filling every echo. The long avenues, paved with marble, presented a brilliant spectacle; for European officers and diplomatists, glittering with orders, Indian ministers and Rajput chiefs, mingled with maharajahs and rajahs, whose attire seemed woven of precious stones. And in and out of the throng moved gracefully the great ladies of the Court of Calcutta.

Suddenly at about ten o'clock was seen, at the farther end of the main avenue, a colossal mass of snow, suspended in the air. It was the Taj, which, previously hidden by the darkness, had just been illuminated with electric lights. The effect was magical. The illumination then became general; and the choubdars proceeded to conduct the guests to the Jawab,—an immense hall, decorated with mosaics,—where a banquet had been prepared, which combined all the luxuries of Europe and Asia.

The supper ended, a display of fireworks took place on the banks of the Jumna, which winds round the base of the Taj in a graceful curve. Numerous rockets shone for an instant, reflected in the clear mirror-like waters. Scarcely was all again shrouded in darkness when a line of fire floated down the stream and bathed it in light. This effect was due to thousands of tiny lamps flung from the Toundlah bridge into the river, which they covered with a sheet of fire. At midnight the English bands gave a concert, and then the crowd gradually dispersed.

On the 16th of November the viceroy reviewed the English army, twenty thousand strong, under Sir William Mansfield (afterwards Lord Sandhurst), on the Grand Esplanade of Agra. The 17th witnessed an assembly of the Order of the Star of India, at which several sovereigns and feudatories were invested with its insignia. The ceremony took place in the Shamiana, or tent of the durbars, which occupied the centre of the Imperial camp,—a spacious pavilion, the khanats of which formed a boldly-curved arch, supported by light and elegant pillars. At one end was raised the viceroy's golden throne, supported by heraldic lions, and crowning an elevated platform which blazed with cloth of gold; and on either side of the throne stretched a row of sofas—those on the left for the lesser, and those on the right for the higher ranks.

The viceroy wore the rich collar, the star, ribbon, and lilac satin robes of the Order. The ceremony of investiture was simple. The prince on whom the honour was to be conferred stood before the dais of the Queen of England's representative; the Imperial letter was read aloud;

AN IMPERIAL DURBAR AT AGRA.

the viceroy then embraced him, and, fastening the ribbon and collar round his neck, proclaimed him a knight; after which he made a short speech, enumerating those services of the new knight which had procured for him so signal a distinction.

We now come to the 20th, the day fixed for the Imperial durbar. From earliest dawn, says an eye-witness, Agra was a scene of tumult and excitement. Everybody desired to see the magnificent spectacle; but so great was the number of Indian princes and nobles and English officials invited to be present, that not more than fifty vacant seats remained in the Shamiana, and these were scarcely sufficient to accommodate the newspaper correspondents and a few other favoured visitors.

At noon the Grand Esplanade in front of the camp was alive with the most dazzling aspects of Oriental magnificence. Each rajah, as he entered, attended by a brilliant retinue, and himself shining with gold and gems, took up the position assigned to him, from which he was to march in state to the durbar. Hundreds of gigantic elephants, emblazoned with inconceivably gorgeous trappings,—some with howdahs of gold or silver, others with standards and royal insignia; thousands of horsemen, Rajputs, Mahrattas, Sikhs, and Boondelas; soldiers in the rich Indian uniforms; thousands of eager spectators from every province of India,—such was the crowd which thronged the Maidan of Agra, order to some extent being preserved by the exertions of the English mounted police.

The procession commenced at about two o'clock. According to the rules of etiquette, the highest in rank came last. Each sowari, in turn, moved slowly up the great avenue; the English troops presented arms; the batteries fired a salute; the royal elephant knelt down at the entrance of the Shamiana; and an English official, taking the rajah by his hand, led him to his appointed seat. For hours the procession continued, the brilliance of the display continually increasing, from the Boondela chief of Alipoora to the mighty lord of Gwalior. At length all were seated,—the Indian princes on the left of the dais, with their nobles and ministers behind them; and on the right the English governors, generals, and officers, their rich uniforms appearing markedly simple in contrast to the full-orbed Oriental splendour of the rajahs. A brief pause ensued, after which the choubdars, clothed in red, and armed with long golden wands, announced the viceroy. All the assembly rose, and Sir John Lawrence, in full uniform, with head uncovered, slowly crossed the pavilion, and, amidst volleys of cannon and the strains of the National Anthem, ascended the steps to the dais.

At a given signal all were seated, and the secretary of state proclaimed the opening of the durbar. Then took place the tedious ceremony of the nuzzur. Each rajah, escorted by his dewân (or prime minister) and the chief thakour (or vassal) of his kingdom, advanced towards the dais, and making a slight obeisance to the viceroy, presented to him a piece of gold, which the latter returned. This piece of gold varied in value according to the rank of the rajah. It was offered to the viceroy as representing the Paramount Power; and subsequently, gifts of equal value were made to the chieftains in acknowledgment of the compliment.

The durbar closed with the distribution of presents from the superior to the vassals, of whom the record showed there were eighty-three.

Agra was one of the places visited by the Prince of Wales in 1876. His reception was a splendid affair. The defence of Agra during the Sepoy Mutiny exhibited in a very striking light the heroic qualities of the English residents.

CHAPTER XI.

THE STORY OF CAWNPUR.

SITUATION OF CAWNPUR—ITS MILITARY IMPORTANCE—THE ENGLISH CANTONMENTS IN 1857—OUTBREAK OF THE MUTINY—SIR HUGH WHEELER'S EXCESSIVE CONFIDENCE IN THE SEPOYS—NANA SAHIB—OPEN REVOLT—THE BRITISH BESIEGED—A GALLANT DEFENCE—NANA'S DEVICE—TERMS OF SURRENDER AGREED UPON—THE BRITISH MARCH TO THE PLACE OF EMBARKATION—A MASSACRE—THE SAVADA HOUSE AND ITS CAPTIVES—A SECOND MASSACRE—THE WELL OF SLAUGHTER—ARRIVAL OF HAVELOCK—CAWNPUR RECOVERED—THE MEMORIAL.

WITH no city in India are more mournful memories connected than with Cawnpur. It will be long before it ceases to awaken painful emotions in the heart of England,—before we can hear its name without being stirred to mingled feelings of pity and indignation.

Cawnpur is situated on the south bank of the Ganges, about half-way between Allahabad and Agra, with both of which cities, as well as with Lucknow on the north-east, it is connected by railway. The river here is about a quarter of a mile broad in the dry season, and about a mile and a quarter when its waters have been swollen by the heavy rains; and yet it has fully a thousand miles to run before it debouches into the Bay of Bengal.

Since 1801 Cawnpur has always been considered a first-class military station; and in the spring of 1857 it attained additional importance, through the annexation of Oudh. It was occupied by three regiments of Sepoys, who, with a force of cavalry and a company of artillerymen, brought up the strength of the native garrison to three thousand men. Of European soldiers there were about three hundred. Add to these the civilians, officials, merchants, shopkeepers, and their families, and it is estimated that the number of Europeans and persons of European extraction then resident at Cawnpur exceeded a thousand.

The English cantonments at that time extended for about six miles along the river-bank, each residence standing in its own compound or paddock of three or four houses. "The house," says Mr. Trevelyan, "like all houses outside the Calcutta Ditch, consists of a single story, built of brick, coated with white plaster. A flight of half a dozen steps leads up to a verandah which runs round three sides of the building. The noticeable objects here will probably be a native tailor, working in the attitude adopted by tailors in all lands where men wear clothes; a wretched being, squatted on his haunches, lazily pulling the string of a punkah that passes through a hole in the brickwork into the Sahib's bedroom—a monotonous occupation, which from time to time he sweetens by snatches of sleep; a Madras valet, spreading butter on the Sahib's morning toast with the greasy wing of a fowl; and, against the windward wall, a row of jars of porous red clay, in which water is cooling for the Sahib's morning bath."

The dreariness of the compound is usually relieved by a well-kept garden; and the cantonments as a whole assume a cheerful appearance, with their race-course, and markets, and racket-court, and library, and the other *agréments* which an Englishman imports wherever he establishes his home. In none of these was Cawnpur deficient; and just prior to the outbreak of the Great Mutiny it was not only one of the most important, but also one of the pleasantest military stations in India.

Great was the change when, in May 1857, the news arrived of the outbreak of rebellion at Meerut, and the famous march of the mutinous Sepoys upon Delhi. At first, indeed, the intelligence was discredited by the British commander,—a veteran of seventy-five years,—Sir Hugh Wheeler; and even when something like the truth was known, he would not believe that the fidelity of his own troops was doubtful. He had lived among the Sepoys, and fought at their head; and he had learned to trust in them implicitly, crediting them with good qualities which existed only in his fond imagination. While the delusion was still upon him he suffered much valuable time to pass by unused; and when he awoke to the fact that treason lurked in his own garrison, he telegraphed to Lacknow for aid, it is true, but he also summoned to his assistance the Nana, or Maharajah of Bithoor,—that most dangerous of Indian characters, a native with a grievance. The Nana, deeply involved in the widespread conspiracy against British rule, and, indeed, its principal instigator, sent forward, with all possible alacrity, ten guns and three hundred men, and speedily appeared in person at Cawnpur. There were officers, however, in Sir Hugh Wheeler's little garrison, who did not share the blindness of their chief; and at their urgent request he at last began to fortify an old hospital, and lay in some supplies of provisions.

To a full perception of the danger, however, he did not awake until it was too late. The mine which the Nana and his fellow-plotters had so long been preparing exploded. On the 4th of June the Sepoys mutinied; and rallying around the Nana as their chief, prepared to overwhelm the gallant little band of Europeans who stood at bay within their feeble entrenchments. The rebel force was speedily swollen by the retainers and tenantry of all the disloyal and bankrupt landholders for thirty miles around; until the British citadel was invested by a numerous army, well provided with munitions, and in possession of several batteries of great guns.

On the 7th these batteries opened fire, and proved at once how unfortunate had been Sir Hugh Wheeler's choice of a site for his fortification. The old hospital was entirely surrounded by large and solid buildings, at distances varying from three to eight hundred yards; buildings from which the assailants derived a protection much more effectual than that which their improvised defences afforded to the garrison. Showers of bullets rained from roof and windows during the hours of daylight, while after dusk troops of Sepoys hovered about within pistol-shot, and made night hideous with continual volleys of musketry.

The annals of warfare, as Mr. Trevelyan remarks, contain no episode so painful as the story of the Siege of Cawnpur. It is not one which needs the graces of language for its embellishment. However simply it may be told, it moves to tears as surely as the deathless pages in which Thucydides has described the last agony of the Athenian host in Sicily. Never before has the sun shone on such a scene; on a crowd of women and children cooped up within a confined space, and for twenty days and nights exposed to the pitiless fire of thousands of muskets and a score of heavy cannon. At first, as each shot or shell struck their asylum it elicited the response of a piercing shriek or a low wail of despair; but before long they grew accustomed to the hell of sounds, and suffered in silence. By the evening of the third day every door and window had been beaten in. Next crashed and splintered the screens, the piled-up furniture, the internal partitions; and shell and ball tore their fierce way unchecked through the naked rooms. Some ladies were slain outright by grape or round shot. Others were stricken down by bullets. Many were crushed beneath falling brickwork, or sorely wounded by the splinters which flew from rent sash and panel. Happy were they, says the chronicler of the siege, whose age and sex called them to the front of the battle, and relieved them from the spectacle of this passive carnage. Better to hear more distinctly the rattle of the Sepoy musketry, and the groans of wounded wife and sister more faintly. If die they both must,—such was the thought of more than one husband,—it was well that duty bade them die apart.

Words cannot do justice to the brilliant valour of the defence. Never on the most illustrious field have English soldiers more heroically upheld the honour of their race. They were few, but they were faithful; day and night they remained at their posts, and endured unshaken the severest labours. They were overmatched in weight of metal; ill-provided with ammunition; and unprotected by an inch of cover. And, what was worse, their provisions failed. Want of water was also a constant and an increasing evil. There was but one well, which at no time could have furnished a sufficient supply for a thousand mouths during the heats of an Indian June; but this well lay in the line of fire of the Sepoy artillerymen. "Guns were trained on to the exact spot; so that the appearance of a man with a pitcher by day, and by night the creaking of the tackle, was the signal for a shower of grape. The framework of beam and brick which protected the drawers was soon shot away. The machinery went next, and the buckets were thenceforward hauled up hand over hand from a depth of more than sixty feet." All this was done under a tremendous fire; and so many gallant lives were lost, that, to a fanciful imagination, the water thus dearly purchased must have tasted like blood.

While the little garrison was diminishing day by day, the ranks of the rebels were constantly being swollen by reinforcements. Yet they made little progress towards the capture of the fort. Every assault was repulsed; and the Nana soon saw that before his artillery killed off every defender, it was probable that relief would arrive from Lacknow or Delhi, and disappoint him altogether of his coveted prey. Moreover, disaffection and disgust were gaining ground in his own ranks from hour to hour; and the men who could no longer be induced to face the heroic Sahibs, might turn their arms upon him and his partizans as easier victims. Since force was unavailing, he resolved to try fraud; and in fraud his cruel, subtle, revengeful nature was fully "at home." He opened communications with the besieged, and addressed to them a written proclamation, setting forth that "all who were in no way connected with the acts of Lord Dalhousie, and were willing to lay down their arms, should receive a safe passage to Allahabad." The message was the subject of infinite discussion in Sir Hugh Wheeler's little council; but after much hesitation, pressed by the approach of famine, and by tender thoughts of the women and children, the gallant old general resolved to accept the offered terms. The representatives appointed by him held a conference with Azimoolah and another myrmidon of the Nana's, and undertook to deliver up the fortification, the treasure, and the artillery, on condition that the little European force should be allowed to march out under arms, with sixty rounds of ammunition to every man; that carriages should be provided for the conveyance of the wounded, the women, and the children; and that boats victualled with a sufficiency of flour should be in readiness at the neighbouring landing-place. These stipulations were accepted.

The Suttee Choura Ghat, or landing-place, lay about a mile to the north-west of the English fort. A picturesque temple is situated close beside it, and at a short distance in the rear it is bounded by a steep rising ground, or natural embankment. Here, with fell treachery, the Nana planted five guns and five hundred musketeers, under the command of a wretch as impervious to all sense of truthfulness or humanity as himself, one Tantia Topee. Sepoys were also drawn up behind the village of Suttee Choura, and a squadron of troopers lay concealed to the south of the Fisherman's Temple. Other arrangements were made, with consummate skill, to ensure the massacre of the little garrison.

At dawn on Saturday, the 27th, the evacuation of the fortification, which had been defended with so much heroism, began. A crowd of carriages and beasts had been assembled; and some of the women and children seated themselves in bullock-carts, some climbed up to the padded back of an elephant. A fine animal, with a state howdah, had been provided for Sir Hugh Wheeler. The wounded were stowed in litters; the others, soldiers and civilians, marched on foot. Through a silent and motionless crowd the strange procession went on its way, and turned into the deep lane that led to the ghat. Then Tantia Topee, who had been anxiously watching for their appearance, saw the white faces and gleaming bayonets; saw the dark tops of the palanquins dancing up and down; saw the howdahs swaying from right to left above the sea of heads. He called to a bandsman who was in attendance, and gave him instructions when to sound his bugle. The last Englishman walked down into the gorge-like lane; and immediately certain troops, appointed to that duty, formed in a double line behind him, and prevented the crowd from following. Meantime, the embarkation was slowly proceeding,—the women, the children, and the wounded had been got into the crazy boats; the officers were preparing to scramble on board,—when the dead silence which had prevailed was suddenly broken by a bugle-call, and instantly a pitiless fire was opened on the little flotilla. The English replied with their rifles; but several of the straw roofs of the barges blazed out into a flame, having previously been ignited by red-hot charcoal, and in the twinkling of an eye the whole fleet was involved in fire. A storm of grape and musketry burst forth from either shore; and the Nana's treachery was complete. To the imagination of our countrymen, oppressed and confused by the bewildering tumult, it seemed that the land was alive with a hundred cannon and a myriad of sharp-shooters.

The details of the foul massacre which ensued we need not repeat. Only one boat got clear, and floated down the main stream. On board the others, the dead soon outnumbered the living; and the murderous troopers, plunging into the river, cut and slashed until their arms were weary with the work. Here is the tale of a half-caste Christian woman who escaped the carnage:—"In the boat where I was to have gone," she says, "was the schoolmistress and twenty-two missies. General Wheeler came last, in a palki. They carried him into the water near the boat. I stood close by. He said, 'Carry me a little further towards the boat.' But a trooper said, 'No; get out here.' As the general got out of the palki, head foremost, the trooper gave him a cut with his sword into the neck, and he fell into the water. My son was killed near him. I saw it—alas! alas! Some were stabbed with bayonets; others cut down. Little infants were torn in pieces. We saw it—we did—and tell you only what we saw. Other children were stabbed and thrown into the river. The schoolgirls were burnt to death. I saw their clothes and hair catch fire. In the water, a few paces off, by the next boat, we saw the youngest daughter of Colonel Williams. A Sepoy was going to kill her with his bayonet. She said, 'My father was always kind to Sepoys.' He turned away, and just then a villager struck her on the head with his club, and she fell into the water." *

When the murderers grew weary of killing, the women and children whom shot and flames had spared were collected and brought to land. They numbered in all one hundred and twenty-five. Some were wet, covered with mud and blood; not a few were wounded; all were faint, and exhausted, and wretched, with a wretchedness that words cannot describe. After a while they were removed to the Savada Kotee, and there confined in a couple of large rooms, under a vigilant guard. Their numbers were soon afterwards augmented by a boat-load of unfortunate wretches intercepted at Nuzzufgurh, and brought back to suffer and die at Cawnpur. Of these all the men were shot down in cold blood; the women and children were thrown into the Savada prison. And soon afterwards a few fugitives were added, who had escaped from Futtehgurh and made their way to Cawnpur, ignorant of the tragedies which had made its name accursed for ever. So that in a couple of rooms, twenty feet by ten, two hundred and six European ladies and children were pent up to endure the burning heat of an Indian summer.

The reader must not suppose that the Indian Government, during all this time, had made no efforts to accomplish the rescue of the sufferers. With all possible speed a force had been assembled under Sir Henry Havelock; but the country was covered with rebel soldiery, and he had to fight his way from Allahabad, which he left on the 6th of July, with desperate resolution—gaining battle after battle against almost overwhelming odds. His march was one long campaign; but, after winning a complete and glorious victory over the Nana's army, Havelock entered the town in triumph on the 17th. Alas, not a single European was living to receive him!

Two days before, all had been massacred; the men first, and then the women and children. The slaughter of the latter was attended with circumstances of peculiar atrocity. Five executioners were employed by the Nana to do the bloody deed; two of whom were Hindu peasants, two Mohammedan butchers, and the fifth a Mohammedan soldier. After some Sepoys had discharged their muskets through the windows, these five men entered the apartments where the poor unfortunates were confined. Shrieks and scuffling made known to those who waited without that the journeymen were earning their horrid wage. By the time darkness had gathered over the scene, the men came forth and locked up the house for the night. The screams then ceased, but groans were heard until morning.

Next day the dead bodies were thrown into a dry well situated behind some neighbouring trees. "The bodies," says an eye-witness, "were dragged out, most of them by the hair of the head. Those who had clothes worth taking, were stripped. Some of the women were alive. I cannot say how many; but three could speak. They prayed, for the sake of God, that an end might be put to their sufferings. I remarked one very stout woman, a half-caste, who was severely wounded in both arms, who entreated to be killed. She and two or three others were placed against the bank of the cut by which bullocks go down in drawing water. The dead were first thrown in. Yes; there was a great crowd looking on; they were standing along the walls of the compound. They were principally city people and villagers. Yes; there were also Sepoys. Three boys were alive. They were fair children. The eldest, I think, must have been six or seven, and the youngest five years. They were running round the well, and there was none to save them. No; none said a word, or tried to save them." They all perished. Before noon on

* We have spoken of one boat as escaping; but only four of its inmates, after undergoing extraordinary perils, reached Allahabad.

the 16th of July, no European remained alive within the circuit of the station. We confess that it is with satisfaction we record the fact that a terrible retribution fell upon all who had taken part, directly or indirectly, in this atrocious massacre. Few of the Cawnpur mutineers escaped the halter or the bayonet; and those few suffered such grievous sufferings, that death had been better for them than life.

We could wish that the innocent had not been involved in the fate which attended the guilty; and that the British soldier, while swift to punish, had been merciful to spare. Yet some excuse may surely be made for men who saw with their own eyes the fresh traces of the massacre, —the women's apartment ankle-deep in blood, and the well choked up with the bodies of women and children. It was difficult to look on these things and not be sensible of a terrible, unappeasable thirst for vengeance. Even now, when Englishmen have learned to regret that the vengeance was so sudden and so indiscriminate, and when the worst memories of the Mutiny have passed away, the cheek flushes, and the eye kindles, and the heart throbs when they read the sad record of the Massacre of Cawnpur!

MEMORIAL AT CAWNPUR.

The fatal Well is now covered with a beautiful Gothic Memorial, enclosing a fine marble statue from the chisel of the late Baron Marochetti. Well may the Angel of Pity extend her wings over so sad a spot! A Memorial Church has also been erected; and the scene of the massacre is occupied by well-ordered gardens, within which no native is allowed to set foot. A magnificent railway bridge of iron now crosses the river; but the bridge of boats which, in 1857, afforded the only means of passage, is still in existence. A recent traveller speaks of the Slaughter Ghat, where the first massacre took place, as the only oasis of greenness along the desolate river-bank. The white walls, with black shot-holes, are now rapidly disappearing; and Cawnpur, with its broad well-kept streets and its neat bungalows, wears the comfortable aspect of a modern English settlement.

There are no public buildings of any importance in the town; no stately palaces, no richly-sculptured pagodas. As a city, it has little to interest or amuse the traveller. Yet to no place in India does the Englishman turn with more eager curiosity. Its associations draw him thither with an irresistible spell. Nor are they wholly painful; for along with its memories of blood and treachery are recollections which make the heart beat proudly,—recollections of the daring courage and heroic endurance of the few defenders who, day after day and night after night, faced the incessant storm of shot and shell, and calmly confronted death, in order that the fame of England might not be tarnished.

CHAPTER XII.

LACKNOW.

VIEW OF LACKNOW—ITS ORIGIN—THE IMPERIAL PALACE—THE MARTINIÈRE—STORY OF CLAUDE MARTIN—THE KAISER BAGH—ITS ASSOCIATIONS—COURT OF THE KINGS OF AÛDH—THE SEPOY MUTINY—SIEGE OF THE RESIDENCY—DEATH OF SIR HENRY LAWRENCE—MEMORABLE PLACES—LORD LAWRENCE'S DURBAR—THE HOSSEINABAD IMAMBARA—THE PRINCE OF WALES'S VISIT.

THERE are few towns in India, says a traveller whose evidence may be accepted without question, which charm the stranger more by their external aspects than Lacknow. On all sides it is surrounded by a spacious park, the green lawns of which are watered by a thousand rills; while its innumerable monuments exhibit their fantastic or graceful outlines above masses of glossy foliage. Nor is this favourable first impression counteracted by anything that one sees on a closer inspection of the city. Its broad streets are regularly built, and lined with handsome houses which are saved from monotony by their wooden balconies and flat terraces; fountains, girdled with tall trees, ornament the principal cross-ways, and cool and refresh the air; the crowds circulating along the sunny thoroughfares are cleanly and picturesquely attired; and the shops are filled with objects which entice and please the eye.

Lacknow—or, as it is more correctly spelt, Lakhnau—was known by the name of Lakchanavati some forty centuries ago, when it was the capital of Lakshmana, the brother of Râma. The present city, however, is of very modern date, and rose into repute and prosperity under the Mussulman emperors of Aûdh (or Oudh) in the seventeenth century. They endeavoured to cover it with buildings surpassing those of Delhi in magnificence; but though the structures they raised astonish by their magnitude, they are soon discovered to possess no architectural merit. They are "eye-deceptions, stage-scenery, mere frameworks covered with tiles and gilding," in which beauty of design and harmony of proportion have been sacrificed to a love of tawdry show and theatrical effect.

The Imperial Palace is really a group of palaces, extending over a very considerable area. Its name, Kaiser Bagh, is a strange compound of the German *kaiser* (emperor) and the Indian *bâgh* (garden); yet it is not inappropriate to the medley pile which a French adventurer designed, and in which Moorish arcades break up an Italian façade, and Chinese bell-turrets cluster round the spire of a Hindu temple.*

* Claude Martin, or Martine, was a poor Breton soldier, who, having been sent with his regiment to Pondicherry, rose to the rank of corporal. The preferment, however, failed to satisfy his ambition; and deserting from his regiment, he plunged into the interior, bent on carving out a fortune. After passing through a succession of marvellous adventures, he reached the court of the King of Aûdh, who was delighted to secure the services of a European, and gave him a captaincy in his army. In some way or other he contrived to gain so entirely his royal master's confidence, that, about 1780, he was both chief counsellor of the Mussulman Cæsar and commander-in-chief of all his forces. To his other talents Martin added a taste for architecture; and all the Mohammedan emperors having been partial to building, he was able at Lacknow to indulge *ad libitum*. He undertook the reform of the native architecture; and the result of his labours, and of those of his pupils, may be seen in the *grandiose* structures of Lacknow. It must be added, to his credit, that he had wise notions of the value of education; and he founded at his own expense the celebrated schools known as La Martinière, where a gratuitous education is supplied to some thousands of children.—*Rousselet*, p. 517; *Russell*, ii.

The Kaiser Bagh occupied many years in its erection, and was finally completed by the ex-king Wajid Ali Shah in 1850, having cost about £800,000. The stranger, on entering, is conducted from one high-walled court to another, where the most interesting features are the huge gates of brass, covered with an infinite variety of richly-wrought devices, including figures of winged mermaids, and fish tied to flowers with a string. Diminutive temples abound, and

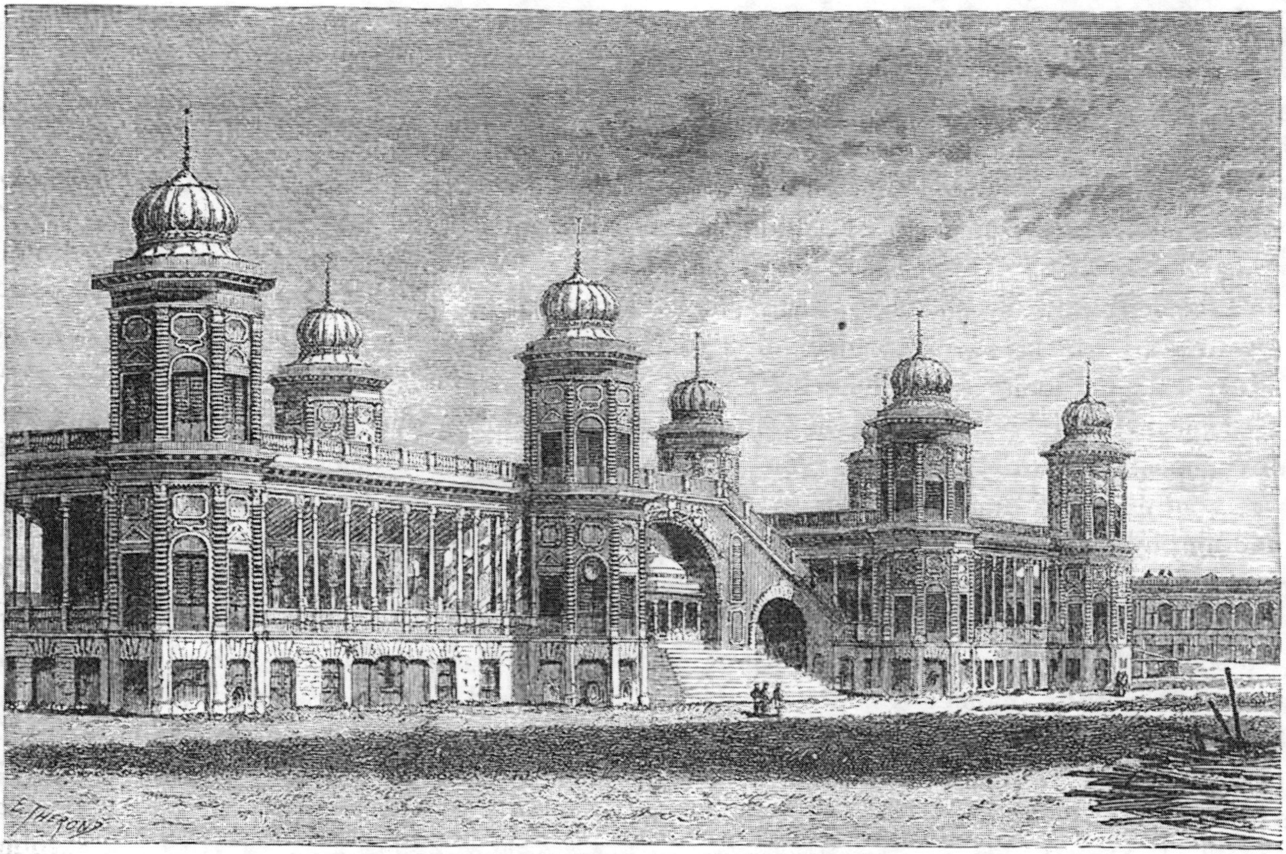

PAVILION OF LANKA, IN THE KAISER BAGH.

fanciful pavilions, prominent among which are the Badshah Manzil, a favourite residence of the last King of Aûdh, and the Chandiwalli Baradari, formerly paved with silver. Through the superb Lakhu Gate, so called because it is said to have cost a lakh of rupees, the visitor enters the grand square of the Kaiser Bagh, where the eye is literally confused by the meretricious splendour of massive pillars and sculptured terraces, and the glittering variety of fountains, water-courses, pagodas, and gilded spires. But a calmer examination convinces him that wide courts, and colonnades, and orange-groves have all a meretricious air about them; and as he wanders among them he feels as if he were assisting at an exhibition of "theatrical properties" on a colossal scale.

Nor does he fail to remember that the darkest memories of unbridled sensuality and moral degradation are indissolubly connected with the architectural pageant before him. If these halls could speak of the scenes formerly enacted within them, the stranger would feel like one who had unwittingly crossed the threshold of Gomorrah. Whether Lord Dalhousie's annexation of Aûdh was politically a blunder, we need not here inquire; but no one who has read Sir William

Sleeman's vivid pages can doubt but that it was high time the infamies of the royal house of Lacknow ceased to be sheltered or connived at by the British Government. The king's court consisted of eunuchs and fiddlers intent on every vice; of ministers and courtiers who pampered the royal appetite and plundered the miserable people; while the king himself was hopelessly sunk in the lowest depths of the lowest debauchery.

To the north of the Kaiser Bagh flows the winding Gumti, and following its course we arrive at the Residency, the palace formerly inhabited by the representatives of British power. It covered a large space of ground, with various buildings within its precincts, such as guard-houses, a banqueting-hall, official quarters, and the Residency proper; all surrounded and separated by lawns and flower-gardens. It was here that, in 1857, the European inhabitants found refuge, and were joined by the small garrison under Sir Henry Lawrence. This able statesman, one of the greatest of our Indian heroes, had anticipated the outbreak of the Mutiny, and prepared for it by the erection of defences and the accumulation of stores and provisions, which enabled him to withstand a siege of several months. As is well known, the garrison were relieved by Sir Henry Havelock after his victory at Cawnpur; but the relievers were in their turn beleaguered by the immense host of the rebel Sepoys, and Lacknow was not finally recovered until the arrival of Sir Colin Campbell's conquering army.

To particularize a little more:—The siege of the Residency began on the 30th of June, and was continued without intermission until the 20th of November. The city and all the surrounding buildings were held by the native troops, who kept up a constant bombardment, firing eighteen-pounders within one hundred and fifty yards of the defences. During the terrific heats of an Indian summer, women and children were crowded into small rooms, or forced to retire to cellars, to escape from the incessant storm of shot and shell. While the soldiers and civilians undauntedly manned the fortifications, and served the great guns, their wives and daughters watched by the side of the sick and wounded, prepared food for their defenders, washed and cooked; and all this while every moment a cannon-ball burst into their place of retreat, or a shell exploded at a few feet distant from them.

Havelock, after losing five hundred men on his march from Cawnpur, and in his four days' desperate fighting in the streets of Lacknow, gained the Residency on the 30th of September, and was received with a tearful welcome. Its defenders originally numbered 1692 fighting men,—that is, 987 Europeans and 705 natives. The fearfulness of the experience through which they had passed is illustrated by the fact that at Havelock's arrival the garrison could muster, including sick and wounded, only 350 Europeans and 133 natives. Early in September the Residency held 220 women, 230 children, and 120 sick and wounded.

Among the dead was the gallant leader, to whose forethought and calm resolution the success of the defence was due. While lying weak and exhausted in his room, he was struck by a splinter from a shell, and the shock was too great for his shattered frame. The last scene of his pure and noble career is thus described by Sir John Kaye. It can never be read without a heart-throb:—

"First of all, he asked Mr. Harris, the chaplain, to administer the Holy Communion to him. In the open verandah, exposed to a heavy fire of musketry, the solemn service was performed,—many officers of the garrison tearfully communicating with their beloved chief. This done, he addressed himself to those about him. 'He bade an affectionate farewell to all,' wrote

IMAMBARA, LACKNOW.

one who was present at this sad and solemn meeting; 'and of several he asked forgiveness for having at times spoken harshly, and begged them to kiss him. One or two were quite young boys, with whom he had had occasion to find fault, in the course of duty, a few days previously. He expressed the deepest humility and repentance for his sins, and his firm trust in our blessed Saviour's atonement, and spoke most touchingly of his dear wife, whom he hoped to rejoin. At the utterance of her name his feelings quite overcame him, and he burst into an uncontrollable fit of weeping, which lasted some minutes. He spoke to several about the state of their souls, urging them to pray and read their Bibles, and endeavour to prepare for death, which might come suddenly, as in his own case. To nearly each person present he addressed a few parting words of affectionate advice—words which must have sunk deeply into all hearts. There was not a dry eye there, and many seemingly hard, rough men were sobbing like children.' He told his chaplain that he wished to be buried very privately, 'without any fuss,' in the same grave with any men of the garrison who might die about the same time. Then he said, speaking rather to himself than to those about him, of his epitaph,—'*Here lies Henry Lawrence, who tried to do his duty. May God have mercy upon him.*' And such is the simple epitaph which is inscribed upon his tomb."

Memorial tablets indicate all the celebrated spots of the Residency, the ruins of which remain in the state in which they were left by Lord Clyde. Thus we read upon one, "Here Sir Henry Lawrence died;" on another, "The site of Mr. Gubbins's House;" and on others, "The Redan Battery," "The Cawnpur Battery,"—and the like. Monuments have also been erected by various regiments to those of their comrades who fell in the Great Siege; and the visitor turns with special interest to the simple, unpretending tombs which enshrine the dust of the heroic Peel, the gallant Havelock, Neil, the bravest of the brave, and the illustrious Lawrence.

With scarcely less interest will his gaze fall upon the ridge or rising ground which connects the plain with the elevated table-land of the Residency; for it was there that the viceroy, Sir John Lawrence, held a grand durbar after the Mutiny, and received the fealty of the Talookdars, or great chiefs of Aûdh. The viceroy, from his chair of state, looked on the grave where his brother lay in peace.

From the Residency we proceed to the fine gateway, the Rumi Durwaza, or Gate of Constantinople, which leads into the Mutchi Bhawan, or Citadel. Here, on the summit of an elevated terrace, stands the Great Imambara, a magnificent pile, with richly-decorated arcades, tapering pinnacles, bell-turrets, and swelling dome, erected towards the close of the eighteenth century by the Nawab Vuzeer Azof-ood-Doulah. Desiring to perpetuate his name by some superb monument, he invited all the architects of India to furnish him with designs, which should exceed in beauty anything achieved by his predecessors. The prize was won by Kaï-fiat-oulla; and it must be owned that his creation shows equal originality and boldness.

Passing onward, we come to the Hosseinabad Imambara, an ample enclosure, containing, in addition to the Imambara, a model of the Taj of Agra, another of the Kootub of Delhi, a mosque, and a bazaar.

Reference must also be made to Claude Martin's own palace, the Constantia, which is imposing enough in the mass, but drives an architect mad when he begins to examine the details. It has been called "original;" and so it is, in the sense that it is an original combination of the features of all the orders of architecture, while the motley façade is overloaded with sculptures of gods and monsters.

The tomb of Ghazi-ood-deen Hyder is another of the "lions" of Lacknow; its interior preserves a collection of miniature portraits of the kings and queens of Aûdh.

The Prince of Wales visited Lacknow in the course of his Indian Progress, and laid the first stone of an obelisk, erected at the cost of the then Viceroy, the Earl of Northbrook, to the memory of the native soldiers who fell, during the siege, under the British flag. This has been described as the most impressive ceremony in which the prince took part in India. "Without the battered and shot-torn walls of the old Residency, the red ensign of England was solemnly saluted with blast of trumpets, raised arms, the rolling of drums, and the firing of cannon. Both European and native troops were present, and formed themselves in three sides of a square before joining in the salute. This effective display of the power and dignity of England was well adapted to produce a strong effect on the native mind."

During his visit the prince was sumptuously entertained by the Talookdars in the Kaiser Bagh; a significant circumstance, when it is remembered that only nineteen years before they had been in revolt against the British Crown.

CHAPTER XIII.

THE CITY OF TEMPLES.

THE HOLY CITY OF THE HINDUS—ITS NAME AND ORIGIN—ITS ANCIENT SPLENDOUR—TEMPLES OF BENARES—BATHING IN THE SACRED RIVER—LIFE IN BENARES—STREET-SCENES—A FESTIVAL DAY—SHOPS AND SHOPKEEPERS—A HINDU TRADESMAN—THE TEMPLES DESCRIBED—THE GOLDEN TEMPLE—WORSHIP OF SIVA—THE SACRED WELL—THE MIRROR OF DOORGA—THE TEMPLE OF GANESA—GREAT FESTIVAL OF GANESA—THE RIVER—A SUCCESSION OF NOVEL SCENES—SCINDIA'S GHAT—A LIVELY PICTURE—RAMNUGGUR—HINDU CEREMONIES OF SEPULTURE—CREMATION—SOME OTHER ASPECTS OF LIFE IN BENARES—THE PRINCE OF WALES'S VISIT.

THE Mohammedans have their "holy city" in Mecca. The hearts of devout Papists turn to Rome. The eyes of the Christian world are more or less steadfastly fixed on sacred Jerusalem. But neither to Mecca, Rome, nor Jerusalem attaches that peculiar odour of sanctity which the faith of the Hindus has attached to Benares. To upwards of one hundred and forty million souls it is the gate of Paradise. Every spot of it is hallowed by the presence and influence of some unseen Power. Its very stones excite the ardour of the pilgrim; and to make a journey to Benares is, in the belief of the Hindu, an action so meritorious as, like charity, to cover a multitude of sins. Its shrines are loaded now, as they have been loaded for generations, with the rich offerings of the noble and the humble tribute of the poor. To die in its holy atmosphere, is to pass at once into bliss immortal. To wash in the cleansing waters of its sacred river, is to purify the soul from all mortal stain. Nowhere else, in a word, is religion so completely *materialized*, and associated with a local habitation, as in Benares. The Christian venerates the earthly Zion as a type of the celestial, and because it witnessed the wonders and love and sufferings of the Son of God. But the Hindu's reverence for Benares has in it nothing of tender sentiment or emotional gratitude; it arises from his implicit faith in the purifying and saving influences of the place itself. It is Benares that he worships, because Benares is to him an embodiment, as it were, of Siva.

There is that in its history which fills even the Christian traveller with astonishment. In spite of the vast revolutions which have swept over India, it retains its old power, its ancient hold upon the minds of men. Even the contact of European civilization seems to have done very little towards shaking its religious pre-eminence. It is still a city of temples; and these temples are still crowded by thousands of worshippers.

The name of Benares is derived from the two rivers, Barana and Asi, which flow into the Ganges on either side of the sacred city. But it is of comparatively modern origin; that is, it has not been in vogue for more than five or five and a half centuries. Ages before, it was the capital of the wealthy and powerful kingdom of Kasi. It flourished as a contemporary of Nineveh and Babylon, and became the centre of Hindu religion and Hindu learning. At first, in the days of the Rig Veda, when Hinduism was a pure and simple monotheism, not a temple, not a shrine, not a place of religious worship was to be found within its precincts. But as the Hindu pantheon increased, temples sprung up in Benares; and its repute for sanctity became so great, that when Buddha undertook to propagate his new doctrines, he selected it as the fitting point of departure, the centre and stronghold of the new faith, the most suitable place wherein to "turn the wheel of the law." It contained at that time about seven hundred schools and colleges, and was the home of the most opulent of the Indian merchants. Its wealth must have been immense, and its inhabitants were famous far and wide for their gorgeous displays. To protect it, a strong citadel stood at the confluence of the rivers Barana and Ganges. The turrets of this citadel were defended by archers with arrows six feet long; its walls by warriors armed with iron-shod clubs, spears, and keen-edged scimitars. And its nobles could muster at need a formidable array of elephants, whose tusks were equipped with sabres, and of war-chariots that rolled forward with impetuous rapidity.

The majority of the one thousand five hundred temples of Benares are situated on the river-bank; and the view from the water is one of great interest and variety, for some are brightly painted, some gay with gilding, some are of elaborately carved stone, others glitter with gilt spires. Behind them rise the flat roofs of the Fakirs' houses, with balconies overhanging gardens of fragrant flowers, and around them thick groves of noble trees. Among these may be seen the shining dome of some private temple belonging to one of the wealthier Hindus, nearly all of whom have their oratories, or private houses of prayer, just as the wealthier Mohammedans have their own mosques. The margin of the river is lined with terraced ghats, or landing-places, where the people come down to bathe, and devotees to reflect, the latter each with a vast grass umbrella extended over his bowed head and bended form; while hundreds are engaged in washing, or in sprinkling holy water, or professing to study the sacred books. Sometimes a thin column of blue smoke ascends from the ghat, and then we know that the funeral pyre has been kindled, and that the greedy flames are quickly consuming the body of the happy pilgrim who came here to die, to die in the sacred city beloved of the gods.

The great majority of the people, we are told, bathe at sunrise, and the ghats then teem with life and motion. Men and women freely enter the water together, and no one is shocked or injured; the daintiest dames, who at all other times veil their faces from the stranger's gaze, and are even borne to the river's edge in close-curtained *tonjans*, to which they will return directly their ablutions are finished, now present themselves in the lightest drapery, perhaps only a sheet of the finest muslin, with their long dark hair "rippling to their knees." It is the custom of the country, and no one turns aside. Thus it is that at every few yards the traveller comes upon beautiful groups in bronze of elegant bathing-nymphs, such as would rejoice a sculptor's heart; and, indeed, of these finely-proportioned bronzes you never think otherwise than as statuary, and no touch of indelicacy or indecency attaches to them.

LIFE IN BENARES.

The visitor feels almost dizzy, as he passes through streets and bazaars which realize the dreams suggested by a perusal of the "Arabian Nights," where the shops are loaded with all kinds of toys and sweetmeats, with dainty stuffs woven by delicate fingers, with exquisite embroideries fit for the adornment of a princess, and vessels of brass and copper, and ornaments

THE MADHORAY GHAT AND THE MOSQUE OF AURUNGZEBE, BENARES.

in silver and gold. On either side are the stalls of the fruit-merchants, their contents reminding him of the spontaneous wealth of the tropical soil,—guavas and pomegranates, plantains and cocoa-nuts, *pumeloes* or shaddocks, fragrant limes, noble pine-apples, creamy custard-apples, and luscious mangoes, with many another fruit and vegetable, appetizing or nutritious. Around these gather the natives, with clear brown skin and garments of different colour, gesticulating and chattering like an Italian crowd; while through the motley multitude stalks, indifferent and undismayed, a great white Brahmanee kite, or a tall grim adjutant-bird.

Let us suppose that it is a high festival day in the City of Temples, and prepare to enjoy it in all its rush of various life. The river-banks, gay with many-tinted clothes spread out to dry, have not ceased to resound with the din of labour; and masons, sawyers, carpenters, toil assiduously in their sheds. A picturesque crowd, glittering in vestments of green, red, or yellow, incessantly move up and down the steps of the great ghat or landing-place, or ripple away in little streams by streets and passages at either side, to mingle with the shadowy perspective of the main street in front. The hour of prayer has struck, and devout Hindus hasten to kneel in devotion on the margin of the sacred river, or to plunge into its turbid waters. Among the thousands of both sexes whom the eye surveys with wonder, not an individual but is or has been engaged in his daily worship. Some are bathing, some stand solemnly in the water with uplifted hands. Hundreds sit shaded by huge umbrellas in covered rafts, either dressing or disrobing—and both processes are very simple; while the bank exhibits a long array of bending pilgrims, filling their brass lotas with holy water, that they may duly asperge the altars of their gods. On a stone pillar, isolated in the stream, a Fakir in long garments kneels motionless in prayer, as if petrified by the wear and tear of centuries. In tiny square cells, raised at intervals along the river-bank, undraped priests of the river-god crouch to receive the gifts of those who desire their blessings for themselves or their kindred. On the flat slabs of masonry forming the roofs of these open vaults, other devotees are busily reciting long prayers, accompanied by numerous genuflexions. Observe yonder enthusiast, erect upon his pedestal, and gesticulating violently at the sun; desisting from this exercise, he repeatedly bows to the ground, and ever and anon strikes his forehead against the stone, before repeating the mysterious gesticulations. His attitude reminds you of the well-known statue of "Ajax defying the lightning." We draw near to the "burning ghat," where the Hindus partially burn the body of their dead before committing it to the Ganges; and we observe that it is black and charred with still smoking cinders,—while a couple of pariah dogs, at the river's edge, are mumbling the bones which have escaped the flames of a contiguous funeral pyre.

Turning to the great ghat, we find the very steps thronged with painted deities—gods and goddesses, black, white, and brown, in every variety of unsightliness; while every available nook and corner, every projecting ledge, presents "some monstrous shape of organized life," or some miniature copy of a temple, into which the people, with many muttered ejaculations, throw marigolds and jasmine-blossoms, together with water from the river.

Again we penetrate into the city, where we are continually meeting with white-robed priests, who beg as lustily as Yogi or Fakir. Far above the turmoil and the dust, prudent men and women calmly parade the flat roofs of their houses, which bloom with fresh plants and flowers, and survey with easy indifference the currents of life that surge to and fro beneath them. More curious are the faces which peep out of the narrow windows on either side. Some of the by-lanes, close enough at all times, are rendered closer to-day by the many-tinted garments hung out to dry on ropes that stretch from roof to basement. And everywhere the eye rests on an animated and seemingly endless panorama of stifling little shops, within which their owners ply their several trades: calico-printers and braziers, handling tiny blocks and hammers; print-sellers, toy-merchants, drapers, and victuallers all busily recommending to prospective customers their different wares,—*dhoolies* and *sarees*, cloths printed and dyed, gods in wood and brass, vestments glittering with gold lace, astrological books and diagrams, jumping-jacks and spinning-tops, grain, seeds, and flowers.

In this rapid survey we must not forget the camels, elephants, and bulls, which form no unimportant part of the population. When a Brahman bull, consecrated to Siva by the priest, and marked with the sign of the trident, stalks through the crowd, it is strange to see with what veneration he is received, and how many hands are eagerly extended to thrust cakes or other dainties into his ample jaws.

Now let us turn aside into this tiny shop, which seems to have been fitted up for doing business with Liliputians. Passing through its dark interior, we ascend a winding staircase to an upper room, where, on our intimating a desire to purchase, rolls of precious *kincob* are spread out before us. Kincob is a certain marvellous brocade of silk and gold, which issues from the dexterous looms of the holy city; and here before us are tissues of the most dazzling hues, wrought with gold and silver in devices very fantastic but exceedingly rich. Brocade fit for an empress, and to be purchased only at prices which empresses can afford! We relinquish our wish to possess a few yards of this wonderful stuff; and we do so all the more willingly because we are forced to own that it could never be fitly worn by English maid or matron,—that it would harmonize only with the bold rich beauty and glowing complexion of a Ranee or a Begum. But it must be said that, as a specimen of human skill and industry, it is perfectly unique. It is surprising, indeed, that the natives, with such imperfect mechanical appliances as are at their command, can ever produce so beautiful and highly finished a work, equally admirable in design and execution.

THE TEMPLES.

But our attention must not be wholly devoted to the streets and shops of Benares, or to the phases of a strange and novel life which they exhibit. In the City of Temples, the metropolis of Hinduism, its shrines and sanctuaries must not be forgotten. And foremost among these, in the estimation of the Hindus themselves, stands the Temple of Bisheshwar, the so-called Golden Temple, dedicated to Siva. "Bisheshwar" is regarded apparently as the tutelary deity of Benares; the god Bhaironath being simply his *khotwal*, or chief magistrate. The spires and domes of his temple are covered with gilded copper, which shine resplendently in the sun, and partly justify the laudatory epithet applied to it. Its domes and pyramids are many; some of these are red, some are gray; all spring aloft out of a mass of sacred peepul-trees.

Close-surrounded by streets and bazaars, and presenting no architectural or artistic beauty that men should love to look upon it, this "filthy little pagoda," as one traveller somewhat too depreciatingly calls it, attracts an immense throng of votaries. You pass into it through a narrow passage which is almost always filled with a surging current of devotees, coming and going, jostling one another unceremoniously, and vociferating with little reverence. Thence you emerge into a court occupied as a bazaar, where the stalls are laden with brazen vessels for temple-use. Brass lotas or pots beautifully engraved with fantastic devices, curious incense-burners, odd spoons, silvery boxes for betel-nuts, brass plates inlaid with shining metal, and every species of idol, great or small, may here be obtained by the curiosity-hunter. The inner court is a high-walled quadrangle, plashing with water, in which a number of sacred bulls contentedly dabble, as they munch the dainties proffered them by the visitors.

Through another close, narrow, and crowded passage you pass into the principal hall, where sacrificial fires burn beneath the golden dome, and wild enthusiasts leap through the flames, like the Baal-worshippers of old, in honour of Mahadéo, the great god.

The central object of attraction is the sacred well through which Siva descended from the light of day into the Other World; a well railed in, and deep, with an iron grating over the water at the bottom, and the lingam, or emblem of phallic worship, affixed to a shaft in the centre. Hundreds of men and women gather round it, dropping in the highly-valued flowers of jasmine and marigold,—or, it may be, the humbler offering of Ganges water from brazen lotas,—muttering the while their monotonous prayers, and touching the iron fence with their foreheads.

Over the well and the well-worship presides a Brahman, seated close at hand, in long robe and skull-cap of scarlet. At his feet lies a vessel filled with water from its gloomy depths; and this having been rendered doubly efficacious by his blessing, he dispenses in precious drops to a constant succession of worshippers, each of whom greedily drinks up his share. At his side is a small box nearly filled with the *pice* constantly pouring into it from grateful hands. For be it observed that they who give nothing receive only the holy (and filthy) water; while they who contribute are rewarded with a blessing, which the priest pronounces aloud, with his hand on the donor's head.

Our next visit may be made to the Doorga Khoond, or Mirror of Doorga, the chief temple of a sanguinary goddess, whose altar reeks with the blood of goats and buffaloes. In front of her shrine, which glitters always with marigolds and other bright blossoms, stands a stone obelisk, surmounted by a dragon; and at the foot lies the great sacrificial sword, used in slaughtering the victims demanded by the goddess's jealous temper.

The temple of Ganesa, god of Wisdom, a many-armed human figure, sitting cross-legged like a Mohammedan, and wearing the head and trunk of the sagacious elephant, is magnificently adorned with ornamentation. The tradition runs that he was born with a human head, but having lost it in a desperate combat, his mother vowed to furnish him with the head of the first living creature she met. This proved to be an elephant, and in this way Ganesa became possessed of the thoughtful elephantine brain. The pillars of his temple are generally carved to represent the limbs of elephants, and their capitals are wrought into huge elephants' heads. It was the old and terrible custom to sacrifice female babes to Ganesa; and the custom was unfortunately popular, because daughters cost much and are worth little in Hindustan,—while, for each daughter thus offered up, the mother was rewarded in due time by the birth of a male child. Such sacrifices were necessarily of the most horrid character; and as the priests exacted heavy fees for performing them, the poorer Hindus satisfied their devotion by becoming the executioners of their own innocent offspring—dipping them into caldrons of boiling milk.

The great festival of Ganesa occurs towards the end of April. It always attracts an immense multitude from every part of India, owing to the popularity of the god, who is regarded as the type of sagacity, prudence, and commercial enterprise, and whose image is conspicuous above the doors of houses of business, because his presence is a safeguard against danger. With the invocation of Ganesa all trade contracts and agreements open ; the invocation being represented generally by a simple sign, indicative of the trunk adorning the god's face. It is estimated that in Benares he possesses two hundred sanctuaries; and early in the morning, on his fête-day, processions are duly arranged in front of each. In a velvet palanquin, which a richly embroidered canopy surmounts, is placed an effigy of the god, made in terra-cotta for the occasion, and glittering with gilded and tinsel ornament. A host of white-robed priests and musicians gather round the sacred litter, and the cortége then moves with measured steps towards the river, preceded by an advanced guard of bayadères, richly attired, who perform a slow dance, waving to and fro their coloured scarfs. These bayadères are "young girls who have been widowed before becoming wives," and have been dedicated by their parents to the service of Ganesa, to prevent their degradation into ordinary nautchnis. Apparently their life is as secluded as was that of a vestal virgin, and they dance only in the temple or at religious ceremonies.

When the different processions reach the terraced river-bank, the scene assumes a truly fantastic character. The crowds, all arrayed in holiday garb, accumulate on the broad stone steps of the ghats, which are soon one motley mass of priests and bayadères surrounding their idols ; while the river is thickly covered with scores and hundreds of boats, gaily equipped with flags. In long skiffs, the prows of which rise sheer out of the water, with bird or quadruped for a figure-head, the Brahmans and bayadères embark with their idols, amid the shouts of the multitude and the clang of musical instruments.

The aquatic display continues until sunset ; but as soon as the golden rim of the great orb of day sinks below the gleaming horizon, the boats lie-to, and the idols are solemnly cast into the sacred waters. This, however, is not the termination of the festival; for as the shadows of evening close over the city the quays blaze out with many-coloured radiance, coruscating fireworks ascend in every direction, and the course of the river is defined by long lines of boats ornamented with lanterns. The Europeans and the wealthy Hindus now enter their skiffs and barges, and, accompanied by nautch-girls and musicians, proceed to share in the revel, and enjoy the strange fantastic spectacle not unworthy of the "Indian Venice."

Following the quay beyond the Munikurnika (or "burning") Ghat, we notice a succession of handsomely decorated palaces, the façades of which rise above immense flights of stairs. Here every rajah has his private residence, which he inhabits on his visits to the religious festivals of the thrice-holy city. One of the stateliest—the palace of the sovereigns of Nagpur—rests on a platform of a hundred massive steps, built up of enormous blocks of white sandstone.

At the further end of this row of palaces, and high above all the Hindu temples, stands the great Mosque of Aurungzebe, with its two shapely minarets, as they spring aloft, seemingly proclaiming the victory of the purer creed of Islam over the dark faith of Siva. Here formerly

FEAST OF GANESA.

stood a celebrated temple of Vishnu, which the Vaishnavas regarded as the sanctuary of their religion, commemorating the spot where Vishnu revealed himself to man. The Emperor Aurungzebe, as a sign of Hindu subjugation, razed it to the ground; and the hundred steps of the Madhoray Ghat, worn by the knees of Hindu devotees who formerly ascended it to prostrate themselves before the image of the god, now lead to the mosque. This, says Rousselet, is a small and even insignificant building, which induces us to regret the loss of the wondrous structure whose site it occupies; yet its minarets, one hundred and forty-seven feet two inches in height, and only eight feet three inches in diameter at the base, are looked upon as architectural marvels. And notwithstanding their comparatively insignificant diameter, they contain a winding staircase of one hundred and thirty steps.

One temple in Benares is very like another, differing only in the types and emblems peculiar to the god to which it happens to be dedicated; and it would be neither interesting nor useful to weary the reader with descriptions which would necessarily present a remarkable sameness. In some are to be seen carved marble bulls, marked with the sacred trident, symbolical of Siva. In many, sacred cows are carefully installed, these being consecrated to Doorga. Peacocks, gleaming in all the brightness of their gay plumage, strut in the open courts of others. And each is filled with a rushing, noisy, gesticulating crowd, carrying their brazen lotas or offerings of radiant flowers.

THE RIVER.

Again we return from the sacred temples to the sacred river, which opens up to our watchful gaze the best and fullest views of the holy city. Each time that the visitor descends it he observes, as he glides along, some object, rare, curious, or interesting, which he had not noticed before.* Some new spire of the fifteen hundred temples attracts the eye, as it flashes in the sunlight; some novel and fantastic combination of pinnacles, domes, balconies, and projecting windows is presented to him; or he is amused with the cooing of innumerable pigeons from innumerable roosts; or with the bright-hued throngs standing, sitting, or lying on the broad landing-places of solid stone; or the gossips—for there are gossips and scandal in Indian cities—clustering on the steep open staircases that rise to heights apparently unguessed-of.

On one or other of the ghats the voyager sees, perhaps, a large, gaudily-coloured image of Ganges mud, "lying like a modern Gulliver among his Liliputian worshippers;" or he sees a devout votary fashioning for his own behoof a little idol of mud or cow-dung, to which he addresses himself in earnest prayer, and afterwards flings it into the river as of no further use. It must not be thought that this is "idolatry," in the common sense of the word; at least, the educated Hindu will indignantly repudiate the imputation, assuring you that he worships an invisible God, and avails himself of his image of mud or wood only to guide and concentrate his thoughts, just as the Papist makes use of rosary or crucifix.

A ghat of magnificent design and construction, built of hewn stone, and enriched with

* "One other ingredient of annoyance mars the enjoyment of most Indian rivers: these are the *dhobies*, or washermen. Perhaps a dozen men, or more, stand in a row along the water's edge, armed with your linen and that of your neighbours, wherewith they scourge the water or some large stone; literally using your nice embroidered raiment as if it were a cat-o'-nine-tails, and as if their one idea of washing were to try how hard they could strike. And at every blow each man exclaims some pet sentence at the top of his voice, generally some one word of two syllables; and this he reiterates till it seems written on your brain. And when a whole troop of *dhobies* thus shout in chorus, the effect is deafening, and suggests some hideous war-whoop, instead of being the peaceful song of those hard-working heroes of soap-suds, who as a class are about the best, and certainly the most diligent, servants in India."—Miss Gordon Cumming.

much carving, is known as Scindia's, and was reared by that remarkable adventurer after he had made his way to a position of absolute power. He intended it to surpass all the other ghats of Benares; but his ambition was foiled in a manner which conveys a lesson to those who care to profit by it. An insignificant stream rippled along the ground where the builders piled their foundations—a stream so insignificant that, instead of diverting its course, they contented themselves with building over it. The consequence was that, silently and slowly, but surely, it undermined the masonry of the new ghat; and before the topmost course was laid, the splendid structure ignominiously tilted backward, as we see it now.

Such, at least, is the story told by the natives, who never allow that earthquakes visit Benares, inasmuch as Siva, who props up the city on his gigantic trident, has carefully guarded it against these calamities.

From a point opposite Scindia's Ghat, a noble view is obtained both up and down the river. Looking back, we see a fine palace of deep red sandstone; the quaint lantern-towers of a group of temples; and, above, on an overhanging bank, the splendid mass of Aurungzebe's Mosque. Beyond, spreads the bloom of leafy gardens; and we count a long series of ghats, and catch sight of the Old Fort impending above the Bridge of Boats. Looking up the river, we mark cluster after cluster of conical towers of elaborately carved stone, most of them bearing the symbol of the golden trident of Siva—that Janus-like or double-faced deity who, under the name of Mahadéo, is recognized as the Author of Life, while under the name of Siva he is dreaded as the great Destroyer. Away beyond these rises the Nepaulese Temple, with projecting eaves, like a Chinese pagoda. Next to it stands a sanctuary dedicated to the goddess of small-pox. On the opposite bank is Ramnuggur, the palace of the Maharajah; while in front of us we take in the sweep of the great city, with its temples, its houses, and its green trees.

In the centre a temple, painted deep red, and bristling with gilded spikes, is partially shrouded by wreaths of blue smoke, which ascend from the burning-ghat just beyond. And this burning-ghat calls to mind the funeral customs of the Hindus. As for the poorer classes, they carry their dying relatives to the river's edge, so that they may pass away in sight of the sacred waters, and happy in the assurance of eternal bliss. Sometimes, it is to be feared, their death is expedited by a dose of Ganges mud; in other cases, a gratuity secures the attendance and absolving prayers of a holy Brahman; in others, again, the living wait in patience, and apparently without regret, for the moment of departure, after which they abandon the lifeless body to the furious appetite of pariah dogs and birds of prey.

Sometimes the affecting spectacle is seen of a Hindu mother bringing her first-born to be committed to the waves on a bier woven of leaf and blossom, while her attendants sprinkle flowers as offerings to the stream.

But the richer Hindus, as soon as the last breath has been offered up, buy as much wood as they can afford: perhaps only just enough to "char the body," which is then cast into the river, and allowed to float slowly down the lazy current; more frequently, as much as will suffice to raise an appropriate funeral pyre.

The corpse is then cleansed in the river waters, swathed in cloth of gold or silver, or attired in a shroud of fair white linen, or it may be scarlet, or, still better, of sacred saffron, on which a little vermilion paint is sprinkled, to symbolize the blood of sprinkling as the atonement for sin. A litter of dry and fragrant grass is afterwards accumulated upon the pyre, and sweet-scented anointing-oil, so that the live flames may leap up with vigorous brightness; and all the preparations being complete, an officiating Brahman hands a lighted torch to the chief mourner, who, taking it in his hand, walks three to nine times round the pile in the direction of the sun's course. The wan lips of the corpse are touched with the holy fire, and then the pyre is lighted. Numerous other torches are immediately applied; the wood crackles; the flames glide from point to point; wreaths of blue smoke coil up into the air; and in a very short time the process of cremation is complete. The ashes are then gathered up, and entrusted to the sacred Ganges, which bears them onwards to the all-embracing sea.

The visitor to Benares is particularly struck—more, perhaps, than in any other Indian city—by the variety, and, so to speak, the abundance, of the life that flows around him. Nowhere does he find a place of solitude or silence; and he wonders how Brahman or Fakir can concentrate all his faculties in a state of self-absorption when so much action and movement obtain in all directions. The river is not less animated than the streets. Throughout the day boats of every kind are passing up and down the stream—sometimes lazily drifting down with the current, sometimes crowding on all their quaintly-shaped canvas, brown, or pure white, or weather-worn, as the case may be; whole families are wafted by in large house-boats, roofed over with straw or bamboo, which form their permanent dwelling-places, as on the Chinese rivers; big barges, with enormous rudders, and piled-up cargoes of rice or cotton, labour heavily along; and gaily-painted pleasure-skiffs carry merry parties up or down, or convey wan-eyed silent pilgrims from bank to bank. Here you will see a raft, loaded with jars of milk, propelled across by a dexterous swimmer. In short, the surface of the river teems with life, and its echoes repeat the shouts and laughter of a continuous throng.

The Prince of Wales visited Benares in December 1875. After viewing its principal "sights," he descended the river to Ramnuggur, the palace of the Maharajah,—being towed thither in a barge, the bows of which were adorned with wooden figures of prancing steeds, painted profusely with white and gold. The chair in which he sat was covered with blue silk, edged by a fringe of golden lotus-leaves. At the palace he was received by a vast array of native warriors on horses, and by a phalanx of elephants and camels. On his return, the river and the ghats were richly illuminated with coloured fires.

One of the London "Special Correspondents" in the prince's train speaks of the river-part of the city, with its terraces of old temples and mosques, and tiers of stone steps looming out through the pale mist, as magnificent. In the European suburb, he says, is a college like the Queen's College at Cork, and surrounded by extensive gardens. The prince laid the stone of a new hospital, and opened a "town-hall;" both of which are of European design, and will form a striking contrast to the native temples, with their domes, and pinnacles, and terraced roofs.

CHAPTER XIV.

IN CENTRAL INDIA.

VISIT TO DHOLEPUR—ITS MOSQUE—SACRED LAKE OF MUCHKOONDO—TEMPLE OF JUGGERNAUT—IN THE BUNDELCUND—DUTTIAH—ITS TEMPLES—THE GOLDEN MOUNTAIN—JHANSI—ITS RANEE, AND HER SHARE IN THE MUTINY—OORCHA—A GARDEN OF FLOWERS—CHUTTERPUR—HINDU FESTIVAL OF THE HOLI.

FROM Futtehpur Sikri, with its memories of Akbar, we may make our way to Dholepur, about thirty miles distant in a straight line. It is situated on the banks of the Chumbul, and is the capital of an independent state, recognized as such by the English Government in 1806. It is divided into three districts, separated from each other by solitary wastes—Purana Chaonee (or "Old Camp"), Naya Chaonee ("New Camp"), and Kila. We shall glance briefly at its principal monuments.

The mosque, built in 1634 by Shah Jehan, is small, but very graceful. A Mussulman cemetery surrounds it; and here is to be seen the Jasjiree, a monumental marble cenotaph, enshrining the remains of a Syud missionary. On the summit of a cliff, washed by the tumultuous waters of the Chumbul, stands an ancient fortress, with massive walls strengthened by circular towers. The interior is a mass of ruins.

Deep among the Pathar peaks, two miles from the town, lies the sacred lake of Muchkoondo,—which, according to the legend, was created by the god Krishna, to reward the hero and prince Mouchou, who had saved his life. It is rather a tank or basin than a lake—about two thousand feet in length, and six hundred and fifty feet in width, and reflecting in its still waters the marble colonnades and cupolas of the temples and palaces which, buried among venerable trees, surround it on all sides.

The principal temple is dedicated to Juggernaut, the "Lord of the World," beneath whose car, on the occasion of his great annual festival, so many devotees were content to fling their despised bodies, in joyful anticipation of a violent death.

THE BUNDELCUND.

By way of Gwalior, we strike onwards to the river Sind, which separates the states of Scindia and Bundelcund. Of Bundelcund the Englishman often hears; but it may be doubted whether many of our readers will have an accurate idea of its position. It is a mountainous region, lying between the spurs of the great Vindhya range and the Jumna, and stretching from the river Sind in the west to the Tonse in the east. Picturesque landscapes are everywhere presented by its successive formations of hill and valley, and by the bright streams which flow into the Jumna, through glens richly covered with wood. In the northern part spread some extensive and well-cultivated plains, which are thickly peopled; but the rest of the country is an

PALACE OF BIRSING-DEO.

almost unexplored forest, producing, among other trees, the mhowah, the bur, and the catechu, besides noble timber trees which belong to our European species. It is a sad association of these immense woods, that in their shade the sanguinary creed of Thuggism first made its appearance. There, too, the Dacoïts, or highway murderers, flourished until hunted down by the British Government; and there the infamous Nana Sahib found an asylum when he fled from the City of Massacre. No great road or railway has yet opened up this wide extent of country, which was formerly included in one powerful kingdom, but is now divided into several independent states, inhabited by races of impure blood and mixed origin.

DUTTIAH.

Crossing the Sind in the track of M. Rousselet, to whom we owe our latest information respecting the Bundelcund provinces, we arrive at Duttiah, the capital of a small kingdom of the same name. It lies amid lakes and woods, at the base of a considerable hill, with the steeples of innumerable temples rising high above the red-tiled roofs of the houses; and, soaring still higher, the domes and clock-towers of the two royal palaces.

There is something characteristic about the Duttiah temples. Each may be described as a square chapel, surmounted by a high conical or pyramidal steeple, which is flanked by four clock-towers. The interior has but little ornamentation; the walls, however, are painted,—and, of course, the altar and the *lingam* of Iswara are always present. Of the two palaces, interest attaches only to that of Birsing-Deo—a quadrangular mass, each side about three hundred feet long and one hundred feet high, with a central dome raising its pinnacle to a height of one hundred and fifty feet above the level of the terrace. Superb balconies of carved stone adorn the four-storied façade, in the centre of which an ogival portico is surmounted by a beautiful loggia. Five other domes crown the summit. The entire pile is of granite, and sits solidly on a grand vaulted terrace, the arches of which are forty feet high.

About six miles to the north-west rises the "Golden Mountain," or Sonaghur, a place of pilgrimage held in high repute among the Jains of Central India. It is surrounded by pyramids of granite, which the action of water has wrought into so many natural *lingams*. At the base of Sonaghur lies a pretty village, embosomed among trees; its summit is crowned by the domes of numerous temples; and temples also cover the whole surface of its eastern slope. They are built of brick, but the walls are coated externally with a smooth white plaster made of shell-lime. A few of them date from the thirteenth century, but they mostly belong to the sixteenth or seventeenth; and the variety of styles—Roman, Saracen, Gothic, modern Jain—is perfectly bewildering.

JHANSI.

Our next halting-place is Jhansi, a place of direful interest in the Great Mutiny. At that time its throne was occupied by the Ranee, a woman of ability, courage, and great personal charms, who chafed under the supervision exercised by the British Government. When the Sepoys rebelled, she thought the hour had come to strike a blow for independence. She put to death all the Europeans of Jhansi, gathered together a small army, and, like another Semiramis, led them to join the forces of Tantia Topee, who owed much to her sagacious counsel. Eventually they were driven back into the forests of the Bundelcund, and enclosed within a ring of avenging British troops, which gradually drew closer and closer upon them, until, in one final battle, the rebels were crushed, and the Ranee perished among her fighting-men. At the same time Sir Hugh Rose, afterwards Lord Strathnairn, captured Jhansi (1858). Stealing from the citadel under cover of night, the mutineers fled to a neighbouring hill which formed a natural fortress of great strength The British troops, however, fought their way to the summit, and drove the enemy right over the abrupt precipice, which has since been known by the name of the Hill of Retribution. No campaigns in Indian military history have been more brilliantly conducted than those in Central India by which Sir Hugh Rose exterminated the remnants of the Sepoy power.

Modern Jhansi dates only from the seventeenth century. It is a place of considerable trade, its bazaars being filled with the famous blue cotton stuffs of the Deccan and the exquisite muslins of Chandêri. The British cantonments are well laid out and strongly fortified; they are always occupied by a considerable military force.

OORCHA.

On the traveller's route to Oorcha, the former capital of Bundelcund, he passes the artificial basin of Lake Barwa-Sâgur, formed by the damming up of the waters of a small tributary of the Betwa. The jungle around is a favourite haunt of the tiger, the jackal, and the hyena; and night is made hideous by the cries of wild beasts in search of prey.

Oorcha lies about eight miles from Jhansi, on the left bank of the Betwa, an arm of which encircles and isolates its citadel. It was founded in 1531, and flourished greatly under the rule of Madhikar Sâh and Birsing-Deo; the latter a sovereign of equal ambition and ability, who extended his dominions from the Vindhyas to the Jumna. Afterwards it became a vassal to the Mogul; and finally it was captured and devastated by the Mahrattas. Its monuments, however, still testify to its former splendour; and its temples and palaces vie in architectural beauty with those of the most powerful Indian cities. The brightest dream of a poet's brain scarcely ever conceived of anything fairer than its Garden of Flowers, with its groves of tropical fruit-trees and its masses of bloom, and its elegant domed pavilion-palace. The Raj Mahal, or royal palace, is an edifice of imposing size; while the Citadel, with its long line of loopholed walls and pointed battlements, conveys an idea of impregnability, which, before the introduction of artillery, might perhaps have been realized. There are also the massive palace, with its enamelled cupolas, which Birsing-Deo erected for the reception of the Emperor Jehanghir; the tomb of Birsing-Deo, a colossal mausoleum ample enough to content even so restless and fiery a spirit; and the grand cruciform temple of Chutter Bhoje, which rests upon a solid granite terrace nearly fifty feet in height.

CHUTTERPUR.

Through Calpee, which is British territory, and by way of Nowgong, a British station, we proceed to Chutterpur, a large but uninteresting town, dating from the close of the seventeenth century.

We may here become eye-witnesses of the great Hindu festival or saturnalia of the Holi, which, to the cultured mind of the scholar, cannot fail to recall the orgies that of old disgraced the worship of Cytherea. It has undergone a degradation similar to that which, undoubtedly, the Greek rite underwent in the course of generations. Holica, at Chutterpur, is not that

THE "GOLDEN MOUNTAIN," SEEN FROM THE VILLAGE.

Goddess of Spring which the pure Rajput intellect imagined, and in which it typified the resurrection of Nature after its winter-sleep; but a female demon, symbolical of lust, who, springing from the head of Mahadeva, introduced dissension and strife into Meruu, the Brahman Olympus. As Vivien beguiled Merlin, so the licentious goddess entangled even Brahma and

MAUSOLEUM OF BIRSING-DEO AT OORCHA.

Indra in her wiles; nor would she set them free until Brahma had bestowed upon her twenty-four titles of honour, and undertaken on his oath to celebrate her name by an annual outburst of the wildest revelry. And when this great festival takes place, the scene is characterized by the coarsest and most loathsome uncleanness. Deeds are done which may not be described; the tenderest feelings of humanity are outraged; while women and children vociferate hymns in praise of the obscene goddess, and shrieking crowds surround the blaze of bonfires, swelling the fearful discord of tomtoms, gongs, and cymbals.

CHAPTER XV.

AJMIR—JAIPUR—BHURTPUR.

SITUATION OF AJMIR—ITS BAZAARS—ITS WOMEN—A SAINT'S SHRINE—A JAIN MOSQUE—KISHENGURH VISITED—JAIPUR—FOUNDED BY JAY SING II. —THE ROYAL PALACE—JAY SING'S OBSERVATORY—ULWUR—ITS ROMANTIC POSITION—BHURTPUR—ABOUT THE JATS—TWO GREAT SIEGES OF BHURTPUR—THE PRINCE OF WALES'S VISIT.

THE province of Ajmir, in Rajputana, is part of our Indian Empire, having been annexed in 1818. It is about eighty miles in length, from the Aravalli Mountains to the Bunas; and forty miles broad, from Ajmir to the Kari Nadi.

Its capital, Ajmir, situated in the midst of abundant gardens of roses which yield the celebrated attar, is sheltered by the strong fortress of Taragurh. It was founded in the first century by the Chohan Aja Pal, who gained possession of the whole country, and left his name to the town, as *Aja Mir*, the "Mountain of the Shepherd," or *Aji Mir*, the "Invincible Mountain."

It occupies the centre of a fair valley, one side of it lying on the edge of the fine broad lake of the Ana Sagur, the other enclosed by the declivities of the fortified Taragurh. We need not marvel that it was a favoured resort of the Mogul emperors, for its position is exceedingly picturesque, and its climate delightfully healthy. They filled it, as was their wont, with gardens and palaces—one of which, now converted into the British Residency, was the Daulat Bâgh, or "Garden of Splendour," of the Emperor Jehangir. The same emperor raised the ramparts which crown the summits of the surrounding hills and join the lofty citadel.

Next to Jaipur, Ajmir can boast of the most splendid bazaars in Rajputana. They are of English construction; fine, broad, well-paved highways, lined with stately houses, the ground-floors of which are shops, and stored with the products of Rajputana. The better houses, built of marble, are singularly beautiful; and though mostly modern, equal the most admirable efforts of Rajput art. They belong to the bankers and merchants of the province, whose taste is not less remarkable than their commercial enterprise. The older portions of the town are thoroughly Eastern, and delightfully picturesque. All the races of India, it is said, jostle one another in the narrow winding streets; and beneath the dark stone arches of the stalls are exhibited the most various manufactures. Here the high-caste jeweller, with the sacred cord round his waist, sits on his elevated bench, working with delicate fingers at the most beautiful jewels, while his sons and workmen around him mould or forge the precious metals. There the musical-instrument maker may be seen at work on his viols, guitars, and tomtoms. Here the bracelet maker sits before a fire, and melting his green or red lacquer, pours it over a conical mould. With a sharp knife he splits the molten substance into thin circles; it cools suddenly, and the result is a score of rings. There the shoemaker plies his trade, embroidering some dainty slippers for the feet of high-born dames; while elsewhere we meet with dyers, potters, and coppersmiths, all busy, and all silent. The bazaars of the clothiers and vendors of manufactured stuffs make the best appearance. The shops are clean and well-lighted; and their owners, enthroned on snow-white cushions, gravely await the coming of purchasers, while their clerks cover endless rolls of paper with interminable rows of figures.

The women of Ajmir do not affect the ordinary native seclusion. They are pretty and graceful, and though allowed much freedom are modest in their manners. Those of the Hindus are recognized by the *kangra* or short petticoat, and the *sari* or scarf; the Mussulman women by their tight trousers.

There are no monuments in the town, except the splendid shrine of the great saint Khoja Moúinouddin Chisti, or Khwajah Saiyad, the first disciple of the Prophet who taught the doctrines of the Prophet to the unbelievers of Ajmir. And there are few noteworthy buildings, except the mosque of Arhai-din-ka-Jhopra, which is at once one of the noblest structures raised by Mohammedan architects, and one of the most elegant specimens of Jain architecture. This twofold character is due to the circumstance that the Mogul emperors, in the construction of their palaces and sanctuaries, employed Hindu architects, and used the materials of the palaces and temples of the Hindu kings. The front is pierced with seven arches, each consecrated to one of the days of the week, and embellished with the finest sculpture conceivable. The interior is astonishingly magnificent, with its graceful pillars and carved roof, its Jain domes, and its decorative work of palm-leaf and pearl; a whole which is not less superb in conception than perfect in execution.

We may notice, also, the massive palace of the Seths, now occupied by a banking firm; it is truly a remarkable pile of white marble, of modern date, yet rivalling in beauty the monuments of the earlier Hindu architecture. The front is richly embellished with finely carved cornices and ornamented balconies of quaint design.

But we must move onward; and passing the sacred lake of Poshkur,—in its valley of shifting sand, with its shores lined by Brahman temples,—and the Naga Pahar, or Rock of the Serpent, we reach the town of Kishengurh, built on a high hill above the lake of Gondola. Thence we proceed to Doudon, a frontier-town of the Jaipur kingdom; and, next, to Jaipur, the capital of the ancient state of Dhoundhar.

Jaipur was founded in 1728 by Jay Sing II., a remarkable man, who, having served Aurungzebe as one of his lieutenants, ascended the throne of Amber, and driving out all the imperial garrisons, laid the foundations of a great kingdom. He was a profound scholar and a wise legislator, and it should be remembered to his honour that he endeavoured to abolish infanticide.

Amber seeming to him unfitted for the capital of a prosperous and powerful state, he founded the city of Jaipur, or Jainuggur; laid it out in noble streets; adorned it with handsome buildings; raised in its centre a splendid observatory; and attracted to the new capital a goodly number of men of science and letters.

The royal palace, or the Chandra Mahal, is a huge pyramidal pile, overlooking an Eden-like scene of gardens, lakes, and fountains. Jay Sing's Observatory is situated to the east of it, and is not, as might be supposed, a building for the reception of astronomical instruments, but a spacious court filled with structures which supported the immense apparatus invented by the king. It is difficult, we are told, to conceive of anything more singular or grotesque than its gigantic dials, the copper wheels suspended between its marble columns, and the walls built in eccentric curves and projections. One might almost suppose it to be the embodiment of an astronomer's nightmare!

Ninety miles to the north of Jaipur lies Ulwur, sheltered by an offshoot of the Aravallis. The state is recognized as in alliance with England, and its Maharajah is "advised" by an English Resident.

The capital, of the same name, is most romantically situated at the mouth of an amphitheatre of the most rugged mountain-peaks imaginable. It is built on a hill, and surrounded by fortifications. Its streets are narrow and densely thronged, and its bazaars are crowded with wares of every kind. Rising above them all is the royal palace, a pile of white marble. picturesque in outline; and on the other side of a small lake stands the Mausoleum of the Rajah Buktawur Sing.

Our course now takes us to Bhurtpur, the capital of the Jât state of the same name, which lies between the kingdoms of Jaipur, Ulwur, Dholpur, and the province of Agra.

The Jâts appear to have been a nation of shepherds, who forced their way into Western India some time before the Rajput invasion, and have always remained foremost in numerical strength and importance. Their native country would seem to have lain beyond the Oxus. To the descent of the Mohammedans they opposed the stoutest resistance. In 1026 they arrested the victorious progress of Mahmoud on the banks of the Indus. In 1205 they strove vigorously with the Emperor Kootub for the possession of the country of Hansi. In 1397 they faced the conquering legions of Tamerlane, who overthrew them with a terrible slaughter; and even from the Emperor Baber their bravery extorted a generous acknowledgment. Allying themselves with the Rajputs, they eventually beat back the Mohammedan power, and seated themselves at Agra and Delhi. Wherever they have settled themselves, they have become formidable through their valour and resolution. In the Punjab, where they are known as Sikhs, they proved the most formidable opponents that the British armies had encountered in the East; and they now furnish our standards with the best and most trustworthy of the native soldiery.

The Jât belongs to the Indo-European family. He has a bright intelligent face, with quick dark eyes, aquiline nose, high forehead, and abundant hair and beard. Tall and well-limbed, he is generally of a very prepossessing appearance. A Sikh warrior is one of the finest types of humanity. The women are mostly comely, and always taller than those of other Indian tribes. When abroad, they discard the veil.

In the annals of the British army, Bhurtpur is celebrated for its two great sieges. In 1804, Runjeet Sing, Rajah of Bhurtpur, was one of the most powerful of Indian princes. Joining Holkar in his opposition to British rule, his army was defeated at Laswari and Deeg, and driven back into the capital, which the British, under General Lake, immediately invested. The trenches were opened on the 4th of January 1805. On the 9th the breach made by the artillery was considered practicable, and Lake ordered a night-attack. This was made with true

GENERAL VIEW OF BHURTPUR.

British vigour, and every inch of ground was fiercely contested. But the attacking force proved too weak to prevail over the desperate courage of the defenders, and, with a loss of four hundred and fifty-six men, retired. Another breach having been effected at a more favourable point, a second assault was adventured. The English soldiers heroically swam across the flooded moat, and essayed to scale the ramparts; but, though they never displayed a more brilliant heroism, they were forced to retreat, leaving behind them twenty officers and five hundred and fifty men. Three other attacks were made, with equal want of success; and Lake, for want of men and material, was reduced to the necessity of blockading the city. This brought the rajah to terms, and a treaty having been concluded, the English general raised the

PALACE OF DURGUN SÂL, CITADEL OF BHURTPUR.

siege—having, in three months and twenty days, lost nearly two thousand four hundred officers and men.

In 1825, the grandson of Runjeet Sing was deposed by the Jât, Dourjun Sâl. As the former was under the protection of our Indian Government, an English army was immediately despatched to restore him to his throne. Lord Combermere opened fire on the 14th of December; and two breaches having been effected, a double assault was ordered on the 18th of January 1826. In spite of the loss and disorder caused by the explosion of a mine, and of the determined resistance offered by the Jât grenadiers, it proved successful, and the English entered Bhurtpur in triumph. Lord Combermere then proceeded to avenge the partial defeat of his predecessor by demolishing the citadel which the natives called the Fortress of Victory, and professed to have been erected on the bodies of Lake's soldiers. He also dismantled the fortifications, which now consist of a long line of ruins.

The Prince of Wales visited the "City of Victory" in February 1876. He entered it at twilight; and one of the correspondents who followed in his train seems to have been much impressed by all he saw in the "soft obscure." The city appeared to him "the daintiest and most classical *native* city in India." The broad regular streets are lined with pavements of white stone, and lighted with gas. The two public squares or parks blossom with flowers, and sparkle with fountains, which refresh with their spray the thirsty shrubs. The houses, built in regular lines and blocks, are prevented from assuming a monotonous appearance by boat-shaped pagodas, perforated screens and kiosks, trellised balconies, and quaintly-carved mouldings. The plaster fronts are painted pink, and embellished with figures and fishes and floral designs in lines of white.

Beneath the upper stories are the shops, all gaily set out with woollen stuffs, brass ware, and armour. At intervals they are shaded by the never-dying peepul-trees, on the knotted clumps of which groups of natives, in white and scarlet, take their rest. The passage of time is noted every hour by musical chimes from lofty campaniles or bell-towers, the fronts of which exhibit handsome clocks. There is a "Mayo" hospital, with English surgeons, erected in commemoration of the friendship borne by the Rajput king to the murdered viceroy; a "Maharajah's College," where two or three hundred little "baboos" are excellently taught; and there is also a school of art.

CHAPTER XVI.

OODEYPUR AND THE RAJPUTANA.

FROM BOMBAY TO AHMADABAD—AHMADABAD DESCRIBED—THE GREAT MOSQUE OF SHAH ALUM—THE "TOMB OF THE QUEENS"—THE LAND OF THE BHEELS—CHARACTERISTICS OF THE BHEELS—TINTOOL, THE RESIDENCE OF A RAJPUT THAKOOR—KHAIRWARA—OODEYPUR—THE MAHARANA'S PALACE—ANOTHER DURBAR.

WE propose to conduct the reader on an excursion into Rajputana, by way of Surat, Baroda, Ahmadabad, and Ajmir, which are the principal stations, as it were, on the road from Bombay to Delhi or Agra. The route also passes through Oodeypur, a town of very considerable interest.

Ahmadabad, the ancient capital of the Sultans, was founded in 1412, by the Sultan Ahmed, on the site of an earlier Hindu city, called Ashawal. In erecting his mosques and palaces, he made full use, it would seem, of the plunder he had acquired in the capture of the Rajput cities of Chandravati and Anhilwara Patan. His æsthetic tastes were inherited by his descendants, with the result that the sanctuaries which they raised for the purposes of Mohammedan worship preserved the characteristics of the purest indigenous architecture. About 1570 the Moguls took possession of the city, and here the beautiful Noor Jehan for some years held her luxurious court. In 1737 the Guikwar of Baroda annexed it to his territories; and in 1818 it fell into the hands of the British.

Ramparts, nearly eight miles in circuit, surround the city; and towers and bastions, reputed to date from 1485, strengthen the fortifications. There are eighteen gates of a massive character, and within these lies a belt of garden-ground and pasture-land, which the visitor traverses before arriving at the city proper. Broad walks, shaded by fine trees, radiate through Ahmadabad in all directions, and afford convenient access to its principal buildings. The life and activity of the place apparently concentrate in the great thoroughfare of the Manik Chowk, which is at once mart and market. A busy crowd constantly circulates to and fro, and elephants and camels stalk along, loaded with motley burdens. In the minor streets dwell the handloom weavers, who, with the simplest and even rudest appliances, manufacture the kinkhub, or gold cloth, for which Ahmadabad is scarcely less famous than Benares. Diving into their low whitewashed houses, the European sees many of the most interesting incidents of native life: a party of hired mourners wailing by the bier of the dead; a woman grinding with a quern, while rocking her baby's cradle by a string fastened to one of her toes; another shelling rice with a club; a third ginning cotton with the rude wheel or *churka;* and a fourth rapidly reeling silk with foot and hand.

One of the sights of Ahmadabad is the great Mosque of Shah Alum, beautiful even in its decay. It consists of several arcades arranged in parallel order, with the pulpit, and the Mecca niche or sanctuary in the centre. Several minor buildings are attached to it, including the tombs of the founder and his queens; the walls being built up of plates of pierced stone, arranged, fifty or sixty together, in the most varied designs.

Ahmadabad contains about fifty mosques, most of them embosomed in grove and orchard, and raised on terraces of stone,—besides numerous mausoleums, of which the most beautiful in its simplicity is the Rani-ka-Rauzah, or "Tomb of the Queens." They belong to the era of the Mohammedan kings of Guzerat (from 1412 to 1572), and are as exquisite in design as in execution. Fergusson says of them:—"In Ahmadabad the Hindu influence continued to be felt. Even the mosques are Hindu, or rather Jaina, in every detail; only here and there an arch is inserted,—not because it was wanted constructively, but because it was a symbol of the faith; while in their tombs and palaces even this is generally wanting. The truth of the matter is, the Mohammedans had forced themselves upon the most civilized and most essentially building race at that time in India, and the Chaulukyas conquered their conquerors, and forced them to adopt forms and ornaments which were superior to any the invaders knew or could have introduced. The result is a style which combines all the elegance and finish of Jaina or Chaulukya art with a certain largeness of conception which the Hindu never quite attained, but which is characteristic of the people who at this time were subjecting all India to their sway."

Crossing a chain of low hills, we enter the Bagur, or country of the Bheels—a wild, rugged, mountainous region lying between Malwa and Guzerat, and forming the south-eastern boundary of Rajputana, or the land of the Rajputs. The mountains that spread over it their ramifications are the *nexus*, or junction-point, of the two great Indian ranges of the Aravallis and the Vindhyas, and to the natives are known as the Doungher. Forests abound, and are composed of stately trees, among which tower the colossal banians and other forest-giants. Nor is animal life less pleasant; and the sportsman may take his choice of game, from the man-eating tiger to the rosy-winged flamingo.

As for the Bheels themselves, they are probably a remnant of the great autochthonous race which formerly peopled the hills and vales of Malwa and Rajputana. The Aryan invasion forced them back into the mountains, where they gradually decreased in numbers, and fell from their original standard of civilization. They now resemble in many respects the Scottish Highlanders of two or three centuries since. They are divided into independent clans, each member of which serves his principal with blind fidelity; and their chief sustenance is derived from their plunder of the Hindus, whom they hate with an hereditary hatred. When they are not fighting or thieving,—and these amusements have been restrained by the strong hand of the Anglo-Indian Government,—they employ themselves in hunting and fishing. Living an Ishmaelite life, they plant their *pâls* or villages on commanding heights; and each house, with its fence of prickly cactus, forms a little fortress. When an enemy approaches, the women and children drive off the cattle into the ravines, while the men remain behind to defend their hearths and homes.

No distinctions of caste are observed amongst them, and members of different tribes freely intermarry. Simple to an excess is the marriage ceremony. On a certain day all the nubile

TRAVELLERS ATTACKED BY BHEELS.

young men choose their partners among the nubile virgins, and each retires with his lady-love into the forest; returning, after a few days' seclusion, in the recognized capacities of man and wife. A like simplicity of principle distinguishes their religion: they worship the elements, and the ills that flesh is heir to, and the *mhowah*—a colossal tree, which supplies them with oil, wood, and a stimulating liquor. Their temple is a rudely wrought flagstone, or a mass of stones daubed with red ochre.

Physically, the Bheels are distinguished by their robust frames, which are generally of the middle height, and their vigour, nimbleness, and strength. Their features are coarse, the cheek-bones being prominent, and the nose flat; they wear their hair, which is black, loose and dishevelled—twisting a single coil round the head by way of turban. Their clothing consists of a fold of cotton round the loins, only a few inches broad. The women are not so dark-complexioned as the men, are of an elegant figure, and move with a considerable degree of grace and dignity. Their attire includes a piece of cloth, which, after encircling the loins, is drawn over the shoulder, so as to leave one breast bare; and such a number of bangles on the arms and legs as to reach from wrist to shoulder and ankle to knee.

The weapon of the Bheels is bow and arrows: the bow is skilfully constructed of two pieces of bamboo, of which the thinner forms the string; the arrows, two feet in length, are made of a light reed, feathered, and pointed with a piece of forged iron, four to nine inches long. Such is their dexterity in the use of this weapon, that they can hit the mark at a distance of twenty-five yards.

At the entrance of the defiles of the mountains is Tintool, the fortified residence of a Rajput noble, or Thakoor, who pays tribute to the Mahrattas, but practically rules supreme over the surrounding country. Thence we enter a well-wooded ravine, where above the leafage rise the tall, slender, sculptured towers of three or four very ancient pagodas. This brings us to the Mookâm, or village, of Sameyra. Continuing our route, we plunge into some difficult passes, whose steep sides are overhung with rocks; and into a fertile valley, buried deep in forest, in the clearings of which are situated the pâls of the Bheels. In old times this was a dangerous place for a caravan; the Bheels issuing in numbers from their secluded pâls, and attacking the surprised travellers with well-aimed flights of arrows.

At Khairwara we find a British advanced post, established by the Government to keep the Bheels in check. Abandoning now the gorges of the Vindhyas, we enter the broader valleys of the Aravalli range, the treasures of which in metals and minerals, marbles, gneiss, and syenite, rock-crystal, amethysts, and carbuncles, are apparently inexhaustible, but as yet have been scarcely touched.

Through a country richly covered with forest we proceed to Oodeypur ("the City of the Rising Sun"), the capital of Meywar.

OODEYPUR.

The distant view of the city is one of great beauty. Forts, pagodas, and palaces stand surrounded by gardens; above which, terraced along the side of a bold pyramidal hill, rise a number of kiosks, bell-turrets, and towers, crowned by a massive palace of white marble, which stands distinctly outlined against the dark blue of the mountains behind it. Lighted up by the glow of sunset, the spectacle is so picturesque that the imagination almost refuses to receive it as a reality; it seems the vision of a poet, suddenly realized at the bidding of a magician.

The town, on nearer acquaintance, proves to be strongly fortified; and it is through a massive gateway, armed with portcullis, and commanded by heavy guns, that the visitor passes into its interior. His first favourable impressions are not weakened by the scenes which then meet his curious gaze. The palaces and the temples are magnificent, and of an architectural style which seems peculiar to the place.

The present ruler of Oodeypur is Sambhoo Sing, the Maharana of Meywar. He is a

SAMBHOO SING, MAHARANA OF MEYWAR.

Rajput Ghelote of the Sesodia clan, and the acknowledged heir to all the glories of the Suryavansas, the celebrated Indian race of the Sun. The supreme authority among the Rajputs, he stands at the head of the Indian nobility, and in the assembly of princes always occupies the seat of honour.

The palace which he inhabits is worthy of so much dignity. India itself can show few buildings more spacious or more magnificent. It covers the entire crest of a hill, the base of which is washed by the blue waters of Lake Peshola; and this crest being insufficient for the

DURBAR OF THE MAHARANA OF OODEYPUR.

full consummation of the architect's design, an immense terrace has been carried out on a level with it, and supported by three massive tiers of arched vaults.

The main entrance fronts the town, and consists of a grand marble gate, with three arches, surmounted by a rich cupola; the balconies and domes being covered with rich but graceful ornament. Thence we pass into the ample courtyard, enclosed on two sides by the royal apartments, and overlooked by galleries on each story. An octagonal domed tower flanks each angle. At the further end of the court a great door conducts to the Zenana, or apartments appropriated to the Rana's wives. A statue of Ganesa, God of Wisdom, is placed above it.

The interior matches well with the exterior in grandeur of effect. There are no fatiguing flights of stairs, but inclined passages lead from story to story. Marble everywhere glitters in the well-lighted apartments; and flowers and fountains meet us at every step. Rich draperies cover the walls of the principal saloons, which are embellished also with frescoes and mirrors; the floors are spread with soft cushions and carpets that yield to the lightest pressure of a woman's foot. But the most attractive and singular feature of this glorious palace is its extensive hanging-garden. The visitor gazes with surprise on blooming parterres and venerable trees situated at so great a height, and occupying so many roofs of different elevations. A sparkling fountain is the central point from which avenues paved with white marble radiate in all directions, and rills of shining water flow in narrow channels until lost in the shade of orange and pomegranate trees. "A marble gallery," we are told, "encircles this enchanting spot, where the grandees of the court, reclining on velvet sofas, indulge in pleasant day-dreams whilst taking their siesta. The view embraces the whole valley; and while gazing on this scene they can call to mind the great feats of arms of their ancestors, who defended their country for centuries against the Mussulman hordes, and converted it into a paradise. When fatigued with the grandeur of this immense panorama, they can turn and contemplate the fairy scene presented by the garden."

Terraced gardens, crowded with summer-houses, pavilions, and fountains, lead to the lake, the shores of which are lined with fairy-like structures, inviting to indolent repose. The arched roof of one of these "bowers of bliss" rests on a thousand slender columns of marble; and all around it is woven a woof of shimmering, rainbow-tinted mist by the leaping waters of numerous fountains.

On the occasion of the visit of Rousselet, the French traveller, to Oodeypur, the Rana held a grand durbar in his fairy-like palace. It was attended by the British Resident, M. Rousselet, and the chief nobles of the Rana's dominions. A huge awning, spread over an open court in one of the upper stories, formed a spacious and cool apartment, in which was placed the Rana's throne—a throne of silver supported by lions of gold. On either side, forming a semicircle, stood the nobles, in gorgeous attire. After a brief conversation, the Rana presented each of the stranger-guests with a packet of betel leaves, called *bira*, and poured a few drops of attar of roses on their handkerchiefs. Then the audience was over.

The neighbourhood of Oodeypur is literally crowded with splendid buildings, temples, tombs, mausoleums, and summer-palaces of the most beautiful description; as for instance that splendid structure the Shah Jehan's Palace in the Island of Jugmunder, which forms the vignette to this volume.

CHAPTER XVII.

GWALIOR—AN INDIAN FORTRESS.

SITUATION AND HISTORY OF GWALIOR—THE OLD TOWN—THE FORTRESS—THE KING PAL PALACE—THE VIHARA TEMPLE—A VALLEY OF SILENCE—THE "TIRTHANKARS"—ABOUT THE JAINS.

THE ancient city of Gwalior is planted on the summit of a steep isolated cliff, 342 feet above the plain at its highest point; a mile and a half in length; and 900 feet in maximum breadth. The fortress-crowned rock stands like a sentinel at the mouth of a valley—a mass of basalt topped with sandstone. Frowning cliffs rise above the slopes at its base, and these are covered with fortifications.

JAIN TEMPLE OF ADINATH, GWALIOR.

If we may believe tradition, Gwalior was founded some centuries before the Christian era, probably by the Indian anchorites. But we gather no certain information about it of earlier

THE KING PÂL PALACE, GWALIOR.

date than A.D. 773, when defensive works were raised around the plateau by Rajah Soorya Sena. The Chohans, in 967, expelled the Kâchwahas, and founded the dynasty of Amber. From 1410 until 1519 it was held by the Tuar Rajputs; after which it was attached to the kingdom of Delhi. When the Mogul empire broke up, it was occupied alternately by the Jâts and Mahrattas. In 1779 it was seized by Scindia; from whom it was captured, about twenty years later, by Major Popham. The treaty of 1805, however, restored it to its Mahratta chief. The present Maharajah Scindia, in the Great Mutiny remained faithful to his alliance with the English, and was driven from his capital by the rebellious Sepoys under one of Nana Sahib's captains. They were dislodged, however, after a series of brilliant movements, by General Sir Hugh Rose (Lord Strathnairn).

The old town of Gwalior extends to the north and east of the citadel, lying between it and the river Suwaranrekha. It has sunk into decay since the new cantonment was founded by the maharajah. The streets are narrow and crooked, but most of the houses are handsomely built. No monuments are extant of an earlier date than the sixteenth century; and those most worthy of notice are the Jumma Masjid, a handsome mosque, and the fantastic triumphal arch known as the Hatti Durwaza, or "Elephants' Gate."

The entrance to the fortress is duly guarded. Hidden among the trees, without, stands a large palace, with a façade of bright blue enamel. Five monumental gates, armed with portcullis and heavy iron doors, afford access to the interior of the citadel. From the first, Saracenic in character, and surmounted by a tier of small columns, begins the causeway—which, though broad and well kept, is a long and wearisome ascent. From this point also begins a series of monuments, bas-reliefs, caverns, and cisterns, of the highest interest. The rocks overhanging the road contain numerous chambers, altars, and statues.

Some huge tanks, excavated from the solid rock, and fed by springs, lie between the third and fourth gates. Opposite the latter stands a small monolith, supposed to belong to the fifteenth century. It forms a temple, chiselled out of a single block of stone; and consists of a single square room, entered by a peristyle, and crowned with a tapering pyramid, the top of which has been replaced by a small dome.

From the very edge of the precipice starts up the mass of the King Pâl Palace, supported by six towers, and pierced only by a few large windows, ornamented with balconies and pilasters. The massive exterior, however, is prevented from being monotonous by a variety of sculptured bands, Jain arches, and indented cordons. Between the Jain arches of the gallery the interspaces are covered with mosaics of enamelled bricks, representing palm-trees on a blue ground; and above each tower rises a lantern with a double row of columns. It is difficult, we are told, to conceive of a grander or more harmonious effect than this colossal palace, with its massive ramparts, produces.

Through a gateway at the southern angle, we pass into a narrow street overlooking the lateral façade of the palace. This façade is one mass of enamel, diversified by broad bands of mosaic, which represent candelabra, elephants, Brahmani ducks, and peacocks in blue, green, rose colour, and gold. Ten centuries have passed over these mosaics, and yet their original freshness seems undimmed. They were designed and executed in the reign of a Rajput prince named Pal.

The royal palace covers an immense area on the east of the plateau, and is the work of successive sovereigns, including the Moguls. Its interior is very simple; the rooms are low, with flat ceilings.

The buildings of the Mohammedan emperors occupied the northern extremity of the plateau.

VIHARA TEMPLE, IN THE FORTRESS OF GWALIOR.

It is easily seen, from their remains, that they were not on so extensive and sumptuous a scale as those of Agra or Delhi.

On a ledge jutting out from the eastern slope of the rocky height is situated the temple of Adinath, a magnificent specimen of the Jain architecture of the sixteenth century. Its ground-

"TIRTHANKARS," IN THE OURWHAÏ, GWALIOR.

plan is cruciform; and the *chaori*, or portion reserved for the faithful, is crowned with a dome. The decorations are superbly rich and fanciful.

In the centre of the plateau stands the Vihara temple, with its monumental tower of stone soaring to an elevation of more than a hundred and twenty feet. In the nave or ground-floor apartment of the temple may be seen, on the wall, the outline of a gigantic palace of Buddha, which once adorned it; above it are apartments corresponding to the five stages of the Pyramids. The real origin of this monument is a subject of dispute; but many archæologists contend that it is Buddhist, and that at an unknown date the Jains took possession of it, and adapted it to their own religious necessities.

The cliffs on the west of the plateau have been split nearly in two by a natural convulsion, which has left the sombre and narrow ravine of Urwâhi between the two precipices. This is a Valley of Silence, where numerous springs maintain a constant luxuriance of vegetation; and it is by no means difficult to understand its attraction for the Jain mystics. It has lost much of its impressive grandeur since the construction of the new road; but even now the grim, weird statues cut out of the solid rock on either hand, and varying in height from one foot to forty feet, burst on the traveller with startling effect. These "Tirthankars" are represented either standing, with their arms hanging down, or sitting with crossed legs, like the Buddhas. They are stiff in design, with nude bodies, pendent ears, thick lips, and enormous eyes. Each wears a circular mitre, ornamented with little balls.

One of the principal figures is that of the Tirthankar Adinath, the reputed founder of the Jain religion; but it is now hidden by the new road. Beyond, in a deep niche, is the statue of Parasnath, sixty feet high. There are also several small cells in the rock, obviously the priests' lodgings; a model of a temple, carved out of a single block of sandstone; and a cavern, approached through several arches, containing three huge figures, twenty feet high. Further groups of Jain sculptures will be found on the south-east.

Of all the religions of India the Jain most merits attention, for it has bequeathed to posterity the most interesting collection of monuments, from the basilicas of Mount Aboo to the Kirti-khamb of Chittur. Its origin, according to the Jain books, may be dated prior to the rise of Christianity. At all events, it existed long before the avatar of Sakya Mouni, who seems to have availed himself of the Jain doctrines in the formation of his own creed. It is, indeed, affirmed by the Buddhists that Mahavira, the last Jain Tirthankar, was the teacher of Sakya. In the twelfth century the Jains lost much of their influence through the secession of the Rajputs, whom the Brahmans won over by the proffer of the title and prerogatives of the ancient Kashatryas. They retained, however, the allegiance of the majority of the mercantile classes, and to this day possess a considerable portion of the wealth of India. Among their adherents are numbered the heads of the principal commercial classes of Bombay and Calcutta. Only the Bhikshus are called Jains, or the "purified;" the faithful are known by the name of Arhât. The former are marked on the forehead with sandal-wood. They are rigid vegetarians; and such is their reverence for animal life, that they wear cloths over their mouths, and carry brooms in their hands, that they may avoid injuring a single insect. They are the great Indian architects, and well deserve their Hindu designation of Vidyavan, or "magic builders." It has been justly said that other religious sects have but copied their earlier monuments.

CHAPTER XVIII.

BHOPAL.

THE BEGUM OF BHOPAL—HER TERRITORY—HER CAPITAL—A MOUNTAIN-BORDERED LAKE—THE MOTI MASJID, OR MOSQUE OF PEARLS—CITADEL OF FUTTEHGURH—THE MOHAMMEDAN NEW-YEAR FESTIVAL—PHASES OF LIFE AT BHOPAL—RECEPTION OF THE BEGUM—ROUTE TO GWALIOR AND AGRA INDICATED—NURSINGURH AND ITS TEMPLE—CHOPAYA-TRAVELLING.

AMONG the illustrious personages whom the Prince of Wales, while at Calcutta in 1875, received at a Chapter of the Star of India, was the Begum of Bhopal, the only woman in the world who can call herself a knight. The present Begum succeeded Secunder Begum in 1863, who, for her loyalty during the rebellion, had been liberally rewarded and

HER HIGHNESS SECUNDER, BEGUM OF BHOPAL.

highly honoured by the British Government. Her successor, displaying an equal measure of fidelity, was decorated in 1872 with the Order of the Star of India. The territory over which

PROCESSION OF THE TAZEEAS.

(*See page 183.*)

she rules covers an area of 6764 square miles, with a population of about 670,000 inhabitants. It includes a portion of the high table-lands on the northern bank of the Narbada, and of the fair rich plains of Eastern Malwa.

Bhopal, the capital, clusters on the eastern slope of a rocky hill, at the base of which sleeps a beautiful lake; and it is enclosed by battlemented walls about two miles in circuit. All around rises a ring of mountain-peaks, and the plain between them and the city is radiant with gardens and well-cultivated fields. A road carried along the embankment which confines the waters of the lake connects the suburb of Jehangirabad with the capital, which is irregularly built, with narrow, winding streets, and high houses rendered picturesque by their numerous small towers and verandahs of carved wood. In the middle of the labyrinth a landmark is afforded by the Cathedral Mosque, or Jumma Masjid; an immense pile, with domes and octagonal minarets,

HER HIGHNESS SHAH JEHAN, BEGUM OF BHOPAL.

and a gigantic central dome, surrounded by arcades and colonnades, all reared on the summit of a massive platform of red sandstone. From this point the visitor may make his way to the Moti Masjid, or Mosque of Pearls, erected by the late Begum; a graceful edifice of white marble, with three domes, one of colossal size, and flanked by soaring minarets, which spring out of a graceful combination of pavilions and colonnades. Between the two run some of the principal streets, where the shops of the pastry-cooks and the armourers, the mercers and the jewellers, make a fine display; and our ears are saluted with a medley of strange tongues, as through the crowd presses a stalwart Afghan or a richly-attired Persian, a Baluchee with brick-red face and mane of tawny dishevelled locks, a Brahman half-naked and shining with grease, a Moulvi with long white beard and robes of decorous flow, and a ragged Gond carrying a heavy hatchet on his shoulder. Among all these the elegant Bhopalese, with finely-cut features and silken beard, is easily distinguished. His dress is that of the Indian Mussulman: an embroidered toque, or a turban placed on one side, like the cap of an English trooper; close-fitting tunic and pantaloons, and yellow slippers glittering with spangles. He carries his sabre wrapped in a muslin shawl; and as he passes, a strong odour of rose-water and sandal-wood is wafted from his flowing hair.

The summit of the hill of Bhopal is crowned by the citadel of Futtehgurh, from which may be obtained a fine view of the Bhopal Tal, a lake that extends to the southward, measuring about four and a half miles in length, and a mile and a half in breadth. Its overflow supplies the eastern lake, or lake of Jehangirabad; and it is itself supplied by the waters of the Bessal.

MOOLLAHS OF BHOPAL.

If fortunate enough to visit this romantically-situated city during the great Mohammedan New-Year's festival of the Mohurrum, the traveller will be entertained by some striking scenes. For days the hills around are covered with stalls, and an immense multitude assembles, bent on no higher purpose than *pour passer le temps.* Troops of bayadères, shining with jewels and attired in radiant silks, are followed by a regular train of musicians and swordsmen; while their movements are parodied by young men dressed in female costume, and surprisingly ready with raillery and epigram. Elsewhere the acrobats go through their feats of agility, and the jugglers deceive the most watchful eye by their adroit manœuvres. Mussulmans, in tunics embroidered with gold and silver, stalk on sedately, disdaining to betray any symptom of curiosity or excitement; while clusters of Hindus, the men in the usual thick white linen dress, and the women in

RECEPTION OF A KHILLUT AT THE COURT OF BHOPAL.

the open bodice and large plaited petticoat, stare open-eyed and wondering at the jogees, or religious mendicants, who, completely naked, and with elfin locks falling free, walk to and fro uttering the most terrible cries, and slashing breast, ribs, arms, and thighs with their long conical-bladed poniards, until showers of coppers allay their seeming fury.

The festival endures for five days, and on the fifth the scene shifts to the borders of the great lake, the waters of which are quickly strewn with tabouts or mimic temples of paper and tinsel,—emblematic of the tombs of the Mohammedan martyrs, Ali and Hussein,—fashioned and deposited by religious hands. In the evening takes place the great procession of the tabouts, or, as they are also called, tazeeas, some of which, raised on the backs of elephants, tower twenty feet in height. Crowds of excited natives, with banners, and matchlocks, and pikes, and torches, follow and surround the train of elephants, raising incessant shouts of "Deen! Deen! Hussein! Ali! Ha Doula!" Above the glare of flaming torches the high towers of the tazeeas glitter with gold and tinsel; while foaming fanatics lead on in front a richly-attired character, who represents the husband of Fatima, Mohammed's daughter. The procession halts at the lake, and, with a renewed outburst of clamour, the multitude begins to disperse, and the Mohurrum is over.

Various are the aspects of life which greet the observant eye in an Indian city. The moollahs of the mosques, grave and reverend signors with keen eyes and flowing beards, ever ready to argue the most trivial points; dancers and dancing-girls, acrobats and jugglers; specimens of different nationalities, all remarkable in costume, manner, and appearance; processions as strange as ever were conceived by a Callot, or as brilliant as ever were imagined by an Oriental story-teller; Fakirs, and other religious mendicants: these supply abundant material for observation and reflection. And it may happen to the traveller to secure the goodwill of the Begum, a woman, it is said, of much intelligence and liberality, and to receive from her hands a khillut of honour. Should he be so far favoured, he will don a glittering costume specially provided for the occasion,—a long tunic of silk gauze, embroidered with gold; ample petticoat-like pantaloons of crimson satin, bespangled with silver; a kumurbund or belt of violet and gold; a rich scarlet cashmir cloak, all gay with gold and silver embroidery; and, finally, a toque of gold and velvet.

Thus gorgeously arrayed, he will enter one of the Begum's carriages, and, through a deferential and salaaming crowd, proceed to the palace; on the steps of which he will be received by a deputation of Bhopal nobles, headed by the dewan or chief minister of state, who will take him by the elbow in true Indian fashion, lead him up the grand staircase, and introduce him into the royal presence. In the hall of durbars, on a raised throne, and surrounded by her court dignitaries, sits the Begum, in silks and velvets, gold, silver, and flashing jewels, a four-plumed diadem on her head, and the Star of India on her breast. Then follow the usual ceremonies,—the hookahs are passed round; a few compliments are exchanged; a title of honour is bestowed on the visitor; a ring placed on his finger; the attar-pân makes its appearance; and he takes his departure.

From Bhopal the traveller may strike through the rich plains of Malwa to Gwalior, and thence to Agra. His first stage will be Sehore, which lies in the centre of fertile fields, studded with leafy villages. Beyond Koundwah he crosses the Parbutti. For this purpose the villagers couple together their *gurhas,* or light, spherical water-pitchers, and attach these to a number of poles in such a manner as to keep their mouths uppermost. On this rough-and-ready raft the vehicle is placed, with the traveller inside; and, entering the water, the natives quickly propel it to the opposite bank.

At Nursingurh, which clusters in the hollow of a beautiful valley, on the borders of a silver lake, and surrounded by noble trees, a handsome temple is dedicated to Vasudeva. At no great distance from this town the traveller reaches a branch of the Great Trunk Road, which connects Calcutta with Bombay and Madras, and is borne onwards by way of Hawan, Rhoteah, and

MAIL-CART TRAVELLING.

Goona. The traveller is now transferred to a conveyance known as a chopaya,—a kind of triumphal car, with gaily-painted body and little sculptured pillars, drawn by a team of oxen, caparisoned with red cloth. It measures about eight feet by five, and is furnished in the interior with mattresses and cushions, a table, a couple of straw easy-chairs, and a lantern, forming bed-room and sitting-room in one. Of course, so cumbrous a machine progresses but slowly, and affords a notable contrast to the mail-cart, which, driven by a lanky Indian, and drawn by a team of three or four horses, dashes past at a tremendous pace, up hill and down hill, across narrow bridges, through brawling streams, as if accidents were impossible.

But, instead of pursuing the road to Gwalior, we propose to conduct the reader to Sanchi, Myhere, and Punna.

FORDING THE RIVER PARBUTTI

CHAPTER XIX.

SANCHI TO PUNNA.

AN ANCIENT BUDDHIST SETTLEMENT—THE LIONS' LAT—WHAT IS A TOPE?—ABOUT THE GAUR OR INDIAN BISON—THE INDIAN FOREST—THE LAND OF THE GONDS—KINGDOM OF MYHERE—GOVINDGURH—A MAN-APE—TIGER-HUNTING—PALACE OF GOVINDGURH—KINGDOM OF REWAH—PUNNA, THE "LAND OF DIAMONDS"—A DIAMOND-MINE DESCRIBED—TWO GREAT FORTRESSES.

SANCHI, on the left bank of the Betwa, has, from a remote antiquity, been the seat of an important Buddhist settlement; and as early as 400 B.C. its community was sufficiently influential to originate a schism of its own, known as that of Chetiya. Its Buddhist memorials, therefore, are extensive and interesting. In the midst of a mass of temples and colonnades, with huge sculptured portals covered with mystic carving, rises the Great Tôpe, a hemispheric dome fully ninety feet in diameter, which rests on a cylindrical basement about fifteen feet high.* Some authorities date it as far back as the sixth century B.C., but the vast colonnade surrounding it, with its monolithic pillars, cannot be referred to so early a period as the reign of Asoka (260–222 B.C.). Not less remarkable is the Lions' Lât, a cylindrical shaft about thirty feet high, surmounted by a dome-shaped capital of three feet, which in its turn is surmounted by a circular plinth, serving as a pedestal for four lions seated back to back. These are so finely executed that General Cunningham believes them to have been the work of Greek artists, sent by Ptolemy Philadelphus II. to the court of Asoka. The archæologist will

* Mr. Fergusson furnishes a very clear and close description of this celebrated tôpe. The principal building, he says, consists of a dome somewhat less than a hemisphere, one hundred and six feet in diameter, and forty-two feet in height, with a platform on the top thirty-four feet across, which originally formed the basis of the *tea* or capital, invariably the "finish" of these Buddhist monuments.

The dome rests on a sloping base, fourteen feet in height by one hundred and twenty feet in diameter, with an off-set on its summit about six feet in width. Judging from the representations of tôpes on the Indian sculptures, we conclude that this was originally surrounded by a balustrade, and ascended by a broad double ramp on one side. Probably it was used for processions encircling the monument, and these seem to have been a common feature of the Buddhist ceremonial. In the centre this great mound is perfectly solid, being composed of bricks laid in mud; but the exterior is faced with dressed stones. Over these was laid a coating of cement nearly four inches thick, which we may suppose to have been adorned with painting or ornaments in relief.

The tôpe was surrounded by a curious fence, composed of stone posts eight feet eight inches high, at intervals of a little more than two feet. These are surmounted by a plain architrave, two feet four inches deep, slightly rounded at the top. So far, says Mr. Fergusson, this enclosure resembles the outer circle at Stonehenge; but between every two uprights three horizontal cross-pieces of stone are inserted, of an elliptical form, of the same depth as the top piece, but only nine inches thick in the thickest part. "This is the only *built* example yet discovered of an architectural ornament which is found *carved* in every cave; and, indeed, in almost every ancient Buddhist building known in India. The upright posts or pillars of this enclosure bear inscriptions indicating that they were all given by different individuals. But neither these nor any other inscriptions found in the whole tôpe, or in the smaller tôpes surrounding it (though there are as many as two hundred and fifty inscriptions in all), contain any known name, or any clue to their age."

The same authority remarks that even more curious than the stone railing are the four gateways. Let us take one of them as an example. We see two bold square pillars, profusely sculptured, with elephant capitals, rising to a height of eighteen feet four inches. They are surmounted by three lintels, which curve slightly upwards in the centre, and terminate in Ionic scrolls. Elaborate carvings cover every inch of surface, and numerous emblematic figures crown them. The total height is thirty-three feet six inches. One of the gateways has fallen; and its removal to England has been advocated, on the ground that it would furnish the student with an admirable specimen of Indian sculpture.

None of the other tôpes of the group, thirty or forty in number, equal in dimensions that which we have described. Some, indeed, do not exceed six feet in diameter; and the enclosures and gateways are never so artistically complete as those of the Great Tôpe. The inscriptions, as we have said, do not enable us to determine the exact date of the erection of these Buddhist monuments; but we know from the characters in which they are written, as well as from the architectural details, that they must date as far back as the beginning of the Christian era. At the same time, they cannot have been raised before the epoch of Asoka (B.C. 250); so that we may conclude they belong to a period between two hundred and one hundred years before Christ. (FERGUSSON, Book I., chapter ii.)

also examine the monumental gates or triumphal arches of Sanchi, which are masterpieces of symbolic carving. There are also the remains of twelve smaller tôpes, a Chaitya temple, three Buddhist monasteries, and numerous chapels and statues.

What is a tôpe, and in what did it originate?

The first monument raised by men, after they had learned to group themselves in tribes or communities, would naturally be designed to commemorate the dead; and the earliest form would be that of a heap of stones piled by reverent hands over the resting-place of chief or hero. In the course of generations the heap grew into a tumulus, which gradually assumed regularity of plan—becoming a *cairn* in Europe, a *pyramid* in Egypt, and a *tôpe* in India. As tradition expanded into legend, the primitive hero was enshrined among the demi-gods, and his tomb

INDIAN BISON.

converted into an altar, above which was elevated the figure of the new divinity. In India Buddhism incorporated this species of idolatry, and invested it with a peculiarly sacred character. It then took possession of the tôpes, and developed out of them a religious architecture thoroughly original in its principal features.

In the neighbourhood of Sanchi, and throughout the higher lands of Central India, the gaur, or Indian bison, is met with. Its range extends from the Himalaya to Cape Comorin, wherever the woods are dense enough to afford it shelter and food; but only in Central India is it found in large herds. Its zoological name is *Bos gaurus;* it is nearer akin to the American bison than to the ordinary bull. It has no affinity to the buffalo.

CHOPAYA-TRAVELLING.

(See page 184.)

Tufts of long reddish hair overhang the broad, high forehead of this powerful animal. The ears are somewhat small, and the strongly-developed muzzle is of a rose-coloured tinge. The horns, which are oval and considerably flattened, curve boldly back from the head, turning upwards in a sharp point. A fleshy hump surmounts the broad sinewy shoulders, extending to the middle of the back: it is generally covered with an abundance of black or nearly black hair, longer than that which clothes the body, the tint of which is a warm chestnut, except on the legs, where from hoof to knee it is almost white. The average height of a full-grown bison is from fifteen to sixteen hands. It feeds upon young bamboo shoots and high grass; and a herd is usually composed of ten to fifteen cows, with their calves, directed and guided by a young bull. The old bulls, for the greater part of the year, live in entire solitude.

The forests which abound in this part of India are mostly composed of magnificent trees, which rear their pillared trunks out of a wonderfully dense and intertangled growth of shrubs and grasses, while flowery creepers frequently hang in bright festoons from branch to branch, and through the glossy foliage dart birds of resplendent wing. Here are found many of those gums and resins which now figure so largely as commercial staples: the *kheir*, to which we owe the well-known catechu; the *babool* and the *sirsa*, acacias yielding the valuable gum-arabic; the *saleĭ* (*Boswellia thurifera*), producing the fragrant resin, labana or olibanum, employed by the Indians as incense; and the *sâl* (*Shorea robusta*), whence is obtained the resinous product known as *dhâk*. The tamarind with its precious fruit, the teak, the wild mango, the mhowah, several species of fig-trees, the *tikur* (a plant which yields the nutritious arrow-root),—these mingle with the celebrated *Bombax indicum*, or *simool*, the seeds of which are covered with a white, textile, silky fibre, capable of being used as a substitute for cotton; the *nîm* (or *Melia aziderachta*), with shoots and leaves much esteemed for their febrifuge qualities; the *Strychnos*, furnishing the potent nux vomica; the ebony *tendoo*, the wood of which is a treasure to the cabinet-maker; the *kour*, a resinous tree, excellent for lighting purposes; and the *jamalkota*, whence is obtained the croton oil of our pharmacopœia.

But we pass on our way, crossing Gondwana, or the land of the Gonds, 20° 10′ to 24° N. lat. and 74° to 80° E. long.; and making acquaintance with a family of Dacoits—the professional thieves and assassins of Central India, who seem to have inherited the evil traditions of Thuggism. Woe to the unfortunate traveller who falls into their clutches! He is first drugged, afterwards robbed; and if he wake in time to offer resistance, is probably murdered. Entirely naked, and their supple bodies well oiled, they glide into tents, and wind themselves to and fro, serpent-like, with such stealthiness as almost always to escape detection.

In the valley of the Tons we find a resting-place at Myhere—a small town romantically situated near the entrance and within the immediate shadow of the Bandair Mountains. Through the valley now runs the railroad from Jubbulpur to Allahabad. It forms the little kingdom of Myhere; and its one hundred and twenty thousand Hindus and Gonds are ruled by a raïs, under the British protectorate. He is described as an intelligent and active prince, and to European visitors always extends a gracious welcome. At a sumptuously-spread table they are entertained with their accustomed viands; and the raïs himself makes one of the party at dessert, drinking a goblet of champagne, and smoking the peaceful hookah.

From Myhere we proceed to Govindgurh, which lies in the midst of rock and jungle, the favourite haunt of the panther, the lynx, the boar, the black bear, while on higher ground are found the neelgau and the stag. It was during his stay here that the French explorer of Central India met with a man-ape, or Bundarlok, as the Indians call him—a representative of the tribe of the Jangals, who inhabit the forest east of Sirgooja, and are perhaps descendants of the aboriginal Negritos. We shall describe him in our traveller's own words :—

"I was struck at once by his low stature—scarcely five feet—and, above all, by the length of his arms; which, united to the animal expression of his wrinkled countenance, fully justified the title of ape given to him by the natives. The low forehead disappeared beneath woolly,

ENTRANCE TO THE PALACE OF GOVINDGURH.

tangled locks; the nose thick at the extremity, and flattened at the bridge; broad, raised nostrils; small, deep-sunken eyes; a fleshless chin; and, to complete the ugliness of this mask, on each side of the mouth wrinkles, running in parallel lines, covering the cheeks. His face, in spite of its ugliness, bore the impress of a profound sadness, which had nothing of the savage in it. The body itself was of a shocking leanness; the skin, of a reddish black, like tanned leather, hung in creases on the limbs; the abdomen, sunk inwards as though withered up, bore in the middle a shapeless protuberance covering the navel, and doubtless proceeding from the umbilical cord."

Govindgurh is a place dear to the sportsman, for game of all kinds abounds in its vicinity; and, if he be so minded, he may essay his skill against a tiger. When the maharajah goes

AT THE TABLE OF THE RAÏS OF MYHERE.

(*See page 191.*)

a-hunting, the spectacle is very striking, and to European eyes exceedingly curious. Shikarees are previously sent out to discover the tiger's lair ; then the *muknas,* or hunting elephants (males without tusks), are duly caparisoned ; prince, nobles, and attendants mount to their howdahs ; and, followed by a long line of soldiers and natives, the procession departs.

On arriving in the vicinity of the tiger's haunt, the hunters dismount and repair on foot to the *hoodi,* a small battlemented building, surmounted by a terrace, and overlooking the mountain-pool to which all the wild beasts of the neighbourhood resort for water. They seat themselves in silence on the terrace, with carbines ready loaded at their side, and wait patiently until the destined victim descends to the border of the lake. Then a discharge of rifles, and the tiger

COURT OF THE PALACE OF GOVINDGURH.

falls with a roar, his body riddled by shot. Attendants hasten up ; the carcass is placed on a litter ; and the procession returns in triumph to Govindgurh.

This, however, is not a sufficiently exhilarating pastime for an English sportsman, who cares not for "hunting made easy," and has no idea of sport without an element of risk or danger.

The palace of Govindgurh is a building of some architectural pretensions. Its principal entrance is a spacious triumphal arch of marble, with three small indented arches in the "best Rajput style." The court inside is surrounded by colonnades of considerable beauty.

Govindgurh is situated in the native kingdom of Rewah, and is the favourite residence of the maharajah, who has deserted his capital for it. Rewah itself is not a picturesque or inviting town: its streets are narrow and crooked, and its houses are built of wattles or of dried mud. The palace lies outside it; and its architect, in designing it, seems to have been desirous of proving his acquaintance with several architectural styles. In the interior, however, are some splendid apartments; especially the hall in which the maharajah holds his durbars—a hall gorgeous with gilding, colours, and glass lustres. The dancing-girls of Rewah enjoy a certain reputation for the elegance of their movements.

Our excursions in this direction will terminate with a visit to Punna, the famous "land of diamonds." On its frontier the English traveller is received by the vakeels of the maharajah,

DANCING-GIRLS OF THE COURT OF REWAH.

and a train of horses and elephants, and, after the usual ceremonies have been performed, is conducted in great state to the capital.

Punna is a city of great antiquity, which some writers would fain identify with the *Panassa* of the géographer Ptolemy. It has no monuments of interest. Its houses, all built of freestone, are perched on the summit of an elevated table-land, and surround the maharajah's palace—a building, or rather an agglomeration of buildings, in the English style—flat-roofed bungalows, surrounded with colonnades, and connected by broad terraces.

At a short distance from the town are situated the mines. The shaft, a circular opening, about sixty feet deep, and from thirty to forty feet in diameter, is sunk through successive strata of gneiss, carbonates, and the adamantiferous ore, a mixture of quartz and silex. The workmen, naked, labour half-immersed in the water which the chain of buckets, though constantly

HUNTING-PARTY AT GOVINDGURH.

(*See page 195.*)

ascending and descending, is unable to exhaust, and send up to the surface a succession of straw baskets filled with a clayey deposit. In stone troughs, erected under a shed, the ore is carefully washed; and the silicious residue being spread on a marble slab, is carefully examined by sorters, under the inspection of overseers. The diamonds thus obtained are cut and polished at Punna, in workshops belonging to the maharajah, and then exported for sale to Allahabad and Benares. They are remarkable for their purity, and flash with extraordinary

A DIAMOND-MINE, PUNNA.

brilliancy. Their colour varies from the purest white to black, passing through all the principal shades—milky, roseate, yellow, green, and brown. Their average weight does not exceed five or six carats; but larger specimens are sometimes found. It is said that very few reach Europe Those so-called Punna diamonds which are sold in our marts are really Brazilian stones: they are sent to India to be labelled with Indian labels, packed in Indian cases, and returned to Europe as Indian gems.

CHAPTER XX.

MADRAS AND ITS NEIGHBOURHOOD.

MADRAS FROM THE SEA — DIFFICULT OF ACCESS — MUSSULAH BOATS — THE CATAMARANS — THE ENGLISH QUARTER OF MADRAS — ABOUT CASTE — A DECCAN VILLAGE DESCRIBED — VISIT TO CONJEVERAM — INDIAN AGRICULTURE— TEMPLE OF SIVA — ITS IDOLS — THE ARRACK-PALM—HOW THE JUICE IS OBTAINED—MAHABALIPUR—TEMPLES OF VISHNU—A CAVE-TEMPLE—ITS SCULPTURES—OTHER ANTIQUITIES—MONOLITHIC TEMPLES—A FRENCH SETTLEMENT, PONDICHERRY — ITS INHABITANTS — ITS HOUSES — TOUR TO TRICHINOPOLI — ITS FORT—THE PRINCE OF WALES'S VISIT— THE GREAT TEMPLE OF SERINGHAM—SECT OF THE VISHNAVITES—TANJORE—ITS TEMPLES—MADURA—TANK OF THE GOLDEN LOTUS.

MADRAS, from the sea, is an enchanted city; it seems as absolutely the birth and offspring of that sea as ever was Cytherea. The voyager sees before him a mass of seething waters, for the Bay of Bengal pours continuously on the long low Madras shore; and out of their glittering foam and snowy surge rise spires, and columns, and temples, and flat-roofed houses, and all the other evidences of a great city. A great maritime city, and yet without a haven or an anchorage for the ships, large or small, which carry on its commerce! It is a strange sight,—that extended range of buildings, stretching far along the open strand, and confronting the apparently boundless sweep of Ocean, which seems as if it would burst resistlessly upon it, and bury it beneath its billows. Even when the outer sea is calm, the white-crested breakers swell and fret near the water-line, and send their echoing thunder along the beach. It is necessary, therefore, that to and from the ships and steamers in the offing the products of the country and the wares of Western civilization should be conveyed in *mussulah* boats, dexterously handled by native rowers. For though Madras can boast of a solid stately pier, stretching into the sea one thousand feet beyond high-water mark, it is available only in calm weather and at low tides, and even then no vessel can lie alongside it. The first stone of a harbour, however, which is to be of such dimensions as to afford secure anchorage to the great steamers of the Peninsular and Oriental Company,* was laid in 1875 by the Prince of Wales.

Hitherto, and at present, passengers have been and are landed in the native mussulah boats, which are built of mango-wood, calked with straw, and sewn or stitched together with cocoa-nut fibre. Ships drop their anchors about half a mile from the shore; the mussulah craft pull alongside, receive their cargo, and are then beached through the surf. Frequently the boat, while lying alongside, will rise and fall twenty-five feet relatively to the height of the ship's deck at each roll of the waves. Ladies are lashed into chairs, and lowered into the boat from the ship's yard-arm.

Infinitely more curious than the mussulah boat is the *catamaran*, a kind of miniature raft, consisting of two or three logs firmly lashed together, on which the native fishermen, an

* It will be formed by piers running out from the shore 500 yards north and south of the present screw pile pier, and will enclose a rectangular area of 170 acres, with a depth at low water of 18 to 42 feet.

TIGER-HUNTING NEAR GOVINDGURH.

(*See page 195.*)

amphibious race, boldly launch themselves through the whirl of waves, propelling themselves by means of a flat piece of wood alternately dipped on either side. These men are adroit and courageous swimmers, and though sharks abound in the Madras waters, they perform the most extraordinary feats,—now diving deep under the dark green tide, now riding fearlessly on a swelling billow.

Mr. Eastwick gives a lively description of the process of crossing the surf-wave, which in calm weather is three feet high, in breezy weather six feet, and in storms fourteen feet high. There are two lines of surf, and between these it is possible for a boat to keep her position without crossing either liquid ridge. The outer wave, or male surf, is the more formidable ; and considerable care and caution are required in crossing it. The great art is to ride in on one wave, keeping the boat's head straight, and then pull away from its successor, so as to avoid being overtaken, which means being swamped. The result is equally disagreeable if the boat should be caught on her broadside, for she is then capsized. And in such an event the peril for Europeans is great; for not only is the most masterly and strenuous swimming requisite, but sharks have to be guarded against. It is true that the hardy rowers of the catamarans are frequently washed from their frail craft ; but they are truly amphibians, with powers of natation equal to those of a fish, and their dusky figures are not so readily detected by the sharks. Yet even to them a terrible death will sometimes come. As soon as the surf is allowed to carry the boat onward, its progress is amazingly swift, and the stem is raised up aloft until it is almost perpendicular. The sensation experienced by the passenger is like that of "taking a leap on horseback." As soon as the first wave has tumbled into spray, the boatmen pull with all their might to elude the next, shouting, "Hillea ! hillea !" ("Pull ! pull !") or, "Javier ! Javier !"—the last a reminiscence of the famous St. Xavier, who prosecuted his missionary work with singular success along the Coromandel coast. The second wave carries the boat to the shore, where, in rough weather, it strikes with so much violence as frequently to split. A number of men, however, are on the alert to seize and haul it up out of reach of the next incoming billow.

Madras, with its suburbs, may be estimated at from twelve to fourteen miles in circuit. It has its native quarter, its Mohammedan quarter, and its English quarter. The English residents, however, chiefly inhabit the suburbs, where, along broad tree-shaded roads, and among open meadows and rice-fields, each house is situated in its own compound or enclosure, and surrounded by groves of feathery casuarinas, date-palms, and banians. Some of the houses are of palatial dimensions, and nearly all are divided into large airy chambers, opening into one another, with a curtain partially covering each doorway, and a verandah projecting on each floor. From every ceiling hangs the universal punkah, which is kept in motion by a cord passing through the wall into an adjacent apartment, or into the verandah, where, reclining on the floor, the indolent workman plies his simple but continuous task. The furniture is mostly made of an ebony wood indigenous to the country, enriched by native skill with a profusion of delicate carving ; while the elegance of the interior arrangements is enhanced by the spotless brilliancy of the walls, due to the chunam, or white lime made from sea-shells, with which they are coated.

Fort St. George, St. George's Cathedral, and the Government House, where the Prince of Wales was entertained on the occasion of his visit in 1875, are the principal edifices of the ocean-city ; but they cannot be said to call for particular description.

Among the Indians the spirit of *caste* takes the place of the domestic tendency: they love their wives and children, but with a love subordinated to certain extraneous principles. The Brahmans and the Sudras, as well as the Pariahs themselves, are divided into a multitude of sub-castes, a member of any one of which can neither eat, drink, nor marry with a member of another. If an Indian lose his caste, he is rejected by his kith and kin; his wife is treated as a widow, his children are regarded as orphans; neither succour nor compassion may he expect from his nearest and dearest, unless he can purchase *back* his caste by heavy payments to the priests. It is probable that English influences, and the labours of our missionaries and teachers, are beginning to tell upon this caste system, which is the great obstacle to the thorough regeneration of India; but as yet the effect is scarcely perceptible. An Englishman is still treated as a Pariah; and the high-caste Hindu, if he has accidentally touched you, washes his hands of the pollution the moment your back is turned. Even the railway division of passengers into classes has been made to subserve the prejudices of caste; and it is caste that stands in the way of more frequent pilgrimages to England on the part of influential and wealthy natives.

A Deccan village is invariably composed of two sections, separated by an interval of some yards. One of these is reserved for high-caste families; the other, enclosed by a hedge, for Pariahs, who cannot enter the streets of the village without the permission of the former, and are forbidden to draw water from any wells but those appropriated to them. Or if there be no such wells, they deposit their empty jars and vessels near the high-caste wells, and wait patiently and humbly for some kind hand to fill them.

If, physically and intellectually speaking, the higher castes can claim superiority over the mass of Pariahs, the latter are much more industrious, more docile, and more accessible to European influences. In the Madras Presidency, they supply the most disciplined and trustworthy of the native recruits of our army.

These details, not, we hope, without some interest and value to the reader, have detained us long at Madras. We shall now conduct the reader to Conjeveram.

As we proceed, we notice that the surrounding country is fairly well cultivated. The banian is very plentiful; and among the fields secluded leafy nooks are scattered, where water shimmers in the thickets, and herds of antelopes disport themselves. Rice is the chief product in an agricultural sense. The fields are divided into a certain number of square plots, enclosed by embankments high enough to prevent the overflow of the waters; the general aspect being that of an immense chess-board. Each square is situated at a different level, so that the irrigating stream may pass from one to the other. The labourer begins by inundating his field, so as to soak the soil thoroughly; then he breaks up the clods, and leaves the grass and stubble to rot. The water having disappeared, the field is ploughed; the plough used being a very primitive implement, and consisting of a coulter without any arm, terminated by an iron point, and fixed to a beam in connection with the yoke. It is the ancient *arera* without any mould-board to turn back the earth, which is simply torn up by the iron; consequently in the muddy soil, wherein the oxen sink to their knees, these animals do more work than the plough does. The ploughing process completed, the agriculturist proceeds to level the ground with a flat piece of wood attached to a long handle; then he sows the seed; and in two days the green shoots are seen above ground. On the fourth day, watering begins; then a tiny rill is introduced every other day until the rice shows three leaves. For a month afterwards the rice-plots are irrigated for two successive days, and then left to dry for a similar interval; and, finally, up to the epoch of complete maturity the soil is watered ten days at a time, two days of rest being allowed between each decade.

The quantity of the crop depends on the fertility of the soil and the plentifulness of the water-supply; so that while certain districts yield but thinly, others will repay the husbandman's labour literally a hundredfold. Again: some species of the grain ripen more quickly than others. The sowing-season differs, too, according to the species sown; but always the best soil, and the best irrigated, must be reserved for the successful cultivation of rice.

Conjeveram lies about forty-five miles from Madras, and derives its fame from its temples dedicated to Siva. It covers a very considerable area of ground, so that its two principal temples are situated at a distance of three miles from one another. The streets are remarkably wide; and at frequent intervals the traveller comes upon small pagodas shaped like a parallelopiped. The square sanctuary, as well as the colonnade which serves for an approach, has a flat roof. Each column is a monolith, with quadrangular base and capital; the pedestals are ornamented with sculptured bas-reliefs, representing bacchanal groups.

Into the outer court of the principal temple, the worshippers pass through two gates, of eight stories, and devoid of carving. Two colossal statues flank each opening. Into the second court none but people of caste are permitted to enter. The sanctuary is spacious, and in front of it is a colonnade, where the visitor is invited to rest himself while the priests display the jewels and precious stuffs which, on great festivals, are employed to decorate the idol. Their value exceeds five lacs of rupees. Diamonds, emeralds, rubies, sapphires, pearls are woven into mitres, collars, bracelets, diadems, and the like. Not one of these stones is cut, though some are of considerable size. The various gems are mounted without taste, and the stones grouped together without any regard to their colour, their shape, or their value. It is a curious fact that one of these ornaments was presented by Lord Clive. To the visitor are also exhibited the secondary idols, such as Hanuman, the monkey-god, and Garuda, the hawk-god; the horse, and the various monsters on which the chief image is enthroned on festal occasions, are all gilded, and all larger than life-size.

HANUMAN, THE MONKEY-GOD.

In front of the entrance to the sanctuary rises a small mandapam, or dais, supported by four columns, and, in its turn, supporting a pyramidal roof, with monolithic chains at each angle. To the left, a rectangular platform, covered by a level roof, is upheld by twelve rows of eight columns each. Under this stately canopy of stone the god, once a month, is exposed to the adoration of his devotees. Behind the six-and-ninety columns which constitute so remarkable an architectural feature sleeps a sacred pool, where the faithful perform their ablutions; and in the middle of which rises another and a smaller mandapam, the shrine, on certain feast-days, of the local divinity.

To the right lies a second sanctuary, with a colonnade in front, literally loaded with sculptures and symbols, such as only an orgiastic creed could admit or sanction.

Every Friday the idol is borne, with pomp of music and procession of priests and nautchni-girls, to a garden adjoining the pagoda; but the grand festival takes place in May. A legion of apes, placed under the protection of Siva, wander to and fro in the sacred enclosure. He would be a rash man who offered them any molestation.

Notwithstanding its great reputation, the Conjeveram temple cannot be regarded as one of the finest in India. Without for one moment comparing it with those of Tanjore and Madura, there are many in Southern India which excel it in grandeur, as well as in beauty of sculptured work.

Proceeding southward, by way of Chingleput, we enter on a country which is dry, unattractive, and poorly cultivated. But wherever in the Deccan the agriculturist ceases his labour, we come upon groves of the arrack-palm. This palm-tree, whose fruit, though not very finely flavoured, is much liked by children, yields a beverage called toddy, a sugar or jaghery, and an alcoholic spirit known as arrack,—all obtained from the flowers, while they are in a rudimentary condition. The inflorescence begins about November or December, and it is then that the sap or toddy is extracted, together with the arrack and sugar. The process is as follows:—The Indian binds his legs together firmly at the ankles, and having passed around the tree a strong leather belt, wide enough to admit of the easy transit of the body, he climbs up the trunk step by step, like an ape, with the assistance of the aforesaid strap, until he reaches the summit. He then presses strongly the base of the floral axil to arrest its development, bruises the blossoms with his fingers, and, in order to facilitate the flow of the juice, cuts the bottom of the secondary axils on which the flowers are, so to speak, incrusted. On the ninth day the sap begins to run, and the end of the spathe is then inserted into an earthen vessel, the contents of which are collected every morning and evening. The outcome continues for three or four months, and amounts daily to two quarts or two quarts and a half. Every third year the palm is allowed to rest and bear fruit; otherwise it would perish. To obtain the jaghery or sugar, a little lime is added to the juice, which is boiled until it is as thick as syrup; then it is poured into small baskets made of palm-leaves. On cooling, it partly crystallizes, and furnishes a sugar of a deep brown tint. Six pints of toddy produce about a quart of jaghery, which is worth threepence.

The arrack is prepared from the toddy, fermented and distilled. The quantity of sugar obtained from the male tree is not more than one-third of that furnished by the female tree.

From Chingleput we proceed to Sadras; and from Sadras, by a salt-water canal, to Mahabalipur, the "city of the great Bali," also known as "the Seven Pagodas." It lies about seven miles to the north of Sadras.

There, on a sandy and silent shore, which is washed by the billows of the Indian Ocean in the season of the monsoons, numerous small temples and caves attract the traveller's attention. The majority appear to have been consecrated to Vishnu, whose worship was widely spread of old along the Coromandel coast.

In the centre of the sand-waste rises an isolated mass of granite, on the western side of which we see a cavern, fronted by a portico of two rows of columns: of the first four the shaft is octagonal, with a cubical base and capital; while the others are polygons, crowned with mushroom-shaped capitals. In the recess were formerly five sanctuaries, each containing a lingam; nothing now remains but the stone basin which held the symbol. The door of the sanctuary is flanked by statues four feet high, which are by no means remarkable in an artistic sense. The whole is carved out of the solid rock. The exterior is ornamented with bell-gables, recalling, as Fergusson remarks, the monastic cells in which the Buddhist monks passed their contemplative lives. To the left of this temple, and on the same level, may be seen a second, the incomplete sculptures of which still exhibit traces of the chisels of the workmen. Attention should also be directed to another small grotto, the façade of which is decorated with two octagonal columns, and two rudely wrought statues. A few paces beyond, and three niches, occupied by shapeless statues, are conspicuous: in the depth of each is sculptured a deity with four arms, the attributes of which are not discernible; and above fly two dwarfs, whose squat bodies, twisted limbs, and hideous heads combine in a monstrous whole exactly like the ugly creatures that figure in the Buddhist monuments of Ceylon—these are the *yakshas* or demons. Below, a couple of men are kneeling in an attitude of prayer. Men, demons, and gods are equally wanting in grace and expression.

When we come to the northern side, our gaze is arrested by a couple of apes—one engaged in scratching his comrade's head—which are truly remarkable for the fantastical character of their attitudes. Afterwards we arrive at a small temple excavated in the rock, of the same style as the preceding. A statue of Ganesa occupies the interior. Other remarkable grottoes there are, of which our limits will not permit us to attempt a description. But we must point to one which rests on a range of four columns having lions for a pedestal. A sculpture in the interior represents a scene from the life of Krishna; and a colossal figure of the god supports with his left hand the temple-vault. Figures of zebus are seen in all directions: one, on the right, reclines in a very natural attitude; further on, another licks a heifer which a man is drawing to her;—these sculptures are well designed and well executed. On the left-hand side are carved numerous monsters, among which is seen a human-headed lion. They have been wrought, it must be admitted, by no feeble or inartistic chisel.

To the north, on the very margin of the sea, are situated two pyramidal temples. The column, generally erected in front of the temples of Siva, has its base now washed by the waves; a proof that the sea has encroached and is encroaching on the Coromandel coast. In the larger sanctuary is a colossal lingam of prismatic form.

About a mile and a half to the south rise five monolithic temples, which are unquestionably the most interesting portion of the ruins of Mahabalipur. Three of them are built pyramidically, and ornamented with quadrangular belfries. A fourth, which forms a square, and is the only one which has been completed, is crowned by a curvilinear vaulted roof. In the sanctuary reigns a four-armed goddess, at whose feet two men are kneeling; round about her fly four plump angels, a couple of whom wear moustaches on their upper lip.

From Mahabalipur we proceed to one of the five resting-places of the French in India. At one time it seemed as if the peninsula would have fallen into *their* hands; but, through the genius of Clive and Hastings, they were beaten back to Pondicherry, where the tricolor still waves disconsolately. A pretty town, is Pondicherry—traversed by broad and well-kept streets—and having about it a curiously French air, or rather a French-Indian air. M. Grandidier speaks of its *Creole* aspect; and adds that it resembles neither a native nor a purely French town, but presents "a happy mixture of those two characters which are everywhere recognized when the French or Spanish race is compelled to live with a foreign population."

It is with the inhabitants, says Grandidier, as with the town: they have made out a life for themselves, adapted to the climate in which they reside; they do not attempt to introduce into India the manners and habits of France, which certainly wither under the burning sun of the Tropics. "The Southern peoples are far from resembling the English, who always tread disdainfully a foreign soil; and, whether in China or Kamtschatka, still think themselves on British ground. The Englishman, in effect, does not travel; he changes his scene, but always carries with him his *home*." We submit, however, that when a stronger but less numerous race is called upon to live with the weaker but more numerous race which it has conquered, it is well that it should retain its own individuality. We hold India by virtue of our superiority, but that superiority would soon disappear if we assimilated ourselves to Indian habits and Indian manners. Pondicherry and Calcutta are each typical of the nations to which they belong; and the difference between them helps to explain why India is British, and not French.

The houses of Pondicherry are nearly all separated from the street by small courtyards enriched with shrubberies and flower-beds. Their appearance, however, suffers greatly from the cryptogamic vegetation which quickly covers them in large patches, and needs to be cleared away every year. After this annual process everything looks clear and bright for two or three months, when the whiteness again disappears under the lichens which extend their myriad arms in every direction, and rapidly spread over the entire surface.

From Pondicherry the traveller may proceed to Trichinopoli, Tanjore, and Madura.

Trichinopoli was formerly the seat of the Chola dynasty, one of the three great ruling powers of the Deccan. It afterwards fell under the sway of the Talingana Naikhars dynasty; and, for a brief period, was the capital of the Mohammedan kings. Here the French made several efforts to establish their authority; and here, too, the foundations of our Anglo-Indian sovereignty were laid by the genius and resolution of Clive and Lawrence.

The Fort is an immense mass of solid masonry crowning the summit of a great rock, with ramparts so solid and battlements so regular that the European is surprised at such a monument of Oriental military architecture. Its white bastions gleaming in the sunshine are visible above a forest of palms from all the country round. Against any native force that can threaten its defences, it is impregnable; and the Union Jack waving from its loftiest tower is a perpetual symbol of the power and glory of England.

On the occasion of the Prince of Wales's visit, both Fort and rock were shrouded in crimson flame, bursting from a myriad jets. The prince witnessed the gorgeous scene from a building which a small lake separates from the base of the great fortress. Showers of rockets were sent up from boats that moved to and fro on the many-coloured sheet of water. A canopy rose above the prince's seat, the splendid tinting of which, in gold and silver and purple, had occupied many weeks of arduous toil on the part of the native artists.

"Behind the prince," says Mr. Wheeler, "upon a rich black and crimson carpet, stood the native dignitaries, in dresses of white and green, gold and scarlet. The military staff of Trichinopoli, and many ladies in evening costume, were also in the brilliant group. His Royal Highness was much impressed as he watched the rockets wreathing round the pinnacles and towers of the citadel, and the coloured fires rolling in clouds down the pallid battlements. On each side of the square lake, beyond lines of fixed lights, were masses of natives, whose peering dark faces, alive with excitement, and picturesque dresses, gave a mystic appearance to the roadways. Outside of the crowd again were troops: native lancers, in light blue, and the attendants of rajahs, in black and red, all of whom held aloft either bannered spear-heads or flashing sabres. Above the whole of the earthly revelry a pale full moon sailed on her course in the misty heaven."

The holiest Indian shrine in the south is the Great Tamil Temple situated on the island of Seringham ("the divine Vishnu"). Its dimensions are enormous, and within its huge precincts it affords accommodation to a numerous company of Brahmans, and others more or less closely connected with the sanctuary. It is needless to repeat a tale already often told, or to dwell upon the details of the courts, and gateways, and colonnades, and sculptures, which generally resemble those of the other great Indian temples. From the summit of the principal gopura, or gateway, may be obtained a gloriously extensive view, northwards towards the mountains which border the Trichinopoli plain, eastward along the fertile and plentifully irrigated level country, and westward to the source of all its fertility, the huge dam which shuts up for purposes of irrigation the rolling currents of the Kaveri. This temple is very rich in precious stones and gems, wrought into a variety of fantastic devices.

TEMPLE AT SERINGHAM.

In this part of India the great Hindu sect of the Vishnavites has split into two divisions, the "men of the north" and the "men of the south." The former wear the symbolical trident on their foreheads, but cut it short between the eyebrows; while the latter lengthen it to a point about half-way down the nose. The Great Temple of Seringham belongs to the "men of the south." They allow the northerners, however, to worship at its altar, but not to carry about the objects of their worship in procession. It requires all the force and moral power of the British Government to prevent the rival religionists from breaking out into sanguinary feuds.

Among other objects of interest in Trichinopoli are the Roman Catholic cathedral; the old palace of the rajahs of Tanjore; the bazaars of the gold-workers, with their singularly beautiful masterpieces of art; the Church of St. John, where Heber, the poet-bishop, preached his last sermon, and lies buried; and Clive's house. Can any Englishman view without emotion the dwelling-place of that foremost among our Anglo-Indian soldier-statesmen?

Tanjore is situated among prolific rice-fields in a burning plain, which only an extensive system of irrigation saves from drought and sterility. It is principally famous for its spacious and lofty temple, which, like that of Trichinopoli, is one of the great sanctuaries of Southern India. A recent traveller, Mr. Grant Duff, says—"Its general effect is not less imposing than, though very different from, that of Edfou or Denderah [on the Nile]. The temples of Benares filled me with something nearly akin to disgust, but this is very different. The famous black bull is a grand beast, of Egyptian proportions and benignity......We lingered long amongst the courts of this splendid temple, learning the uses of its different parts, and strolled a little in the till lately neglected garden, which is gradually being put into order by the local British providence."

The palace is large, with some good architectural features; it commands a fine picturesque view of the city, the roofs of which, unlike those in Northern India, are not flat, but pointed. The arsenal is now empty of weapons; but the library is rich in Sanskrit manuscripts.

Madura, on the Vaiga, is largely frequented by pilgrims, inasmuch as it lies on the route to the sacred island of Rameshwaram, and is in itself a sacred city, with several splendid temples —the chief (the Great Pagoda of Minakshi) being that built by Trimal Naik, a former Nayak of Madura. It is dedicated to Siva and his wife Parvati. The interior is magnificent, with long-drawn corridors and arched roofs, and images of the two deities in gold and silver placed at frequent intervals. Beyond the pagoda lies the celebrated tank of the Golden Lotus, the lily sacred to Siva; to bathe in the waters of which is the aspiration of the faithful in the Southern Deccan.

Adjoining the tank is a magic seat, upon which the candidates for places in the Council of the University of Madura, to which students from all parts of India formerly resorted, were made to take their places. The story goes that if the aspirant were in very truth worthy of the honour he sought, the bench, when he sat down, extended so as to accommodate him. But, on the other hand, if his ambition exceeded his deserts, the bench contracted; and the unlucky candidate, after coming to the ground, was flung into the tank to cool the fever of his desires.

CHAPTER XXI.

HURDWAR: AND THE GANGES.

THE SACRED CITY AND THE SACRED RIVER—THE INDIAN GRASSES—THE PLANTAIN—IN THE JUNGLE—THE "GATE OF HARI"—DESCRIPTION OF THE CITY—THE TEMPLES—THE GREAT GANGES CANAL—A BATHING-GHAT—THE GREAT FAIR OF HURDWAR.

THERE is much that is beautiful in the aspect of the Ganges near the sacred city of Hurdwar. It is of considerable width, with a light sandy soil; bounded on the left by the lofty Himalaya, their white peaks sharply defined against a sky of intensest blue, and on the left of the lower summits of the Siwalik range, waving with green woods of pine. In the neighbourhood of Dehra the great upper valley seems to reach its highest fertility. The sunny slopes bloom with all kinds of crops, which are diversified by extensive tea-plantations, and brightened by breadths of fragrant blossom, among which conspicuous shine the flowers of the rosy hibiscus, pure white as snow in early morning, and at noon as crimson as a lake in the sunset. At frequent intervals dense clumps of bamboo lift high their feathery foliage, like colossal plumes of ostrich feathers. Can anything be more gracefully attractive than these tall grasses? Each reed is about four or five inches in diameter at the base, and springs upward, in points of two to three feet each, to the height of forty or even fifty feet. Tall and strong as they seem, at the impulse of the wind they sway their feathery crests in graceful curves, while each separate bright green leaf quivers as at the touch of an unseen finger. Surely it was out of one of these that Pan, of old, made to himself the melodious pipe with which he charmed the echoes of Arcadia. At least the Malays are cunning now-a-days to convert them into musical instruments, breathing the sweetest sounds imaginable as the wind plays upon them. For this purpose, holes are bored in each hollow joint, holes varying in size according to the diameter of the bamboo; and as the breeze steals through them, each organ-pipe responds with melodious tones, some soft and dulcet as those of a distant lute, some rich and full like the swell of a summer sea.

Besides these groups of bamboo we see the towering plantains, with each broad shining leaf, eight or ten feet long, crowning a low stem, from which depend the large full crimson blossoms and the clusters of luscious, creamy fruit. The plantain enters largely into the Hindu peasant's daily fare; yet it is not so precious to him as its neighbour, the bamboo,—which, indeed, in this Ganges valley, plays a part as important as the cocoa-nut or the bread-fruit in the isles of Polynesia. The young sprouts, which are carefully pruned in order to facilitate the growth of the main shoots, can be eaten as a vegetable, or boiled with sugar into a sweetmeat, or made with vinegar into a pickle. Cut up small, mixed with honey, and exposed to the action of a wood-fire, it furnishes a very agreeable confection. A decoction of the leaves supplies a mucilaginous drink, useful as a cough-mixture; and its outer rind serves as a febrifuge. From the young buds is obtained a cooling diaphoretic; and the root supplies a valuable salve. The cane is turned to account for an infinite variety of purposes. Every kind of article, from a fishing-rod to the mast of a vessel, is made out of it; and not only the mast, but the hull, the rigging, and even the canvas. The rafters and floors of houses are bamboo; bows and bowstrings, bamboo; arrow-

BAMBOOS.

shafts and pens, bamboo; buckets and water-wheels, bamboo; mats, blinds, water-pipes, musical instruments, bamboo. In a word, if every other tree were swept clean out of the Ganges valley, the Hindu would still be immeasurably rich in his possession of the bamboo.

Through this scene of abundant crops and feathery foliage we pass into a tract of jungle, where the palms are fantastically festooned with wreaths of emerald-tinted parasites, studded all over with starry blossoms. Here we realize, for the first time in our lives, the true beauty of the grasses. Grasses of all kinds are around us: tall, plume-like grasses; silky grasses; short, spiky grasses; tufted grasses; grasses light and feathery; grasses waving like wild oats; and tall, pink, sirkee grasses, which rear their rosy plumes twenty to thirty feet in height. Through a fluttering, bending, whispering, rustling world of grasses we make our way; and the effect is as novel as it is beautiful. At this point the two mountain-chains approach each other very closely, and it is in their deep, silent shadow that the Ganges pours downward its clear, fresh, bright blue waters, in vivid contrast to the turbid stream which washes Agra and Benares.

At length we arrive at Hurdwar, or Haridwar—that is, the Gate of Hari (or Vishnu), the Indian Sun-god, the subject of as many myths as the Greek Hyperion or the Latin Apollo. It is a small and ancient city, presenting the usual Oriental characteristics. Every house is more or less ornamental; not a few are richly carved and painted; and each window has its littlo overhanging balcony. In the middle of the chief street a row of paltry booths, thatched with brown straw, is built up on either side of the road against the tall stately houses, producing a very curious and picturesque effect of colouring. The thoroughfares are crowded with people, numbers of whom carry great baskets of flowers, and radiant wreaths of roses and marigolds, to deposit at the shrines of their idols, or with which to festoon the sacred river. Others are busy sealing up its holy water in tall, thin bottles, so that happy pilgrims may take it home with them, for the purpose of anointing their household gods. This sealing process is singular enough; no ordinary fire is used, but the workman kindles one end of a large tree, and allows it to smoulder gradually. Groups of women, close by, prepare cakes of the fuel of the country, and plaster them over the fronts of the houses that they may dry in the sun.

The main support of the inhabitants of Hurdwar is cotton-picking. All other avocations are more or less closely connected with the temple-worship. Many stalls are wholly confined to the sale of all kinds of brass idols, brass bells (such as are rung in the temples), flower-vases, incense-burners, mirrors, lotas, toys, and phials and vases for holy water. Others are appropriated to sweetmeats and beads.

The temples here, as elsewhere, line the river-bank, and though neither of graceful nor imposing design, are rendered attractive by their tall, pyramidal, elaborately carved domes. Generally they are enclosed in a grove of peepul-trees, and these are tenanted by countless monkeys, chattering incessantly, and doing whatever they list; roaming about the temples and the town, perching on roofs and balconies, and carrying off from the stalls, without let or hindrance, any object on which they happen to set their fancy.

In the immediate neighbourhood of Hurdwar begins the great Ganges Canal, which has done so much to avert the evils of the prolonged droughts that frequently afflict India. Works of irrigation on an extensive scale occupied the energies of the Mogul emperors; but none of these could compare with the grand achievement of English engineering skill. It was designed by Sir Proby Cautley; and extends from Hurdwar to Cawnpur, a distance of four hundred miles, transforming a parched desert into a blooming garden, and supplying life and freshness to an area of six hundred thousand acres. The difficulties overcome in its construction were enormous; and immense tunnels, aqueducts, and embankments, and a vast system of locks weirs, and sluices, will long perpetuate in India the memory of the English *raj*.

Close to the head of the canal a spacious bathing-ghat has been built by Government, with the view of diminishing the pressure of the crowds of pilgrims who assemble at Hurdwar on the occasion of its great annual fair.

For Hurdwar, being the city nearest to the source of the Ganges, is reputed almost as holy as Gangotri itself, where the river issues from its parent ice-cave at the base of the colossal glacier.

Once a year, then, pilgrims resort to it from every part of the empire, on a day appointed by the Hindu astrologers. For it is necessary that the fair should be held when Jupiter is in Aquarius, at the time of the sun entering Aries—Hurdwar being, as we have already stated, consecrated to the Sun-god, Hari.

For weeks previously the pilgrims arrive in a continuous stream, pitching their camps on every available spot. They come in entire families, so that all alike may cleanse themselves of their sins in the river of purification—Kashmirians, Paharis, Hindus, Persians. Thither, too, drawn by the hope of gain, flock Tartars, Afghans, Cabulees, and Mohammedans of many nations.

The fair is a great horse-fair, where you may find every variety of breed, from the fleet Arab and the stout, heavy draught-horse of New South Wales to the sturdy ponies of Kashmir and Cabul. But it is not only a horse-fair; it exhibits a tolerably complete collection of the world's zoology,—elephants, buffaloes, camels, bears, leopards, cheetahs, cats, dogs, cows, sheep, and monkeys. Then, among other merchandise, we find choice boxes of dried fruit, sweetmeats, mats, shawls from the most dexterous looms of Kashmir and India, jewels in infinite variety, beads and toys, woollen goods, perfumes, silks, cottons, and all kinds of European wares. The hubbub is tremendous when the fair is at its height; for vendors and purchasers never complete a bargain without an extraordinary amount of "palaver," accompanied by a no less extraordinary amount of gesticulation.

According to Miss Gordon Cumming, who visited the fair in 1875, a certain ghat, just below a favourite temple, is esteemed the sacredest spot in all Hurdwar; and thither, on the great day of the festival, every one rushes to bathe—half a million of people contriving to plunge in at this consecrated spot within a few hours. Men, women, and children bathe indiscriminately, but without any indecency, from their absolute unconsciousness of wrong-doing or cause for shame. "They plunge joyously in, as if thoroughly enjoying themselves in the clear rippling stream, and the women washing their long raven hair; and all coming out again as fresh as—well, we cannot say as fresh as daisies, more like glossy horse-chestnuts! The richer pilgrims are led into the water, supported on either side by a venerable Brahman, who carefully takes them to the mid-stream, plunges them in thrice, silently and solemnly, then escorts them to land once more; a very grave proceeding, much in the style of the solemn three dips and out again of the genuine health-seeker at the sea-side."

The average yearly attendance at the Hurdwar festival is computed at about two hundred thousand persons; but every twelfth year, when Krishna himself is supposed to revisit the earth and favour his worshippers with his unseen presence, it swells to a million and a half. The sacredness of the river-city on such occasions is almost inconceivable and indescribable. It becomes the very gate of heaven; and the air of sanctity abroad is such as to secure the salvation of all who are present, not even Christians being excluded!

CARAVAN ON THE ROAD TO HURDWAR.

CHAPTER XXII.

CALCUTTA: THE CITY OF PALACES.

SITUATION OF CALCUTTA—ITS GENERAL ASPECT—DESCRIBED BY M. GRANDIDIER—THE ENGLISH QUARTER—THE NATIVE QUARTER—NATIVE HOUSES—ABOUT THE BABOOS—THE BURNING-GHAT—THE TEMPLE OF KALI—SANGUINARY CULTUS OF THE GODDESS—THE CHURUK-POOJA—ANIMAL SACRIFICES PRESENTED—THE ADJUTANT-BIRDS—THE HACKRIE, OR BULLOCK-CART—CALCUTTA MERCHANTS AND SHOPKEEPERS—"PIECE-GOODS" MERCHANTS—AFGHAN TRADERS—THE MAIDAN, OR ESPLANADE—THE BOTANICAL GARDEN.

CALCUTTA, the so-called "City of Palaces," the capital of British India, is situated on the Hugli, one of the principal streams of the Gangetic Delta. Though thirty leagues distant from the sea, the estuary is so deep that ships of the largest size can lie close to its quays. Unfortunately, the current is very rapid, and bringing down with it great quantities of soil, accumulates at the mouth of the river a number of shifting sandbanks, which seriously obstruct navigation.

The impression which the first view of Calcutta produces on the visitor is decidedly favourable. He suddenly perceives, says M. Rousselet, a stately line of palaces fronting an immense esplanade. Columns and belfries rise in all directions; the harbour is thronged with a forest of masts; the quays seem to heave and swell with tumultuous crowds; while carriages and palkies of novel aspect incessantly pass to and fro. Nor is the impression diminished by a closer inspection. The squares are not unworthy of London; streets containing sumptuous shops are lined with houses having the porticoes of Greek temples. Dr. Macleod remarks that Old Court-house Street is so fine and wide, with shops so brilliant, that no part of London would be ashamed of it; and he adds that the breadth of the great thoroughfares, the size and imposing style of the residences which line them, and the arrangements necessitated by the climate, which demands air and shade, and gardens with their flowers and verdure, all combine to extend the European portion of Calcutta over a really imposing area. And Mr. Matheson, an accurate matter-of-fact observer, asserts that the appearance of Calcutta is decidedly that of a "city of palaces." It may be described, in a sentence, as an immense crescent (perhaps two miles in extent), mainly formed of elegant white buildings, with flat, ornamented roofs and broad balconies,—this view, adorned by several spires and enriched by abundant foliage, forming the magnificent boundary-line of a wide, noble park, stretching down to the banks of the river. "Here the eye takes in at a glance the best portion of the city, including Chowringhee (the handsome 'West-End'), Government-House, and other public edifices. The Maidan—which, in consequence of being the public exercise-ground, has been appropriately styled the 'lungs' of Calcutta—might with equal propriety have been called its strong arm; for here stands Fort William, encircled by green ramparts and wide intrenchments—an impregnable little city of soldiers, bristling all over with guns, and well stored with British means and appliances of offensive and defensive warfare. Here, too, is the 'Course'—the scene of that afternoon gathering, which of itself is something worth visiting Calcutta to witness."

One of the liveliest descriptions of the city with which we are acquainted has been furnished by M. Grandidier; and it is interesting to see the effect its various phases produced on the mind of a quick and intelligent Frenchman. He speaks of the English division of the city as composed of numerous gardens, enclosed within low walls or hedges, with the bungalow in the centre. The offices, stables, and servants' apartments are arranged along the sides, like wings. These houses have a special style of their own, being carefully adapted to the necessities of the climate. If not very elegant in appearance, they are pre-eminently comfortable; and their internal

THE PORT OF CALCUTTA.

arrangement is suitable to a tropical life. They are mostly of two stories, raised on a platform of bricks, and surmounted by a pyramidal roof. A verandah is carried all round the bungalow, where the inmates, safe alike from sun or rain, may contrive to breathe and live during the hottest hours of the day. The chambers are spacious, and divided only by thin partitions, which, in order to allow of a free circulation of air, do not reach the roof. To each chamber is attached a bath-room, where morning and evening the languid European refreshes himself by abundant ablutions.

The furniture is simple: cabinets and tables of mahogany, a piano, lustres, lamps, beds, spacious fauteuils of bamboo with raised backs and long arms,—these are the principal articles. The beds are placed in the middle of the room, and draped with gauze curtains, which fit in closely, so as to shelter the sleeper from the attacks of mosquitoes and the other insect-plagues of the East. The flooring usually is of bricks, cemented in a layer of white lime : this, too, is designed as a defence against insects, and has a cool, clean look which is very pleasant.

Let us now direct our steps to the native quarter. Here the streets are dark and dirty, and lined by dusty brick houses, utterly devoid of architectural merit. The shops, as in all Indian bazaars, are entirely open, and generally on a level with the pavement. The owner sits within, cross-legged, in the midst of his wares, patiently awaiting the arrival of a customer, when he suddenly bursts out into activity, and recommends his goods with the fluency of an English auctioneer.

Sooth to say, the bazaar would not be very interesting but for the various costumes of the people which throng it. The different races of India here mingle together, and the artist finds a

LOW CASTE BENGALEES.

constant succession of subjects for his pencil. The aborigines differ from the Bengalees, as the Bengalees differ from the Europeans; and the eye soon learns to distinguish between diverse tribes and races.

Entering one of the native houses, we find it divided into low, small, close, and unhealthy rooms, the furniture of which exhibits the very essence of simplicity. The mat rolled up in yonder corner will be spread on the ground in the evening, to serve the purpose of a bed. A few earthenware or copper vessels to cook the food and hold water—some large green leaves for plates—a metal dish resting on a tripod, or deposited in a niche of the wall, and filled with oil for lamps—and a hookah in the corner,—these articles may be said to complete the furnishing of an Indian "interior."

The rich Baboos have adopted, in their more spacious but equally dirty abodes, the European style of furniture. The luxury is useless, however, since they never inhabit the apartments in which are accumulated, like so many precious relics, chairs and couches of mahogany, clocks, musical boxes, and vases of gilded porcelain.

We must not quit the native quarter without paying a visit to the ghat, on the bank of the Ganges, where the natives burn the bodies of their dead before flinging their ashes into the waters of the sacred river. On three sides the place is surrounded by a high wall; and along the parapet assemble a crowd of vultures and marabouts, prepared to contend with one another for the morsels of flesh which the flames of the funeral pile may spare. While we are looking on several corpses are thus consigned to the elements ; and the details of the ceremony interest us sufficiently to enable us to endure the nauseous odour that impregnates the air. So little influence has the sentiment of death upon the Hindus, as Grandidier remarks—so impassive and unconscious are they rendered by their faith in the doctrine of the metempsychosis—that the funeral preparations, singularly distasteful as they are to the European mind, produce not the slightest impression upon them, in spite of their domestic attachments. Father, son, or wife is given to the consuming fire, and the ashes distributed on the wind, if not with actual joy, at least with an indifference which the English observer is apt to misunderstand. But this indifference is not a want of feeling ; it is the result of a fatalistic resignation to things independent of the human will.

It will be appropriate enough to pass on, from this place of the dead, to the temple of Kali, the Hindu goddess of Death. It is situated at Kalighat,—now a suburb of the city, but probably the original of the modern Calcutta,—and consists of a spacious chamber, dimly lighted from the door, enshrining an image of the goddess. And anything more hideous it would be difficult to imagine. The black face is crowned with long hair, and from the mouth projects a red tongue, descending to the chin. The body has four arms, one of which grasps a scimitar, while another holds a giant's head by the hair. Round the neck hangs a chain of skulls, and the figures of two dead bodies depend from the ears. And, finally, the eyebrows are coloured with red paint, which flows like blood down upon the breasts.

No divinity in India is more dreaded than Kali ; and no *cultus* is more sanguinary than hers. There is nothing logical, indeed, in addressing one's prayers to Brahma, the Creative God, whose work is finished, or to the Preservative God, Vishnu, who, by his very essence, is specially occupied in the preservation of every living creature, while poor Humanity is in constant terror, if not of disease, at least of that death which is ever threatening and ever terrible. From their point of view, then, the Hindus are justified in directing their petitions towards the sole goddess of their pantheon who holds their destiny in her hands, or towards her husband, the ferocious Siva. Who has not heard or read of the feasts celebrated in honour of Kali, when maddened enthusiasts pierce their tongue with red-hot iron skewers, and others go through the *Churuk-Pooja* (or ceremony of the circle)? A hook passed through the skin of the back raises them at the extremity of a swing, and they hover in the air above the heads of an admiring crowd, offering, with a smile upon their lips, their sufferings to the implacable goddess.*

* The British Government have forbidden this custom, and the Baboos have endeavoured to give a new direction to it. M. Rousselet describes the festival as he saw it:—"On arriving at the place where it was held, I saw a respectable assemblage of Baboos occupying a circle of chairs round a large piece of turf, in the midst of which rose a scaffolding provided with trapezes, bars, cords, rings—in short, a complete gymnastic apparatus. Soon after, a number of boys and young men arrived, who very cleverly executed some excellent feats of agility, under the direction of two English soldiers. To the gymnasts succeeded an orchestra, also composed of young Indians, who played us several pieces; and finally there came a chorus of children, who sang hymns in Bengalee. When the representation was over, prizes were distributed to the children, who were afterwards invited to sit down to a copious repast. 'The greater part of these children,' said my companion, 'belong to the poorest classes of the town, and yet there are numbers of young Baboos among them. By providing for them pleasures and recreations which were unknown to them before, we wean them from the sanguinary spectacles to which they would otherwise have become attached; we elevate their minds, and prepare them to become men.' It will thus be seen that the Baboos of Calcutta deserve all sympathy from Europeans, and they are most steady and praiseworthy people."

At one time human sacrifices polluted with their blood the altar of Kali; but these have been sternly prohibited by the British Government. Animal sacrifices have been substituted. Dr. Macleod saw several goats presented. "A few ceremonies were performed over them by a Brahman, who received the head of each as a small fee. The head of the animal was inserted in

THE GODDESS KALI, OR DURGA.

a square frame, made secure by a pin, and then severed at one blow by the executioner. The priest received the head, and the body was removed by the offerer—to be eaten, I presume, by him and others. These animals are thus offered every day. On great festivities oxen are killed, and hundreds of goats."

The image of the goddess as given in the plate is very different from the favourite form in

Bengal. Nearly all the horrid accompaniments are absent. There is, however, a prostrate figure, on which a lion is trampling. The lion would indicate the goddess Durga; but the four arms indicate Kali—Durga having ten.

Let us now glance at some of the most interesting features of Calcutta, without pretending to take them in any particular order, or to do more than bestow upon them just that amount of observation which a stranger would bestow in passing through the city.

Our attention is first arrested by the *arghilahs,* or adjutant-birds, which stalk through the crowded streets, or perch upon the roofs of the houses, with a wonderfully amusing dignity. They are almost as tall as men; and their bald heads, with two reddish, round, little eyes, support a huge pointed beak, capable of disembowelling a fowl, and furnished with a violet-tinted pouch, in which the said fowl may be accommodated before it passes into the capacious stomach. Hence the bird is vulgarly known as "the bagged-stork." The curiousness of its appearance is increased by its motley colouring: it has a white body, two black striped wings, which cross behind the back, and a couple of tawny legs. It is the natural scavenger of Calcutta, carefully cleansing the streets of every morsel of dirt, offal, and refuse; and in such a city, where the climate is oppressively hot and always more or less malarious, its presënce is more useful than that of a Board of Health. Kites, buzzards, and vultures assist it in its work; but supreme among them all moves the philosophical arghilah, impressed with the wise belief that "dirt is matter in the wrong place." At the breeding season it leaves Calcutta, but punctually returns after an absence of three months.

WATER-CARRIERS OF CALCUTTA.

Another civic institution is the bullock-cart or *hackrie,* the creaking, rasping noise of which adds greatly to the discordant music of the streets. It is rudely constructed of bamboo, with an axle of the same material; and is drawn by a pair of bullocks, fastened together by a pole laid across the neck immediately in front of the hump. As the whole weight of the burden rests upon this pole, the animals suffer greatly; and the hackrie may justly be regarded as an effective engine of torture.

A large staff of men is employed in watering the streets, and keeping down the dust, which would otherwise be insupportable. They are called *bheesties,* or water-carriers, and each is provided with a *mussak*—a bag of skin or leather—filled with water. As the Hindu shrinks from all vocations however remotely connected with animal life, the bheesties are Mohammedans, and their yearly wage is about £8 or £10.

In London we are well aware that a profitable business is not necessarily connected with an

THE MAIDAN, CALCUTTA.

imposing exterior, or a great display of plate-glass and gilding; and in Calcutta we may learn the same lesson as to the folly of judging by appearances. Prosperous traders will squat throughout the day, year after year, on the earthen floor of a little dusty den which is barely large enough to accommodate the owner and his wares; and extensive dealers in goods and produce whose annual transactions amount to several lacs of rupees, dwell in tiny garrets which English philanthropists would pronounce unfit for paupers. A traveller describes a visit which he paid to the "emporium" of a prominent merchant, or dealer in "piece-goods." Through a narrow lane and up a shaky stair he was conducted to a large open gallery, overlooking a court below in which a number of men were engaged in packing bales and boxes. Above this gallery, on projecting ledges thick with dust, large flower-pots, in every stage of dilapidation from wear and tear, held plants which were drooping and withering from the heat; while a cloud of pigeons, esteemed birds of good omen, hovered in the sunny air. Around it, within a series of tiny chambers, or rather cells, the several dealers, alone, or with their partners in trade, were engaged in the various departments of their business. Each apartment might be compared to a child's toy-house; "something, or rather anything with a glitter, being stuck into every available crevice and corner. Even the iron safe which held the receipts and rupees, did duty also as the gilded ornament of a wall that was embellished with a hideous crew of paint and porcelain divinities staring down upon the inmates."

The "piece-goods" merchants are principally Marwaris, or "up-country" men, and are usually attired in a long toga of white linen, with a turban or head-dress of various designs. Their hands invariably blaze with jewels.

"In the business haunts of Calcutta," says Matheson, "as the nucleus of North-Western commerce, we naturally encounter a fresh variety of race and costume. Some brown faces now mingle with the black; and, side by side with the feebler form of the Bengali, strong, thickly-clad, bearded figures of Afghans, who have travelled thus far with shawls from Kashmir, and fruits and spices from Cabul, afford in their own stalwart persons a striking example of the wide difference existing among Indian communities. These men leave their camels to await their return at Delhi, more than one thousand miles behind, whence they now take the railway to Calcutta; and there, following in a troop at the heels of an interpreter, perambulate the European 'go-downs' in social parties, to select the cotton stripe prints and the few other articles which they carry back to their country in exchange for its own merchandise. The bargaining process is here also frequently conducted between the broker and buyer by signs made with joined hands under cover of a cloth,—the purchaser first making his offer."

To the burning-ghats it is unnecessary to make further allusion. They are at Calcutta what they are at Benares, and at all the great Indian cities. No dead bodies are allowed by the British Government to be consigned to the Hugli; and even the poorest are compelled to resort to the practice of cremation. For their behoof a large tower is provided at the public expense, where a brazier is constantly flaming; and every precaution is taken to ensure the entire consumption of the corpse.

The centre of the out-door life of Calcutta is the celebrated Maidan, or Esplanade. Its shape is that of a parallelogram; at one end stands the spacious and stately Government-House.

with its memories of Dalhousie, Canning, Lawrence, and other great statesmen and rulers; and near it the Town-Hall, Treasury, and High Court. Opposite, in the centre of the broad plain, rises the huge mass of Fort William; and beyond may be seen the steeple of the beautiful Cathedral, sharply defined against the glowing sapphire sky. Along one side runs a noble street with the "palatial mansions" of Chowringhee; on the other the broad Hugli, with its innumerable ships and boats, mingled together in apparently inextricable confusion.

MARWARI MERCHANTS, CALCUTTA.

The Maidan is embellished with flower-garden and lawn, with several memorial equestrian statues, and the tall Ochterlony Column. But its chief attraction is to be found in the crowds that assemble in its open spaces: Brahmans, Sikhs, Afghans, Europeans, merchants, soldiers, sailors, equestrians, carriages with prancing horses,—all pass by the stranger like the shifting scenes of a panorama, and forcibly impress upon him the strange contrasts and varieties of Indian life.

On the right bank of the river, at a short distance above the town, is situated the celebrated Botanical Garden, founded by the late eminent botanist, Sir Joseph Hooker. Within its precincts, flourishing under the blue warm sky, grow side by side all the wonders of "the African, American, Asiatic, and Oceanic Floras."

CHAPTER XXIII.

IN THE NEIGHBOURHOOD OF CALCUTTA.

THE ROAD TO ORISSA—WAYSIDE RELICS—SCENES ON THE ROAD—AT PURI—TEMPLE OF JUGGERNATH—THE SACRED BULLS—WITHIN THE TEMPLE—MONSTER IMAGES OF THE GODS—JUGGERNATH'S DAILY RATIONS—A CURIOUS SPECTACLE—THE APE-GOD—A SACRED POOL—THE TRIUMPHAL CAR—THE SUNDARBANS—CHANDERNAGAR—GHAT OF TRIVENI—PANDOOAH—BURDWAN—MURSHIDABAD—THE RAJMAHAL MOUNTAINS—PATNA.

FROM Calcutta the road strikes in a westerly direction to Midnapur, and then southward to Balasore, crossing an immense area of rice-fields, studded with Bengalee villages, and groves of cocoa-palms. Beyond Balasore the traveller enters the plain of Orissa, which, a few years ago, was the scene of so terrible a famine. The road then leads to Cuttack; and from Cuttack to Puri, the sacred city of Juggernath, situated on the sea-shore.

Along the route the traveller is not a little surprised to see numbers of large earthen vessels, intact, or only slightly injured. People of caste hold that there is pollution even in the glance of a Pariah, and when travelling, however great their indigence, never cook their food in a vessel which, after having been used, may be exposed to the eye of a casteless wretch; they prefer to reduce their ration of rice so that they may buy every day a new dish or pan. This rule, however, like all other rules, has its exception. Certain stuffs, such as silks, and certain vessels,—namely, vessels of copper,—possess the curious virtue of becoming purified, after a series of washings, from the pollution inflicted upon them by having come in contact with even the vilest Pariah. It is not difficult to explain these subtle distinctions; articles of little value, and, owing to their cheapness, within the reach of all, are the only articles which can be absolutely polluted. Here is an illustration of that arrogance of caste which admits nothing in common with the unprivileged orders. Though sometimes compelled by pecuniary conditions to adopt the same social economy, it still finds means to erect a barrier of demarcation.

Some such spectacle as the following will also meet the traveller's gaze: an old man prone in the dust, enduring the last agonies of death, and near him his son or wife, looking on with an air of resignation amounting almost to apathy. The old man, it may be, feeling his end approaching, has desired, notwithstanding his weakness and his sufferings, to drag himself to the sacred city of Puri, and in sight of the Temple of Juggernath to breathe his last sigh. But his desire may not be fulfilled, and he will pass away while still at a distance from the goal of his weary pilgrimage. It is the belief of the Hindus that, if they render up the spirit while their dying gaze is fixed on a sacred river or some celebrated shrine, they will go straight to heaven. Hence, along the road from Calcutta to Juggernath, according to M. Grandidier, the traveller frequently meets with the skeletons of pilgrims who have perished before their task was completed. He adds, that at the epoch of the great annual festival the air is so poisoned with the odours exhaled by decomposed corpses, as to constitute a serious danger to the public health. Cholera has frequently originated in this hotbed of pestilence, and thence spread in blackness and gloom over India and Europe.

Wonderful are the works of fanaticism! Enthusiasts may be seen engaged on a journey of several hundred leagues, measuring with their body the intervals between one famous pagoda and another. They grovel, face and stomach, on the earth—spring to their feet, and start again from the point touched by their hands; and this process they repeat until their goal is reached. Such, at least, is the statement made by several authorities; though it may be doubted whether the painful penance is not chiefly limited to the circuit of some renowned temple.

Puri is situated on the sea-shore; in front of the Hindu city, and scattered along the beach, extend the bungalows of the English inhabitants. They are connected with one another by causeways of brick, which enable the pedestrian to avoid the fatigue of plunging through the loose shifting sand of the shore. The native town is dirty and ill-built. In the long narrow street which leads to the temple, most of the houses are decorated with brightly-coloured designs,—rude representations of bayadères, Hindu divinities, and fantastic animals such as never were found on the earth or in the waters under the earth. All the thoroughfares are more or less obstructed by the sacred bulls, which visit the different stalls, and banquet without let or hindrance on the fruits and vegetables exposed for sale. No one dares to interfere with them; they are under the powerful protection of Juggernath, the "ruler of the world." It is singular, we are told, to observe the hatred which they seem to cherish against "the whites." Europeans penetrating into the sacred city are obliged to obtain the protection of the native police against their attacks. "In one of my walks abroad," says Grandidier, "I was accompanied by no fewer than four soldiers, in the midst of whom I walked gravely. I have often seen the noble beasts turn their horns even against their benevolent adorers, though it must be said with much courtesy, and in a manner not unworthy of well-fed divinities in a good humour. These bulls are very handsome; and I greedily admired the haunches of fat on their backs, which might have furnished me with a truly succulent dish!"

The bulls are not the only animals with an odour of sanctity, and assuredly they are not the most troublesome. On house-tops and temple-walls, and among garden-trees,—everywhere, in fact,—may be seen troops of apes, gambolling, grimacing, and teasing, and evil-doing, without any person assuming to interfere with their manifestations. There are two species—one with a long tail, one without that ornamental appendage, but, by way of compensation, embellished on the naked parts with vivid colours. Then, again, the ponds are teeming with crocodiles and sacred fishes, so tame that they take from the hands of the devotees the food they offer them.

The temple is surrounded by a handsome crenelated wall, which encloses within its rectangular precincts, it is said, numerous sanctuaries, porticoes, and sacred pools. As no European is suffered to cross the threshold, the traveller sees only the Bara-Dewal, a massive tower in which are enshrined the three divinities of the place. From a distance it resembles a colossal landmark; but it is, in reality, a square building, the walls of which as they rise describe a curve, and form towards the summit a semi-ellipse. Each face is supported by a buttress rising about two-thirds of the total elevation. The angles are slightly rounded. There is little carved work or ornamental sculpture about this pagoda, which is more striking from its magnitude than from its architectural merits.

Through the principal gate you pass into a vestibule with a pyramidal roof. On each side frowns a monster, a kind of lion, its head crowned with a tiara. Along the pediment are figured the images of the sun and the planets, as in all the religious edifices of Orissa. Four small and grotesque caryatids support a cornice, in the centre of which is Juggernath, the "master of the world." The sanctuary measures about two hundred and twenty-five feet in height. Therein the devout Hindu may daily prostrate himself before the monstrous figures of Juggernath or Vishnu, his brother Balarama or Mahadeo, and his sister Soubadea or Kali. These figures are plain wooden busts about seven feet high, of which the head does not offer even a rude resemblance to humanity; they are painted white, black, and yellow. The sister is armless, like Miss Biffin; the two brothers raise stiff in air their wooden arms, like those of dolls.

Every day three repasts are served up to the triad of deities; and the amount provided is stated at four hundred and ten pounds of rice, one hundred and twenty-five pounds of flour, three hundred and fifty pounds of clarified butter, one hundred and sixty-seven pounds of molasses, sixty-five pounds of vegetables, one hundred and sixty-six pounds of milk, twenty-four pounds of spices, thirty-four pounds of salt, and forty-one pounds of oil. Such a supply must surely be sufficient for the stomachs of the three gods, even were they Gargantuas, as well as of those of their priests and acolytes. During each repast, which lasts about an hour, the gates are carefully closed, and only a few servants of the temple—such as the Rajah of Khoorda, the high priest of the pagoda, and the Brahmans sanctified by a prolonged practice of asceticism and penance—are privileged to be present at the Olympian feast, during which the shrill sounds of music swell continuously, to the great satisfaction of the "faithful."

Should the traveller regret his inability to penetrate within the sacred precincts, he will find ample compensation in the curious spectacle presented in front of the pagoda. Here, in the middle of the open space, rises a monolithic, polygonal column, of graceful outline, surmounted by a small statue of Hanumān, the ape-god, or Hindu Mercury. Among a hundred bulls and other animals presses the fantastic crowd of ascetic votaries; while a few cabins, constructed of reeds or dry branches, afford shelter to men whose nakedness assuredly is not sufficiently concealed by the chalk with which they whiten their limbs, and who prove their surpassing piety by spending their lives in contemplation of the walls of the holy pagoda.

About a mile from the town, and approached by a broad avenue thronged with pilgrims and traders, is a sacred pool or tank, in the centre of which stands the pleasure-house or pavilion of Juggernath. Thither he is supposed to retire every year to spend a few days in the enjoyment of bathing. According to Mansbach, there are two principal fêtes,—one when the "master of the world," after certain ablutions, assumes the form of Ganesa, the elephant-god (the metamorphosis being very easily accomplished, to the great joy of his worshippers, by means of a simple mask of pasteboard); the other, and more important, in March, when the sun enters the constellation of Aries.

Three triumphal cars are employed to transport the divinities to the border of the sacred lake. That of Juggernath, mounted on sixteen wheels, and plentifully covered with sculptures of an indecent character, measures about twenty-six feet in width and as many in length. On this immense platform rests the idol, surrounded by a legion of priests, under the direction of the Rajah of Khoorda, and overcanopied by costly stuffs. In front the statue of a charioteer conducts a team of gilded horses. Amidst deafening shouts and the blare of trumpets, onward rolls the cumbrous, sumptuous mass, drawn by thousands of infatuated pilgrims.

Returning now to Calcutta, we propose to make an excursion in a different direction. We might find much to interest us in the Sundarbans—the low, marshy country of the Gangetic Delta, which a network of canals divides into little islands, covered with thick jungle and cocoa-palms, and peopled with water-fowl, crocodiles, and tigers. The inhabitants of this malarious district are called Molanghis, and supply the Calcutta market with fish, especially the exquisite mango-fish. Some English planters, however, have successfully introduced the culture of rice, indigo, and sugar. At the mouth of the Hugli lies Diamond Harbour; and at the mouth of the Mutlah—another and a broader arm of the Ganges—is Port Canning, founded by the Governor-General whose name it bears.

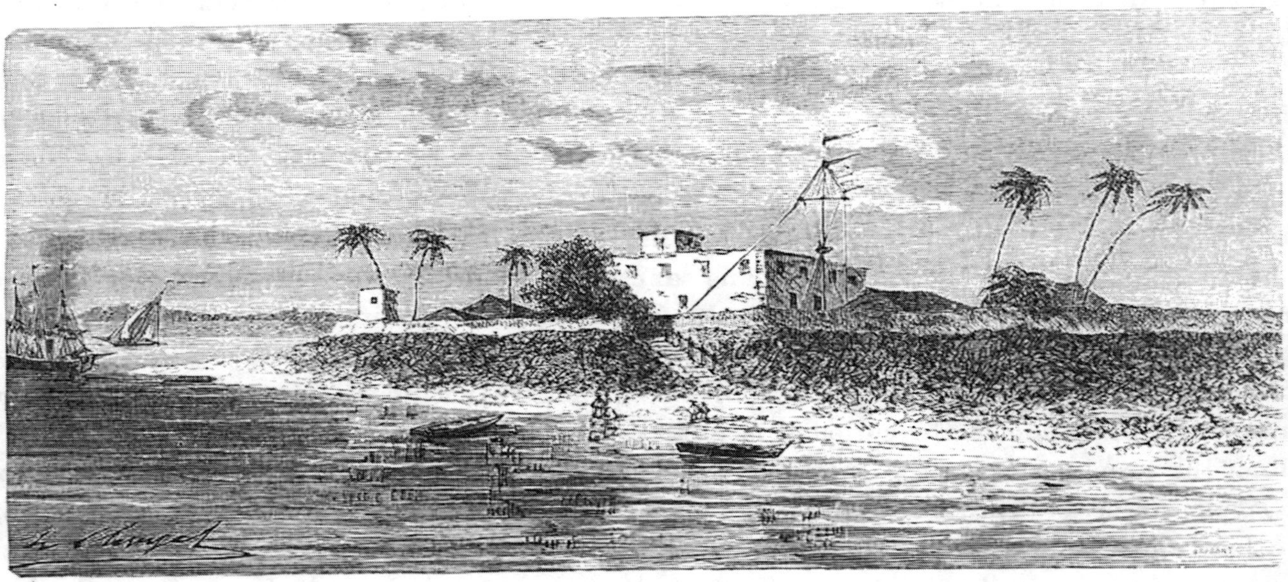

DIAMOND HARBOUR, AT THE MOUTH OF THE HUGLI.

Another interesting journey, by means of the Eastern Bengal Railway, takes us to Barrackpur—a great military station, with a fine park—and thence to Goalando, on the principal arm of the Ganges. But our final excursion will take us up the great river to Behar.

The first station of importance is Chandernagar, picturesquely situated on the right bank of the Hugli. It belongs to the French; though why they should retain it, or why the British Government does not purchase their rights and interests in it, is not easily understood. To the French themselves it is of no value. "Dull streets without life, bazaars without trade, a harbour without vessels,—such, at the present day, is Chandernagar, which in 1740 eclipsed Calcutta and governed Bengal." The garrison is limited by treaty to fifteen soldiers; but generally consists, according to the wits of Calcutta, of *two and a half*. It was occupied by the French in 1700; captured by Clive in 1755; restored to the French; again captured; and finally restored in 1816. In the neighbourhood are Hugli, celebrated for its spacious and stately mosque; and Chinsurah, an ancient Dutch colony.

THE GRAND MOSQUE OF HUGLI.

At Muggra we find ourselves close to the ghat of Triveni. Like Allahabad, this is supposed to mark the confluent, or rather divergent point, of three rivers. It is esteemed one of the most sacred places in Bengal. It is much frequented by pilgrims.

A cylindrical tower, one hundred and twenty feet high, at Pandooah, commemorates the great victory which was won here by the army of the Mogul emperor, Feroze Toghluk, over the Hindus. At its foot a stately mosque presents an accumulation of two hundred brickwork cupolas.

At a distance of seventy-four miles from Calcutta we reach Burdwan, the capital of a small state, ruled by its own maharajah under English protection. It occupies the centre of a wide extent of plains and rice-fields, dotted with rich green clusters of taros and palm-trees. The district is densely populated, and celebrated for its abundant fertility. Burdwan itself consists of a mass of primitive-looking huts—separated from one another by dense thickets of arecas and cocoa-palms—and stagnant pools, on which the broad green leaves and pearly corollas of the sacred lotus lie outspread. The maharajah's palace is a handsome building, in a fine garden, which abounds with lawns, groves, and shining sheets of water.

Murshidabad is one of the largest and most populous towns in Bengal, and stretches for several miles on either side of the Ganges. "Imagine," says a traveller, "an assemblage of huts of the most wretched appearance, with walls made of straw matting suspended to stakes, and with roofs of palm-thatch, half battered in by the rain; muddy streets without pavements, overrun with water and weeds, in which it is scarcely possible to make a step without slipping; and above the huts, rising at intervals, high-terraced brick houses. To these add, by way of monuments, vast buildings of strange design, wherein stately rows of columns enframe arched Moorish windows; and the uniform blackness produced by the damp reminding the traveller of the architectural perspectives of Pall Mall. Such is Murshidabad; and such are all the towns in English Bengal. What an immense difference from the handsome bazaars, elegant dwelling-houses, and sumptuous palaces of the towns of Rajasthan, and even of Hindustan!" Nor is the difference less striking between the meagre, slender, small-statured Bengalee, and the vigorous up-country Hindu or robust and well-made Sikh. In many respects the inhabitants of Bengal are closer of kin to the Chinese than the Aryan, though retaining the language of the latter, and his delicate features.

Beyond Murshidabad we may visit the Rajmahal Mountains, inhabited by the primitive races of the Sontâls and the Mâlers. Here the adventurer may make acquaintance with the peril and excitement of tiger-hunting. Following the course of the Ganges, we proceed by way of Bhagulpur to Monghir; and thence to Patna, the celebrated rice emporium, and the capital of Behar. It is identified by antiquarians with the ancient Palibothra, the seat of the Maurya emperors, visited by the Greek ambassadors of the successors of Alexander. It was made known to the Western World by the narrative of Megasthenes, the envoy of Seleucus. Here was planted the first English factory in the Eastern provinces; but the town did not come into our possession until 1763. The country all around is "a vast sheet of cultivation."

Between Patna and Benares lie Buxar, the scene of Sir Thomas Munro's great victory in 1764; and Arrah, celebrated for the gallantry with which its little garrison repulsed the Sepoys in the Great Mutiny. The railway is carried across the Sône by a splendid tubular bridge.

CHAPTER XXIV.

THE ISLAND OF CEYLON.

DIMENSIONS—PHYSICAL CHARACTERISTICS—VEGETATION—ANIMAL LIFE—INHABITANTS—THE CHIEF TOWNS—A COFFEE-FARM—LAKE OF KANDELY.

OUR general survey of British India cannot be brought to a close without some notice of that rich and valuable "natural appendage" to the peninsula, the island of Ceylon. It lies within the Tropic of Cancer, being situated between 6° and 0° N. latitude, and 80° and 82° E. longitude. Between it and the Coromandel coast intervenes a channel, the Gulf of Manar, which at its narrowest part is about thirty miles across. In figure it is nearly heart-shaped, the apex pointing northward; in length it measures 271 miles; in extreme breadth, 137 miles; and its superficial area occupies 25,742 square miles. The Gulf of Manar widens towards the north into the Palk Strait, the two being divided by a chain of rocks and sand-banks, which prevents the passage of large vessels; is known as Adam's Bridge; and in Hindu mythology is represented to be the route pursued by Râma, the warrior-god, in his invasion of Ceylon.

The shores are almost everywhere low and flat, and lined with groves of the cocoa-nut; the perennially verdurous slopes rising gently inland in undulating hills, clothed with the most luxuriant vegetation. Above these in the south is elevated a fertile table-land, between fifteen hundred and two thousand feet in height; out of which towers the bold conical summit of the Pedrotallagalla Mountain, 8260 feet, the culminating point of the island. Not far distant is Adam's Peak, the *Samennella* of the Cingalese, 7420 feet; on the crest of which is shown the footprint of Buddha—a slight depression in the rock, five feet long and two feet broad, protected by a circlet of brass, studded with a few trivial jewels. The legend runs that Buddha's object in visiting the island was to deliver its natives from the tyranny exercised over them by a host of demons. So numerous were they that, on his arrival, he could not find a free space on which to set his foot. Buddha, however, directed his discourse to a portion of the vast crowd before him, who immediately gave way before his inspired fervour, and fell into a panic at the superiority of his power. Availing himself of their confusion, and perceiving a vacant spot, Buddha straightway descended and occupied it. As he continued to preach, the demons gradually fell back before him, until at length they were driven into the sea. Locally this sacred mountain is, therefore, known as "The Footstep of Fortune;" and the Buddhist pilgrims ascend it as an act of special devotion.

Geologically speaking, Ceylon is composed of primitive rock, granite or gneiss, traversed by strata of quartz, hornblende, and dolomite. Shell limestone, mixed with a coral formation, is found in the district of Jaffnapatam. Along the shore a gray and blackish sandstone is found.

The metallic ores are iron (in great abundance), manganese, plumbago; and numerous precious stones in the alluvial plains—such as sapphire, ruby, garnet, topaz, rock-crystal, and amethyst.

The vegetation of the island is not less luxurious than that of the richest parts of the peninsula, and necessarily exhibits the same general characteristics. The breadfruit-tree attains to an immense size, with gigantic leaves, like those of the banian. The wild pine-apple is plentiful; and in the southern table-land the cinnamon-laurel grows more profusely than in any other part of the world, furnishing commerce with three important staples,—the aromatic cassia buds, the dried bark or cinnamon, and an essential medicinal oil. The plant thrives best in a light sandy soil, with a humid atmosphere. In its wild state it grows to the size of a large apple-tree, but when cultivated is pruned down to ten or twelve feet in height. Coffee is now cultivated extensively in the south of Ceylon. In the north, a prevalence of palms—such as the palmyra, taliput, and cocoa-nut—gives colour and character to the landscape. The mountain-sides rejoice in heavy masses of forest-trees, including teak, ebony, and satin-wood; and the scenery is all aglow with the most splendid creepers and flowering shrubs of the greatest brilliancy. The cocoa-nut palm is as much prized and as ingeniously utilized by the Cingalese as it is by the islanders of the South Seas. At all times of the year its fruit is available; bud, flower, and nut, in their various stages of growth, being found simultaneously growing on the same tree. The bud, or *spathe*, when an incision is made into it, yields a liquor called toddy, which a due amount of fermentation and distillation converts into arrack; or it may be made into vinegar, as well as into the coarse sugar called *jaggery*. The *coir*, or fibrous husk enveloping the nut, supplies the material of stout cordage and carpeting. The kernel, as everybody knows, is good eating; and it furnishes an admirable oil, which human ingenuity has applied in many different ways. Then, as for the shells, they are readily adapted for the purposes of goblets and other domestic utensils; the leaves are woven into mats, or employed to thatch the roofs of the native huts. Scarcely less valuable is the palmyra palm, the leaves of which supply a substitute for paper, and the fruit of which is convertible into a nutritious jelly.

BREADFRUIT-TREE OF CEYLON.

BRANCH OF THE CINNAMON-LAUREL.

The areca-nut is another of the island products; so also is the kittul-tree, with its saccharine sap and farinaceous fruit. Tobacco of excellent quality is largely raised; and fruits and culinary vegetables seem to grow almost spontaneously. But we must refer to Sir Emerson Tennent's exhaustive work for a variety of details in illustration of the extent and variety of the island's natural products.

The Ceylon fauna corresponds with that of the mainland, with the exception that it is entirely free from the tiger, the wolf, and the cheetah, or hunting-leopard. Elephants are numerous, and being caught and tamed in the "corral," are trained as beasts of burden for home use or exportation. Of late years, however, a marked decrease has taken place in the herds. Among the several species of deer, the elk and the fallow-deer are the most numerous. Bears, leopards, tiger-cats, monkeys, wild boars, and a fierce species of baboon, are also met with. The

AN ELEPHANT CORRAL, CEYLON.

so-called flying-fox is a pertinacious visitor; while the sportsman will rejoice in the opportunities of "sport" afforded by numbers of squirrels, raccoons, mangooses, armadilloes, snipe, pigeons, pheasants, red-legged partridges. The woods and groves are frequented by birds of the most splendid plumage; but it must be admitted that less welcome guests abound—such as serpents, snakes, and alligators. The Reptile World is also well represented. In the Gulf of Manar extend several banks on which was formerly found the pearl-oyster. This was at one time the object of an extensive fishery, which, after a protracted period of decay, owing to causes not satisfactorily explained, has recently shown symptoms of fresh activity.

The inhabitants of Ceylon consist of Cingalese (or Singhalese), Malabaris, Veddas, Mohammedans, Europeans, and Negroes. The Veddas, a wild and untamed race, are supposed to be descendants of the aborigines. They are now few in number, and have withdrawn into the most inaccessible districts, where they live on fruit and wild animals, and dwell in huts or arbours constructed among the branches of the forest-trees. The Cingalese form the bulk of the population. A writer describes them as differing from Europeans less in features than in colour, size, and form.

The early annals of Ceylon are shrouded in obscurity. But two facts stand out with some distinctness: first, that Buddhism at a very early date became the religion of the islanders; and, second, that the numerous small principalities into which the island was divided were gradually absorbed into the one kingdom of Kandy. Europe knew little about either until the beginning of the sixteenth century, when the Portuguese opened up commercial relations with the King of Kandy, who purchased their aid against the Arab pirates by a tribute of cinnamon. The new allies soon became dangerous enemies, and established themselves in the island; whereupon the Cingalese sought the assistance of the Dutch—who, in their turn, claimed and exercised supreme authority. The Dutch were driven out by the British in 1769, when Ceylon was placed under the administration of the Madras Presidency; but in 1796 it was formally transferred to the British Crown.

For some years the King of Kandy retained his throne, but his intolerable tyranny provoked his subjects to revolt, and the English were solicited to depose him. Our troops accordingly took possession of Kandy, and in 1815 the whole island was declared a part of the British dominions. It is now administered as a Crown colony, and enjoys the advantages of a firm and equitable government. Nor is it an exaggeration to say that the Imperial Crown has few brighter gems than this rich and prosperous island.

For administrative purposes, the island is divided into seven provinces,—the Northern, North-Western, Western, Southern, Eastern, North Central, and Central. The principal towns are Colombo, Point de Galle, Trincomalee, Kandy, Jaffna, and Kornegalle.

Colombo is seventy-two miles distant from Point de Galle. It is a handsome, well-built town, nearly divided into four parts by two broad thoroughfares. The description which Bishop Heber gave of it some forty years ago applies to it now with but little alteration. There are fewer Dutch houses now than there were then, but they may still be distinguished from those of the English by their glass windows, instead of venetians, for the Dutch seem to shut up their houses at all seasons; they have large verandahs to the south. The houses of the Europeans without the town are very beautifully situated, especially those near the sea; they are all, with one or two exceptions, lower-roomed—that is, one-storied—houses, and built on the same plan as those of Bombay. "The floors are almost universally of brick, very unsightly and disagreeable from the dust which they occasion; but this is unavoidable in an island where no chunam, or mortar, is made but by a most expensive process from shells, and where the white ants immediately destroy timber."

The trade of Colombo is now very considerable. The exports consist of the island products—such as cinnamon, cardamoms, coffee, coir cordage, ebony, pepper, plumbago, satin-wood, and cocoa-nut oil. The shops in the town are well-supplied, and an abundance and variety of provisions, with tropical herbs and fruits, render the bazaars interesting to a stranger. The air is loaded with the perfume of cinnamon, nutmegs, citrons, limes, and other delicacies of the Vegetable World. The commerce of Colombo will be considerably benefited by the construction of the massive breakwater, which will protect shipping from the heavy surf always rolling on its exposed shore.

A Ceylon coffee-farm is a picturesque scene. It is invariably situated at an elevation of not less than three thousand feet above the sea, where the air is sufficiently fresh and cool. The coffee-trees, no taller than gooseberry-bushes, are of a vivid green, and their bright scarlet berries sparkle everywhere about them. They are planted in regular rows, like the hops in a Kentish hop-garden. Below the fields grow deep vast masses of bamboo, lantana, and citron-trees—masses so dense and closely set that men shrink from plunging into them, lest they should disturb some wild beast in its secret lair. "The labourers, everywhere moving amidst the coffee plants, heighten the bright and diversified character of the picture; for their bodies, naked save at the waist, are copper-coloured, and their turbans are of the deepest scarlet. These men are not Cingalese, but Tamils, and natives of Southern India. In the same way as the Irish reapers cross St. George's Channel every autumn to make a harvest in English cornfields, so the Tamils every year traverse the Palk Strait to eke out a livelihood in Ceylon."

Railway communication has been established between Colombo and Kandy, and the line runs through scenery of the most picturesque and varied character. After fifty miles through a level stretch of fragrant cinnamon gardens, it ascends the hills by a steep incline, passing among apparently endless groups of shapely palms, and, at one thousand feet above the sea, reaching a bold projection known as Sensation Rock. Thence it is carried round the mountain-summit in a picturesque gallery, which opens up the most enchanting views of the country beneath—the slope being luxuriantly embedded in palms and coffee-bushes, breadfruit and nutmeg trees, and glorious masses of roses.

The Prince of Wales, on his visit to Ceylon, made this most delightful and novel journey. On reaching Kandy, he was received, says Mr. Wheeler, by two new orders of human beings—one a group of chiefs descended from the old Kandyan kings; the other, a motley assemblage of Veddas, or wild men of the woods. "The attire of the chiefs," it is said, "made the prince smile. The men were like so many Vandycks, with gold four-cornered pin-cushion hats. Each man had a dress of scarlet and gold, covering a mass of rotundity—stuffed to such excess as to outrival the stomach of any ancient burgomaster. The hose was of coloured silk, and all over the body were suspended medals, daggers, and chains of antique gold."

Kandy, or *Maha-neura*, "the great city," is situated at the head of a noble valley, about fourteen hundred feet above the sea-level. Standing on the border of a beautiful artificial lake, within a glorious belt of wooded hills and mountains, it almost merits the eulogistic title which has been applied to it, of one of the Seven Heavens. Its principal buildings are the royal palace and the Buddhist temples. The former has a long low façade of about six hundred feet, terminating in a hexagonal building of two stories. The largest temple forms a quadrangle, with sixteen pillars of solid masonry supporting the roof. The sanctuary contains a colossal figure of Buddha, about thirty feet high, carved out of the rock, with several small figures grouped around it—some standing, others sitting with their legs crossed—many of them painted a bright yellow. In another temple are preserved some bones removed from Raja Singh's tomb at the time of the British occupation of Kandy. The cemetery lies close at hand; here the tombs are of stone, with rude coarse carving—those of the kings and queens facing one another in the shadow of some venerable peepul-trees. One celebrated temple boasts of the possession of the tooth of

Buddha—truly an astonishing souvenir, for it measures nearly two feet in length! It is kept in a dagoba or shrine, curiously wrought of gold and crystal, studded with precious stones, and festooned with jewelled chains. Needless to say that it attracts crowds of devout admirers, who strew the pavement around with their offerings of flowers.

To the north-east of Colombo, on the east coast of the island, stands Trincomalee. It is fortunate in its harbour, which is deep, spacious, and accessible at all seasons. It is fortunate in its scenery, which a Scotch traveller not inaptly compares with that of Loch Katrine; and, indeed, the bay is so land-locked as to appear like a lake, from the edge of which gradually rise the swelling hills bright with perennial verdure. The town possesses few buildings of interest, but it has a busy and prosperous aspect, and is rapidly growing into importance as a commercial station and naval arsenal.

In the level country between Trincomalee and Battikaloa, extending to the mountain-terraces, are found many striking remains of well-constructed tanks and temples, testifying to the existence in former days of a much larger population than the district now owns. About sixteen miles from Trincomalee lies a stupendous reservoir, the formation of which must have cost years of labour. The Lake of Kandely, as it is called, measures nearly fifteen miles in circuit. In several places it is solidly embanked with a wall of huge stones, each from twelve to fourteen feet in length, and proportionately broad and thick. The portion of the majestic work most deserving of attention is the parapet,—nearly one hundred and fifty feet broad at the base, and thirty feet on the summit,—which connects two hills, and prevents the overflow of the waters into the valley between them. When this great enterprise was designed and executed, and how and by whom, are questions which the archæologist is unable to answer satisfactorily.

CHAPTER XXV.

VEGETABLE LIFE IN INDIA.

COTTON—OPIUM—CEREALS—FRUIT TREES—SPICES—FOREST AND TIMBER TREES—THE BANIAN—THE BAMBOO—THE DEODAR—THE MHOWA.

FROM a remote antiquity India has been famous for the extent and variety of its vegetable resources. It seems to comprehend within its borders an epitome of the Botanical World, from the humblest grasses to the most majestic forest-trees. In the plains it revels in a profusion of Tropical plants; on its mountains it exhibits the species characteristic of the Temperate flora. Hence it has in all ages been "the fountain of mercantile wealth and the focus of commercial enterprise."

Of late years, and more particularly since the outbreak of the American Civil War, it has largely supplied the European markets with cotton. Very recently this branch of trade seems to have undergone a new development. We read of a large cotton-mill, started with native capital, at Barrackpur, near Calcutta; its trade-mark being the figure of the azure-coloured god Vishnu. There are now, it is said, upwards of twenty mills at work in Bombay; and their tall chimneys, towering high above the palms, are among the objects which first catch the eye of the traveller as he descends the Ghats by rail from Upper or Northern India. Ten or twelve more are in course of construction; and outside Bombay nineteen others are now in constant activity. The cotton-growing districts of Central India and the Deccan will soon be equally well supplied with mills. The erection of one at Haidarabad is another sign of the rapid progress of the manufacturing industry of India. The Maharajah Holkar has established a mill—the first of the kind in Central India—at Indore; and this great prince is now a cotton-spinner, and keeps his own books.

The cotton-plant is small and shrubby, seldom above six feet high, with a yellow flower, and seeds enveloped in a kind of short grayish down.

An important article of Indian produce, contributing largely to the revenue of the Government, is opium. It is obtained from the *Papaver orientale*, or Eastern poppy, which flourishes in almost every province, though the best opium comes from Behar and Bengal. The opium poppy is an erect annual plant, slightly branched, about two feet in height, with a glaucous green stem, and leaves of an oblong shape, which clasp the stem by their base. The flowers are violet-coloured, with a purple centre.

The process of preparing the drug, which Paracelsus is said to have introduced into the European pharmacopœia, may be thus described:—

As soon as the flowers are in bloom, the petals are removed, to be used in packing the prepared drug. After a few days the half-ripe capsules are scarified from above downwards by two or three knives tied together, and called "nushturs." The milky juice which exudes from these slight incisions is allowed to harden, and then collected in earthen pots. The hour chosen for slicing the capsules is three in the afternoon, when the great heat of the sun quickly covers the exuded juice with a protecting film.

THE OPIUM POPPY.

The slicing operation is repeated twice or thrice at intervals of a few days; and the drug is then conveyed to the Government factory, where native workmen busily knead it into a homogeneous mass. A careful analysis is afterwards undertaken by competent authorities to determine the quality of the opium, to ensure its freedom from adulteration, and also its reduction in strength as nearly as may be to a uniform standard. It is then pronounced in a fit state for exportation; and, by means of earthen cups, moulded into spherical masses of the size of a child's head, closely invested on the outside by the dried petals of the flower, and rendered thoroughly compact by pressure and by immersion in the viscous residuum drained off from the more solid opium during its preparation.

CAPSULE OF THE OPIUM POPPY.

The chief market for Indian opium is China, notwithstanding the vigorous efforts of the Chinese Government to prevent its importation. It cannot but be a matter of regret that for financial reasons the Indian Executive permits and encourages a demoralizing trade, and supplies the Chinese population with a deleterious drug.

Those cereals which are most common in Europe flourish abundantly in India; but the chief food of the natives is rice, and rice is cultivated in almost every province. In Orissa and Bengal a failure of the usual crop threatens millions of industrious families with starvation. This important grain is supposed to be of Asiatic origin; though recent travellers in South America report that they have found it growing, apparently in a wild state, on the banks of some of the rivers. Among the Mahrattas the holcus (sorghum) is extensively cultivated. Instead of our potato the Indians use the yam, the arachis (a kind of legume), and the katchil root. We may also enumerate the moong, a species of bean; the murhus, the grain of which is like mustard-seed, and employed in making cakes; and the toa, a shrub yielding a favourite kind of pea. The roots of the red lotus are also used for food. This is the *Nymphæa rubra;* a different species from that of the *Nymphæa alba*, which covers the waves of the Nile, and is also found in the pools and tanks of India. The flowers of the latter have a peculiar property of collapsing their petals, and of submerging them during the night; a property to which Moore alludes in some well-known lines—

> "These virgin lilies, all the night
> Bathing their beauties in the lake,
> That they may rise more fresh and bright
> When their belovëd sun's awake."

For the Brahmans and the Indian philosophers generally the favourite food has always been the banana (*Musa sapientum*), the sister-plant, as it were, of the plantain. It is highly nutritious, though less so than wheat or the potato. On the other hand, it occupies less space, and does not require so much culture; so that Humboldt has calculated the produce of bananas compared to that of wheat as 133 to 1, and to that of potatoes as 44 to 1.

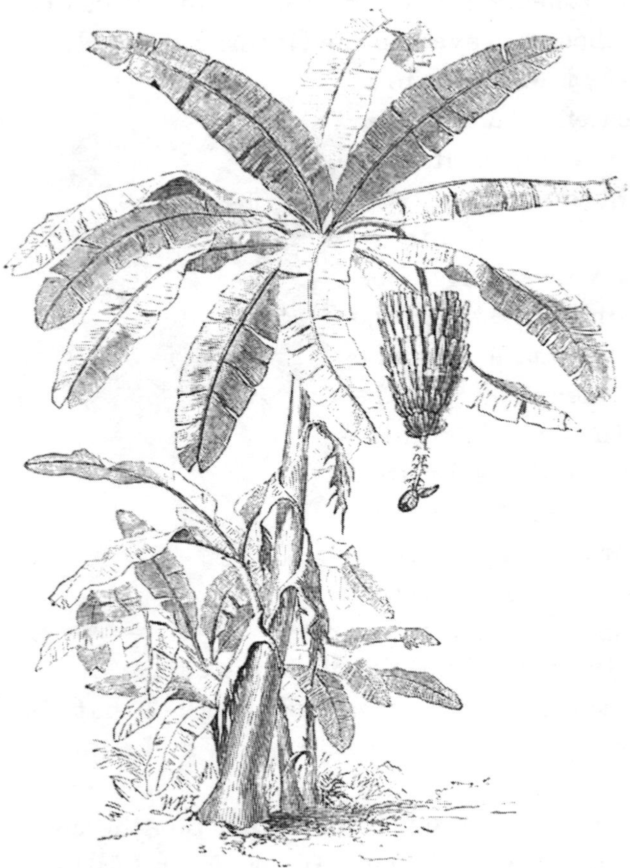
BANANA-TREE.

In the Eastern Ghats, the agave, or great American aloe, grows abundantly. The sap yields an agreeable vinous beverage. In the warm dry sands of the Carnatic thrives the bread-tree, its "unadulterated loaves" ripening spontaneously in the liberal sunshine.

As to fruits, India is rich in the most delicious varieties that ever tempted the epicurean palate. In almost every part grows the luscious mango; which, in its mature state, furnishes the dessert with an additional attraction, and, in its unripe, forms the staple of an extensively used pickle. The mango-tree is one of those which contribute most freely to the supply of human wants. Its leaves and leaf-stalks furnish the natives with tooth-brushes; the leaves are employed medicinally; and the gum-resin that exudes from its bark is an external remedy for certain skin diseases, and an internal cure for diarrhœa and dysentery. The wood, with that of the sandal, is used by the Hindus in burning their dead.

In Northern India thrive many of the most esteemed fruits of Europe; such as the apple, the pear, the apricot, the plum, the orange, the mulberry, the walnut, and the almond. A finely-flavoured plum, called the *alorcha*, is cultivated at Battalah, in the Punjab. The jamboo, a species of rose-apple, is valued not only on account of its fruit, but for the beauty of the crimson flowers which depend from every part of the stem. Reference may also be made to the pillau, an almond-flavoured nut; and the Averrhoes Carambora, or Caramba, which thrice a year bears a crop of gherkin-shaped fruit; and the elephant-apple,* to which the animal whose name it bears is not less partial than the Hindus themselves.

It will be seen, then, that if any Indian Porphyro, on a St. Agnes' Eve, desired to prepare some such delicate repast as the poet Keats has set forth in his beautiful poem, there would be no lack of variety or resource. Yet we have said nothing of the delicious guava, of the custard-apple, or the water-chestnut, which is eaten so largely in Kashmir.

Let us now go further afield, and see what trees or plants are available for the purposes of the perfumer or the physician.

* *Feronia elephantum.*

The *malabathrum* with which, according to Horace, the Roman youths anointed their shining locks, is by some authorities identified with the betel-leaf; which, together with the areca-nut and quick-lime, forms a digestive masticatory, largely employed by the natives of the East. The guettarda yields a delightful perfume; and the jalamansi has an odour faintly sweet,

COCOA-NUT PALMS—A SCENE IN THE NEIGHBOURHOOD OF BOMBAY.

like that of violet. The areca palm, for the sake of its nuts, is cultivated all over India. But palms are profuse everywhere; including the noble fan palm, the beautiful and useful sago palm, and the multifarious cocoa-nut palm, which yields food, lamp-oil, cordage, thatch, and a stimulating liquor. It is Nature's *multum in parvo*, and man's resource in almost every kind of position.

How valuable a production is the sandal-tree of India, it is needless to say. There are red, and white, and yellow species; and the last is the best, having an agreeable smell, and yielding an aromatic bitter. Reduced to powder, it furnishes an unguent with which the Persians and Chinese, as well as the Hindus, anoint themselves. When burned, it evolves a delightful fragrance; and for this reason it is used in the temples and on funeral pyres. A fragrant essential oil is distilled from it, which hardens into the consistency of a balsam. The dragon's-tree, or *Dracæna draco,* which in India seldom exceeds thirty feet in height, exudes a resinous astringent known as dragon's-blood. Gum-ammoniac is obtained from the *Dorema ammoniacum* of Bengal, gum-lac from the *Mimosa cinerea,* and gamboge from the *Garcinia pictoria* of Mysore.

Cassia-trees are a characteristic feature of the Indian landscape. The *Laurus cassia* bears the Malabar cinnamon; but the *Laurus camphora*—the camphor cinnamon-tree—is not found in the peninsula. In the mountain-districts the acacia catechu rises to the height of about twelve feet. In the Deccan a common tree is the acacia arabica, or babul, the gum of which is sometimes used by the poorer natives for food: the bark is used for tanning leather. The sugar-cane is very largely cultivated. Two species of pepper are found; and, indeed, the Malabar coast is called by the Arabs *Beled-el-folfol*—"the pepper-country." Indigo grows spontaneously in Gujerat, and forms an article of extensive culture in Oudh, Agra, Behar, and Bengal. We send to the slopes of the Ghats for the cardamoms which our physicians so frequently prescribe; while in cases of intermittent fever the native doctors "exhibit" a decoction of the astringent and tonic bark of the *Swietenia febrifuga,* which flourishes among the mountains of the Rajahmundiry Circar. The ginger-plant and zedoary (*Curcuma zerumbet*) are natives of Malabar.

Nor does India merit less particular notice as a land of forest and timber trees. Besides those which it has in common with Europe—the oak, the pine, the cypress, the fir, the poplar—it possesses many valuable indigenous species. Our shipbuilders long ago learned the value of the teak-tree as a substitute for oak; it furnishes a wood which is firm, hard, and almost incorruptible. A native of Southern and Central India, it extends as far north as the province of Bundelcund, and its range includes also Burma, Pegu, and some of the islands of the Eastern Archipelago. It is an evergreen, and almost a sacred tree. From the tender leaves is obtained a purple dye; also a syrup of certain medicinal properties; and the flowers, mixed with honey, are prescribed in cases of dropsy.

The *Valeria indica,* or ponna, also called the poon or mast-tree, which grows to a height of sixty feet, furnishes wood well-adapted for the masts of some "tall ammiral." Smaller timber, good for building purposes, is obtained from the koru of the Northern forests, the djissoo, and the nagassa or iron-wood. The Indian ebony is found in the neighbourhood of Allahabad. Gum-trees are scarce, but among them the *Eucalyptus pendula,* with its scent of peppermint, seems likely to be naturalized. In Bengal a common tree is the great Bombax, or silk-cotton, which, in the season of inflorescence, becomes a mass of crimson flowers. Its fruit is a large woody capsule, containing numerous seeds arranged in five cells, each seed being surrounded by a quantity of beautiful silky fibre; when ripe it bursts into five pieces, allowing the seeds to be wafted abroad on the wings of the wind.

From the Sulea pine a pure turpentine, called *kota,* is extracted. The mountain-slopes of Nepal and Lahore are richly clothed with magnificent forests of this noble tree. The Scotch fir rears its familiar trunk on the colder slopes of the hills beyond Delhi; and on the high grounds of Kumaon thrives the Phutwarrah, attaining a height of sixty feet and a girth of six feet, and producing a quantity of nut-like fruit, from the kernels of which a fatty substance is extracted. Much smaller, but perhaps more useful, is the *Salvadora persica*, or mustard-tree, which grows to a considerable height, and by some authorities is identified with the mustard-tree of our Lord's parable.

In the neighbourhood of Sealkote, and on the borders of Kashmir, the traveller passes through great thickets of buteas and acacias, with the *Euphorbia Royliana* towering high above them. Euphorbias, or spurges, abound in many parts of India, however, though none of such colossal dimensions as the Royliana. The Hindus use the juice of *Euphorbia antiquorum* as an external remedy for rheumatism and neuralgia. The physician has discovered the astringent and aromatic properties of *Euphorbia thymifolia;* while an important commercial staple is the admirable caoutchouc yielded by the juice of *Euphorbia cattimandoo*, a native of the Madras presidency. When the branches of this tree are cut off, the milk-white juice flows freely. It is collected and boiled on the spot, at which time it is very elastic; but after being formed into cakes or cylinders, it turns resinous or brittle, and in this state it is sold in the bazaars, and employed as a cement for fixing knives into handles, and other similar purposes. It is also used medicinally as an external application in cases of rheumatism. The gum, however, is inferior to gutta-percha in one respect, in not being ductile at all times. When first boiled, it can be moulded to any shape; but afterwards it ceases to be plastic, unless softened over the heat of a fire or lamp.

Every reader of "Paradise Lost" will remember Milton's fine description of the celebrated Banian, or Indian fig-tree:—

"Such as at this day, to Indians known,
In Malabar or Deccan spreads her arms
Branching so broad and long, that in the ground
The bended twigs take root, and daughters grow
Above the mother-tree, a pillared shade,
High over-arched, and echoing walks between.
There oft the Indian herdsman, shunning heat,
Shelters in cool, and tends his pasturing herds
At loopholes cut through thickest shade."

Tavernier, the quaint old traveller, says:—"The Franks call it the Banian's tree, because in those places where these trees grow the idolaters always take up their quarters, and dress their victuals under them." According to Dr. Fryer, the Portuguese aptly called it *Arbor de rais*, because its branches bear their own roots; and the Banian-tree, because the banians adored it—"holding it as sacred as was the oak to our old Druids, painting it daily, and making offerings of rice, and praying to it." Two famous banians are spoken of as existing—one in an island of the Narbada, near Broach, and the other not far from the town of Mangi in Behar. The natives assert that the former is three thousand years old—an unquestionable exaggeration: it is said to be the largest in the world, and capable of sheltering seven thousand persons. It has no fewer than three hundred and fifty trunks—that is, branches which in their turn have taken root—and each exceeds in girth most English trees; and upwards of three thousand smaller branches, measuring nearly two thousand feet in circumference. The other can boast of nearly sixty stems; and at noon the shadow which it casts extends over an area of eleven hundred and sixteen feet. These are enormous and extraordinary specimens; but in all cases the tree presents a remarkable aspect, with its central trunk and subsidiary rooted stems. Its branches, covered with heart-shaped leaves, about five or six inches long, afford a home to bats, and birds, and monkeys. The last-named eat both leaves and fruit, which grows in pairs, is larger than a cherry, and of a rich scarlet colour. The wood of the banian is light and porous; its bark is a strong tonic, and the Hindu doctors administer it in cases of diabetes.

Not less characteristic of India is the bamboo, which in many places grows in complete forests, and erects its straight knotted stem to a height of sixty feet, crowned with tufts of leaves and panicles of flowers. It is applied to a singular variety of purposes. The larger shoots and

THE BANIAN-TREE.

the trunk are used by the Hindus in building their houses and constructing their articles of furniture. The young shoots are pickled for eating. The indurated juice, called *tabasheer*, is used medicinally; the first and smaller shoots form the once-popular walking-canes; the larger shoots are converted into vessels for carrying water.

India, we may add, is rich in Grasses. The korsa, or *Poa cynosuroides*, has a sacred character, and is almost constantly in the hands of the very devout. Its roots are woven into *tatti*, a kind of mat which, placed against door or window, and well watered, renders the air of a room refreshingly cool. The jungle grass, in Bengal and elsewhere, shoots up to the height of eight or ten feet, and is crested with a downy blossom, not unlike a swan's plumage. Sandy soils produce the augeah grass, which grows to even a greater height—twenty-five to thirty feet—and is as thick as a man's wrist. In some parts of India the grasses are succulent and nutritious, affording an excellent pasture. This is especially the case in the provinces of Ajmir and Delhi, in Rajputana, in Gujerat, and on the downs or table-lands of Mysore.

But our description, so necessarily brief and rapid, of the vegetable life of India, shall not conclude with these notes upon its humbler forms. We prefer to recall the reader's attention, in conclusion, to the mighty forests which clothe the spurs and offshoots, and the slopes and higher terraces, of the Himalaya. We would have him fill his mind with images of the colossal

A THICKET OF BAMBOOS.

trees which there stand defined against a deep-blue horizon, in vivid contrast to the perpetual snows of the virgin peaks above them. Let him think of the gigantic deodar, which furnishes so striking an emblem of perfect strength and perfect beauty; of the *Pinus excelsa*, or "weeping fir;" the ubiquitous cheel, or *Pinus longifolia;* the aspiring *Pinus morinda*, or *Pinus khutrow;* and the loftiest of all its congeners, the *Pinus morinda*, or *Abies pindrow*. None of them, however, can compare with the "tree of God," the deodar or kedron—*Cedrus deodara*. "There was something very grand," writes Mr. Wilson, "about these cedars, sometimes forty feet in circumference, and rising almost to two hundred feet, or half the height of St. Paul's, on nearly precipitous slopes, and on the scantiest soil, yet losing no line of beauty in their stems and their graceful pendent branches, and with their tapering stems and green arrowy spikes covered by a clinging trellis-work of Virginia creepers and clematis."

CEDRUS DEODARA.

Had Camoens seen this glorious cedar, he might have said of it, much more justly than of the cypress, that it stands forth as a

> "Preacher to the wise;—
> Lessening from earth her spiral honours rise,
> Till, as a spear-point reared, the topmost spray
> Points to the Eden of eternal day."

In the Himalaya the deodar flourishes between five thousand and nine thousand feet high; and, except in the loftier regions where it wants heat, it prefers the shady northern and eastern sides of the mountains. The cedar-forests of the Sutlej are the most extensive and valuable of

India; but they spread along the whole line of the Western Himalaya, furnishing an exceedingly useful wood for building and railway purposes.

In Nepal is found the Indian Butter-tree, or Phulwara, which, though not a giant in size, is a tree of no little importance. Its botanical name is *Bassia butyracea.* From its seeds, when bruised and pressed, is squeezed out a fatty substance of the consistency of hog's lard, but whiter. It is used to adulterate ghee, and as an unguent for the hair, and as a remedy for rheumatic pains. It makes, moreover, a very good substitute for soap.

Another bassia is the *Bassia latifolia,* or well-known Mhowa-tree, which furnishes a hard, strong, durable timber. The sweet-flavoured flowers are eaten raw, but more frequently are employed in the distillation of an ardent spirit like whisky, which the natives of Gujerat and other parts consume in liberal quantities. From the seeds is extracted an oil for lamps, which is useful also in the manufacture of soap, and for culinary purposes. The Bheels collect the mhowa flowers, and, after drying them, store them up as a staple article of food. Hence, in expeditions undertaken for the punishment or subjugation of these restless people, the invading force, it is said, generally ensures their submission by threatening to cut down their mhowa-trees. In Malabar and Coromandel the flowers are roasted and eaten; also, bruised and boiled to a jelly. The leaves and the milky juice of the immature fruit figure in the native pharmacopœia, and the resinous product of the bark is valued by rheumatic sufferers. If, then, we take the deodar as a type of strength and beauty, may we not see in the mhowa-tree an emblem of humble usefulness?

CHAPTER XXVI.

ANIMAL LIFE IN INDIA.

ITS FAUNA—BIRDS—REPTILES.

AS we are not writing a zoological treatise, our review of the Animal Life of India will be little more than an enumeration of some of its principal forms. Here, as in the Flora, any attempt to generalize is baffled by the wide extent of the area with which we are concerned, and the radical differences induced by climatic variations and physical influences. Certain animals there are, however, which the popular mind at once identifies with India—such as the tiger, the elephant, the hunting leopard, the gavial. But of the Indian Fauna it may be said, as of the Indian Flora, that though generally and principally Tropical in character, it also includes numerous forms belonging to the Temperate regions—such, for instance, as the horse, the ass, the ox, the sheep.

If we were called upon to represent India by any particular animal, we should unquestionably select the elephant. It is the elephant that figures in state processions, that stalks conspicuous in the "ranks of war," that serves both as a beast of burden and a beast of draught. Though no longer employed to charge the battalions of the foe, it carries into the battle-field the necessary stores of ammunition, and light pieces of field-artillery are frequently mounted on its back. In the tiger-hunt it provides the sportsman with a secure and commanding position. Nor has the increase in the number of conveyances, nor the extension of railway-communication, done much to lessen its popularity or usefulness. Mrs. Murray Mitchell, describing a grand ceremony of which she was an eye-witness, observes, that elephants in their gay trappings were at least as common as horses. She herself went on one of these huge creatures two or three times "to see the sights." "I felt myself," she says, "a Ranee at least, as we sat in dignity on the back of our elephant, resplendent with gilt howdah, and saddle-cloth of scarlet velvet embroidered with gold."

The Indian elephants differ among themselves in size, and colour, and the length of their tusks; but though the differences are sufficient to constitute varieties, they are not important enough to constitute species. The general hue is a blackish brown; the sacred white elephant being the product only of Indo-China, and, in the opinion of many naturalists, owing its distinctive colour to disease. In the thick woods of the Ghats elephants are still found in herds of two to three hundred. The average height of the male is eight to ten feet; of the female, seven to eight; but the individuals in the north of India are much smaller. It is said that the largest elephant ever seen in India measured ten and a half feet at the shoulder; it was caught in 1796, and belonged to the Nawab of Oudh. The largest tusks of the Bengal animal rarely exceed seventy or eighty pounds in weight.

In Bengal the one-horned rhinoceros is scarcer than it used to be, thanks to the extending influence of British civilization and love of sport; but it still frequents the islands of the Gangetic delta, and is frequently seen in company with the tiger. The two are not naturally fond of each other's company, but they are here brought together by causes which overrule any

THE INDIAN ELEPHANT.

instinctive mistrust. The tiger finds food and shelter among the dense jungle-growth of the Sundarbans; and the rhinoceros resorts thither for protection against the burning heat.

If the elephant be a fitting type of India itself, the tiger has been taken as an emblem of its people. It has, at all events, the sleekness and suppleness of the Hindu, though the Hindu can hardly be said to possess its ferocity! Of all living animals, surely it is the handsomest; with its bright glowing eye, its brilliant skin, its compact, powerful, and lissom frame. The force and swiftness of its bound is something terrible; the rapidity of its course justifies the ancient application of the name Tigris to an arrowy river. It will clear fifty feet at a leap; it will outrun the fastest horse; it is so strong that it will seize in its jaws and carry off a bullock. Hunting such an animal is, therefore, no tame or paltry pastime, but needs, in most cases, the possession of great courage and singular presence of mind, with the addition of a keen eye and a thorough command of one's nerves. But it is seldom that the native challenges the tiger "face to face." He leaves the hazard and glory of

THE INDIAN RHINOCEROS.

such an encounter to the English *sahib;* and, for himself, is content with the adoption of cunning devices, or with a shot from some absolutely secure position. The trap, or "string-bow," is a favourite invention. He makes an immense bow, some eight or nine feet in length, and strings it with good strong gut line. Usually the path by which the tiger leaves his den is very narrow; on each side of it a post is firmly driven into the ground, and to these posts are attached the two ends of the bow. Further: a blunt stick is inserted between the bow and the bowstring to extend the latter, just as if it were going to be discharged; and between the end of the stick and the inner side of the bow is driven a long wedge, to which is fastened the thick extremity of a long string, and the string is then trailed across the tiger's track. In the bent bow is placed an arrow, dipped in some deadly poison. When the tiger comes in contact with the string, the wedge and blunt stick are forced out by the shock; and the poisoned arrow, released from the bow, speeds straight to the animal's heart.

Another and bolder manœuvre may be thus described:—In the dense jungle-depth, a cage made of bamboos, with tolerably wide intervals between the reeds, is erected between a couple of trees. Therein the hunter, armed with a well-tempered *tulwar*, or sword, takes up his post and waits. The tiger, prowling in search of food, is drawn to the ambuscade by his sense of smell. He throws himself upon the cage, endeavours to rend it in pieces, and with greedy

THE ROYAL TIGER.

teeth and cruel claws to seize the solitary hunter shut up within it. The latter, cool and wary, watches until his assailant presents his ample breast, and then drives his tulwar into it,—generally with so much skill and strength that the tiger falls to the ground, mortally wounded.

That every man's hand should be against the tiger, is not to be wondered at, when the extent of his ravages is taken into account. Not only does he prey on the flock of the shepherd, but, when pressed by hunger, on man himself; and after he has become "a man-eater," nothing but human flesh will satisfy him. He will allow the cattle to pass unmolested, in order to pounce upon their drivers. Abandoning the secure recesses of the jungle, he prowls about and around the villages, and seizes the child at play, or the woman going to the well. Some idea of the havoc annually committed by this ferocious animal may be gathered from the fact that, in a single district, during a period of three years, five thousand head of cattle and three hundred human beings were destroyed by tigers. The Indian Government, therefore, pays a reward to every man who rids the earth of one of these rapacious creatures.

Ancient Indian records speak of the lion, or *singh*, as formerly existing in most parts of India; but not a few authorities believe that the animal meant was really the leopard. At all events, he is no longer to be found except in menageries. The serval, or panther-cat, ranges from the Deccan to Tibet, and proves a formidable enemy to the cattle. In the central districts of the Deccan, and in the province of Gujerat, is found the ounce; and Bengal owns a peculiar species of the panther, distinguished by the deep black colour of his skin, which is varied with spots of still deeper black. Several species of leopards exist, and the *cheetah*, or hunting-leopard, is carefully trained for hunting wild deer. Panther and leopard spring probably from the same stock; and the only distinction between them is, that the *ocelli* or spots of the former are larger and more conspicuous than those of the latter. Both are supple, sleek, and handsome; and their skins are highly valued. The panther, by many, is regarded as a more dangerous animal than the tiger; for he is not less crafty than ferocious.

THE PANTHER.

Hyenas, jackals, wolves, wild boars,—these are among the Indian beasts of prey, and in some districts their numbers render them no slight nuisance to the tiller of the soil. The black bear of Coimbatore is described as comparatively inoffensive, and as living chiefly on the fruit of the palmyra palm, and on white ants or termites. Bengal produces a kind of fox, with bare, dog-shaped head, and a short, smooth coat; while all over India are to be found the jerboa, the musk-rat, the civet, the badger, the ichneumon, and the raccoon. Nor must we omit the scaly ant-eater, or short-tailed manis, with its curious faculty of coiling up into a compact ball, by bending its head towards its stomach, curving its back into a bow, and securing its body in this —attitude, shall we call it?—by a tenacious grasp of its mail-covered tail. It is encased, as the reader knows, in a kind of body-armour, composed of sharp-pointed, keen-edged, horny plates, placed with their points towards the tail, and overlapping each other like the tiles on the roof of a house.

The native princes of India have always sought a relief from the tedium of their useless lives in the enjoyment of the chase, and various species of deer, scattered all over the peninsula, have offered them a convenient quarry. The favourite sport of Tippoo Saib was hunting the neelgau with the cheetah. The beautiful oryx is also found, and the Chinese antelope, the common deer, and the graceful gazelle, which figures so frequently in Eastern poetry. The musk-deer seems to be confined to the Himalayan range. In Kashmir, the hunting-dog is not uncommon. He is usually of a brown or yellow colour, and not unlike a Newfoundland in hair and shape. His courage and strength are extraordinary, and he will hunt down and overcome even the leopard and the wolf. The wild dog lurks in some parts of the Jelum valley, hunting in packs, and, when hunger-driven, destroying children or grown persons.

We might well devote a chapter to the monkeys of India, so numerous are their species, and so full of interest their "manners and customs." In many parts they so abound as to do much damage by their depredations. In Bengal and on the Coromandel coast dwells the gibbon ape; and it is said that the orang-utan has been seen in the Carnatic. The lion-tailed ape, the pigmy ape, the green monkey, the talapoin, the tawny,—all these are numerous enough,

THE ORYX.

and the courts and roofs of the Hindu temples are always alive with the chatter of one species or another. A peculiar sanctity attaches to the so-called Radjakada ape, with red face and black beard, for it is regarded as a representative of the god Hunooman, or Hanuman, who himself is reputed to be an incarnation of Siva. Having assumed that form, Siva placed himself at the head of an army of monkeys, and, marching to the assistance of the god Râma, brought about the defeat of Râwan, king of the giants and ruler of Ceylon. At Benares one of the "sights" is the Monkey Temple, which a recent traveller describes as a very curious but rather revolting place, from the colonies of monkeys, of every size and age, which inhabit it. Monkeys scramble over every wall and fill every tree; and it is amusing to watch the grotesque creatures swinging down to the court, as the worshippers continually throw them offerings of rice or fruit. They seem quite to understand that they are privileged, and walk impudently about among the people, grinning and chattering, and nimbly clambering up the fretted pillars if they seem to be in danger from the crowd.

The ox and the cow are treated with much veneration, and every temple has its sacred bull.

THE ZEBU.

Brahma, it is said, created the Brahmans and the cow at the same time; and the latter is honoured with the title of "mother of the gods." The reverence paid to the ox and the cow arises probably from an early recognition of these animals as symbolizing the productive powers of nature. This species is the zebu, or *Bos Indicus* of naturalists; is of a small size, active, well-

YAKS.

knit, with a hunch or fatty protuberance on the back, and strong erect horns. In the neighbourhood of Surat and in Ceylon a breed of oxen is kept, no larger than mastiffs. The buffalo is a native, chiefly, of Southern India; and among the Ghats, as well as in the Himalaya, we find the arni, a fine large species, with horns of enormous length. In Tibet the yak, or wild ox, thrives in the cold snowy regions, but quickly dies when brought into the lowlands. Mr. Wilson speaks of it as a magnificent animal, and one of the finest creatures of the bovine race. The shortness of its legs takes away somewhat from its stature; and so does its thick coat of fine black and white hair, though this is no mean addition to its beauty. The head is not large, and the horns are poor, but its shaggy hair and wild, dark eye give it a striking appearance. The tail is a splendid feature, and is much prized in India as an emblem of dignity. Wild yaks exist, it is said, on the plains of the Upper Sutlej and in some parts of Ladák. The manner of hunting them is unique. Two holes in the ground, communicating with each other beneath, are prepared for the hunter in a place frequented by the yaks. "If the wild yak is only wounded, it rushes, in its fury, to the hole from whence the shot came; on which the hunter raises his head and gun out of the other hole and fires again. This rather ignoble game may go on for some time, and the yak is described as being in a frenzy of rage, trampling in the sides of the holes, and tearing at them with its horns."

Mr. Wilson furnishes a graphic account of the miseries of Tibetan *yak*manship. He advises any one who wishes to form an idea of riding upon a yak, to fasten two Prussian spiked helmets close together along the back of a great bull, and take a seat between them. This will afford a tolerable notion of a yak's saddle; only it must be understood that the helmets are connected on each side by ribs of particularly hard wood. The sure-footedness and the steady though slow ascent of these animals up the most difficult passes are very remarkable. "They never rest upon a leg until they are sure they have got a fair footing for it; and, heavy as they appear, they will carry burdens up places which even the ponies and mules of the Alps would not attempt. There is a certain sense of safety in being on the back of a yak among the mountains, such as one has in riding on an elephant in a tiger-hunt; you feel that nothing but a very large rock, or the fall of half a mountain, or something of that kind, will make it lose its footing; but it does require some time for the physical man to get accustomed to its saddle, to its broad back, and to its deliberate motion when its rider is upon it, and not in a position to be charged at."

In the delta of the Indus camels are bred; and some, of an inferior description, are found in a half-wild state in the sandy tracts of Gujerat. Horses are numerous; from the small, ill-tempered *goot*, or *gunt*, of Bengal, and the swift, lithe, and active Mahratta breed, to the draught and saddle, or *cuttoo* horses, of Bengal. At one time the province of Lahore was celebrated for its breed, which the Mogul sovereigns are supposed to have introduced. The Emperor Akbar, if chronicles may be trusted, kept a stud of no fewer than twelve thousand horses, which he imported from Arabia, Persia, and elsewhere. In Aurungabad and on the borders of Nepal, large numbers are bred for the service of the British cavalry; and the horse-fairs of Hurdwar and other places attract buyers from all parts of India.

The argali, or wild sheep, is included in the abundant fauna of the peninsula. In Assam, a species of ram, with four horns; in Moultan, the *bhara*, or thick-tailed sheep; and in Kashmir, the delicate breed that furnishes the fine wool used in the manufacture of the celebrated shawls, —are the objects of careful cultivation. In the woods and highlands of Orissa, Telingana, Berar, and Malabar, we meet with the goat which yields the morbid concretion called bezoar.

What a subject for the fertile pen of the naturalist is presented by Indian Ornithology!

The birds of the peninsula are not very remarkable for number and variety, but for beauty of plumage ; and an enthusiastic ornithologist would quickly dazzle the reader with his descriptions of glowing colours and diverse dyes. India is the native country of the peacock ; and the Greek writers have not forgotten to record the delight and surprise which Alexander the Great felt on first seeing "the bird of Juno." Prior to his epoch, however, it was known in Palestine ; for it

THE PEACOCK.

is mentioned as one of the treasures imported by the fleets of Tarshish in their expedition to Ophir (2 Chron. ix. 21). Notwithstanding the ravages committed by bird-dealers, the peacock is still found in large companies in the forest-glades ; and in some localities is so abundant that Colonel Williamson, in one day, counted between twelve hundred and fifteen hundred.

An important gallinaceous curiosity is the horned turkey, the head of which is furnished with a couple of callous horns, besides two long and broad dew-laps, pendent one from each side of the bill. This is more properly called, perhaps, the horned pheasant, or tropogon, a native of Nepal. To Nepal and the Himalaya belongs the splendid lophophorus, or Impeyan pheasant, with its plumage glittering like precious stones in rare combinations of bronze, violet, green, and blue.

THE IMPEYAN PHEASANT.

We have no space to dwell upon the numerous species of kingfishers, vivid with the brightest plumage; of flycatchers, shining with a rich metallic lustre; of shrikes, which seem to have assumed all the colours of the rainbow; of calyptomenes, clad in a coat of emerald green; of drongos, attired in deepest blue—which inhabit the hills, plains, and valleys south of the Ganges. We might rise higher in the scale of animal life, and tell of the lordly eagle and rapid falcon, of the hawk of Kashmir, and of the Brahmany kite, or Coromandel eagle, which the Hindus regard with high veneration as an incarnation of Doorga. As to the crows, they are as familiar and audacious as the monkeys. They frequent the European bungalows, and, when the servants are carrying in dinner, alight on the dishes, and bear away the meat, unless driven off by persons who attend with sticks for the purpose. The Hindus look upon rooks and ravens as receptacles of the soul when dissociated from the body: the souls of Brahmans are supposed to be embodied in the *ardigigas*. Then, as to owls, they are numerous in the more secluded woody districts, and on the Malabar coast assemble in flocks composed of several thousands. Among the various species we may enumerate the well-known white owl, the great horned owl, and the double-eared, the prevailing tint of whose plumage is gray.

"Nearchus tells us," says Arrian, "of a parrot bred in India as a great rarity there, and takes much pains to describe the several qualities of that bird, particularly its imitation of men's words. But as I have seen many myself, and know them to be common enough, I shall forbear speaking of them as anything marvellous." They are certainly no rarity, as every visitor to the Indian temples, or to the gardens of the Taj Mahal, can easily determine. It is said that upwards of fifty species have been recognized in the Deccan. Cockatoos, white as the snow of the Himalaya, are also met with, even in the streets and thoroughfares of busy towns, if, as is often the case, they are planted with trees; and they are so tame, and familiar with men, that they do not fear to breed under the eaves of the houses. Their name, kakatuas, is an instance of onomatopœia. Parroquets are also numerous; most of them are handsome birds, with plumage of green, and red, and purple, and blue. The Alexandrine, of a bright emerald colour, was the only species known to the Greeks, and it is said that the warriors of Alexander the Great introduced it into Europe. A rose-red band on the back of the neck is the distinctive mark of the rose-ringed species, which commits great havoc among the grain crops.

Still handsomer than the handsomest parroquets are the cuckoos, which rejoice in a very varied and dazzling plumage. The trogons also claim our notice. The fasciated trogon, about ten inches long, with black head and neck, a white band on the breast, and gray and dusky tail and wings, frequents the lofty trees of the jungle-wildernesses. The Malabar trogon inhabits the forests of Malabar, its range extending to an elevation of about three thousand feet. It has a habit of sitting with its head nestled between its shoulders, as if it had no neck, or rather as if it were covered with a Fakir's kufori, or cowl. Hence it is known to the natives as the *kufori churi*.

The paradise drongo elevates its head proudly, crowned with a crest of feathers. The two outer feathers of the tail are considerably elongated, so as to form two long naked shafts, which terminate in small palettes composed of barbs. Its food is the larger coleoptera, but it also preys upon flying insects. It has a very characteristic note, distinctly divided into two parts; the first a kind of harsh chuckle, and the second a metallic sound like the creak of a heavy wheel. From its aptness in imitating the strains of other birds, the Hindus call it the *huzar dastan*, or "bird of a thousand tales."

Among native Indian birds are many which form the delight of our English groves and glades; such as the thrush, the creeper, the wheat-ear, the nut-hatch, the yellow wren, the house-swallow, the snipe, and the woodcock. The *mango*, so called because it feeds on the fruit of the mango-tree, is a well-known European bird, the golden oriole. Among the balmy flowers of imperial gardens may often be seen the honey-sucker, perched on the sweetest blossom, and extracting its nectar with its long slender tongue. The bright-plumaged bee-eater arrives in the Ganges valley about the end of autumn; and it is worth while to watch it on its hunt after insect-food, its aerial movements are so rapid and so graceful.

THE RHINOCEROS HORNBILL.

Of shrikes there are several species. As, for instance, the Malabar shrike, which inhabits most parts of India; is as large as a jackdaw in Bengal, and as small as a thrush in Malabar; is always clothed in black, and has its head crowned with a graceful crest, the feather-tips of which are backward inclined. The Bengal shrike is known as the butcher-bird, from the dexterity it shows in dissecting its victims. This genus of birds is held in unfavourable repute for its strident voice, yet one species has been named the "fighting bulbul,"—a bit of popular irony, perhaps, as the bulbul, or nightingale, is famed far and wide for the beauty of its song. Its bellicose epithet refers to the fact that the natives train it to fight for their amusement, as we English of old trained game-cocks.

Nor is India without its extraordinary or curious birds : such as the so-called coppersmith bird, whose voice at a slight distance is easily mistaken for the sound made by a man in hammering metal ; and the elegant sarus crane, which dies of a broken heart, it is said, if its mate be killed, and is, therefore, spared by all but the cruellest-hearted. The buceros, or hornbill, with its huge, strong, and boldly curved beak, presents a remarkable appearance. The male is accustomed to confine the female in the hollow of a tree, plastering her up, and feeding her, while she hatches her egg, and brings up her young. The hole chosen is generally at a considerable height from the ground, and is stopped up with clay or mud, which the male bird carries in his beak. The *Malacocercus terricolor* deserves notice on account of its strange habit of flying about in flocks of seven ; whence the Hindus call them " the seven sisters,"—a name reminding Englishmen of Wordsworth's beautiful ballad.

The grosbeak is celebrated for the pendulous nest which it weaves with so much skill and patience. This social bird, the *baya* of the Hindus, is about as large as a sparrow, with yellowish brown plumage, and a thick conical bill. Preferring a lofty position for its nest, it frequents the cocoa or palmyra palms, or the Indian fig-tree, selecting one that overhangs a rivulet or well. Its nest is woven, or felted, of grass, or the long fibres of plants, until it assumes a texture like that of cloth, and the shape of a gourd, or large bottle. By means of a stout fibre, eighteen to twenty inches in length, this marvel of ingenious industry is suspended to the end of a slender branch, with its mouth or opening downwards, as a security against snakes and birds of prey. There it waves with the wind, but undergoes no injury.

NESTS OF THE GROSBEAK.

> " Behold a bird's nest !
> Mark it well, within, without !
> No tool had he that wrought, no knife to cut ;
> No nail to fix, no bodkin to insert ;
> No glue to join ; his little beak was all !
> And yet how neatly finished ! What nice hand,
> With every implement and means of art,
> Could compass such another ? "

Internally, the nest exhibits three compartments ; in the first of which the male keeps watch, while in the second the female incubates, and in the innermost are accommodated the young. It is said that in the outer cell a little tough clay is fixed to one of the sides, and here two or three fire-flies are held in captivity ; not, as the natives believe, to afford the inmates light, but to provide them with food.

The grosbeak is gregarious, and not seldom the nests of a whole community will be found among the branches of a single tree, with a sloping roof like that of a thatched barn erected above them, as a protection against tree-snakes and other reptiles. It is one of the most industrious of birds, and better fitted in this respect to point a moral than the proverbial ant. All day long it seems to be engaged in building or repairing its nest, or collecting food. As the number of the settlers increase, so do they increase the amount of accommodation, until the tree can no longer bear the burden imposed upon it, and, by giving way, compels the birds to go in search of a new home.

With the Hindus the baya enjoys a well-deserved repute. A native naturalist says of it: "This bird is remarkably sensible, faithful, and docile; it never willingly abandons the place where its young were hatched; but, like many other birds, it shows no aversion to the society of mankind, and is easily taught to perch on its master's hand. It may also be taught to fetch a piece of paper or any small object its master may indicate. It is a well-attested fact that, if a ring be dropped into a deep well, and a signal given to the baya, it will fly down with wonderful swiftness, catch the ring before it reaches the water, and bring it up with apparent exultation; and it is confidently asserted that, if a house or any other place be shown to it once or twice, it will carry a note thither on a proper signal being made. One instance of his docility," says the writer, "I can myself mention with confidence, having frequently been an eye-witness of it. The young Hindu women at Benares, and in other places, wear very thin plates of gold, called *ticas*, slightly fastened by way of ornament between their eyebrows; and as they pass through the streets it is not uncommon for the youthful gallants, who amuse themselves with training bayas, to give them a sign which they understand, and send them to pluck the golden ornaments from the foreheads of their mistresses, with which they return in triumph. The baya, when free, feeds on grasshoppers and other insects; but when tamed will subsist on pulse macerated in water. The female lays many beautiful eggs resembling pearls: the white of them, when boiled, is transparent, and their flavour is delicious. When a number of bayas are assembled on a high tree, they fill the air with their lively strain; but it is chirping, rather than singing. Their lack of musical talent is, however, amply compensated by their natural sagacity, in which they are not excelled by any of the feathered inhabitants of the forest."

ARGALIS, OR ADJUTANTS.

Among Indian birds it would be unpardonable not to notice the pigeons, which are truly remarkable for the variety and beauty of their plumage. The domestic pigeon is found in great numbers, and in the time of Akbar, whom Pennant describes as the greatest pigeon-fancier of his day, great attention was paid to their breed.

Passing over the pied flycatcher, so much esteemed in Bengal for its melodious song that it is named *shawbul*, or king of the singing-birds; the pagoda-thrush, which frequents the courts of the temples, and charms the air with its minstrelsy; swallows, goat-suckers, and other passerine birds,—we come to the aquatic tribes, which we can notice only with the utmost brevity. Argalis, or adjutants, are familiar enough in the streets of Calcutta. Some persons suppose them to be *Garuda*, the deified carrier of Vishnu. They are held in great repute, probably on account of their usefulness as scavengers. They wage war against snakes and noxious reptiles generally, and complete the work which the jackal and vulture begin. The Hindus believe them to be animated by the souls of Brahmans; which is hardly flattering to the Brahmans, as they are birds of unpleasing aspect, with a red, naked, pendulous craw, and plumage of an iron colour—the legs and half the thighs quite bare.

In Bengal the ibis is a common bird. There are at least three species: the white-headed, the black-headed, and another with long yellow bill and pale brown wings. The banks of the Ganges are haunted by the flamingo and the pelican; and at night the booming cry of the bittern echoes across the marshy plains of the Delta.

In the Reptile World we are at once confronted by the serpents, which are unpleasantly numerous in every part of India. On the Coromandel coast alone upwards of forty species have been distinguished. The royal serpent, or *boa constrictor*, which frequently attains the length of twenty-five to thirty feet, has an odour of sanctity. According to Sir Robert Ker

COBRA DI CAPELLA.

Porter, it is not venomous, nor is it known to injure man; however, the natives of the plains stand in great dread of it, never bathing in waters which it is known to frequent. Its usual dwelling-place is chosen near a lake, swamp, or river; and it lurks also in the close and wet ravines produced by inundations of the periodical rains. Fishes, as well as the animals which repair there to drink, become its prey. It waits and watches secretly under cover of the water, and, while an unsuspecting animal is drinking, suddenly dashes at its muzzle, and, with a grip of its back-reclining range of teeth, never fails to secure the terrified beast beyond the power of escape. In a moment the sluggish waters are lashed into foam. The whole form of the serpent is in motion; with its huge coils it rapidly encircles the struggling victim; and but a short interval elapses before every bone in its body is broken.

Sometimes the boa conceals its length in the depth of the marshy jungle; or attaches its tail to the branch of some overhanging tree, and, while thus suspended, allows its head and body to float supinely on the surface of the water.

What shall we say of the dreaded *cobra di capella*, or hooded snake—the *nága* of the natives? It has been described so frequently and so amply that another description would tax the reader's patience. As he is aware, this formidable reptile receives its name from the dilatable membrane on the top of its head, which it has the power of expanding into a kind of cap or hood. In the middle of the said dilatable skin may be seen a mark, in black and white,

SERPENT-CHARMERS.

resembling a pair of spectacles; whence the cobra is also called the spectacle-snake. It distends this membrane only when agitated by fear or some other passion. Then it rears the fore part of its immense body erect,—spreads it out,—moves its head around,—projects its forked fang,—and darts in every direction a fiery glance. Its poison is very virulent; but it never attacks man, except in self-defence. It lives almost entirely upon rats, frogs, and toads, with a young chicken occasionally by way of variety.

The Indian snake-charmers make use of the cobra, as they do of the cerastes, in their surprising performances. The *modus operandi* is thus described by one authority :—

The juggler takes in his hand a root, regarded popularly as a preservative against any ill effects from the cobra's bite. Drawing the reptile from the basket in which it is kept confined, he excites its passion by presenting a stick to it; immediately the creature, after the manner of its kind, elevates the fore part of its body, swells out its neck, opens its jaws, and projects its forked tongue; its eyes begin to blaze, and it hisses violently. Then a kind of struggle ensues between the serpent and its charmer; the latter, intoning a low monotonous chant, opposes his closed fist—sometimes his right, sometimes his left—to the reptile, which, fixing its gaze on the threatening hand, follows its various movements, and, balancing its head and body, simulates a dancing measure.

On the Coromandel coast the bungarum and the kerait are found in considerable numbers. They are like the cobra, but without the hood; they prey upon small mammals, toads, lizards, and probably on other snakes. It is said that the bungarum's bite is very dangerous; but the danger with this, as with all other species of venomous snakes, depends on various collateral circumstances, such as the size and energy of the snake, and on the place of the wound.

In the wooded districts abound the leaf-green, arboreal, viperine snakes, called trimeresmi. Slow and lethargic, they make no effort to move out of the path of the stranger; and as, owing to their colouring, they very closely resemble the branch on which they repose, frequently they are not perceived until they prepare to dart, vibrating the tail, and emitting a low, faint, hissing sound. Accidents, therefore, are by no means of rare occurrence; and it is a fortunate circumstance that these snakes are seldom above two feet in length, so that the consequences of their bite are less to be dreaded than that of other poisonous species. When angered, they are remarkably fierce; they strike at whatever is within their reach; and, in their frenzy, will fix their fangs even in their own bodies. They live upon birds, frogs, and small mammals.

The bite of the cobra marrilla, or cobra morril, is very formidable, and its poison has been known to kill a bull-terrier in twenty minutes. The natives call it *Tic-plonga;* it has a bluish-coloured body, a non-prehensile tail, a broad head, and is beautifully marked with a triple row of oblong brown spots, bordered with white. As it enters the houses, and creeps upon the beds and chairs, it is specially dangerous; and European and native are equally eager to kill

> "This small close-lurking minister of fate,
> Whose high concocted venom through the veins
> A rapid lightning darts."

To describe or even to enumerate the Insect tribes is beyond our province. A volume might well be devoted to the beautiful butterflies, dragon-flies, beetles, cicadas, and other insects which animate the groves and gardens with their various tints, and fill the air with their continuous hum. These are the creatures of the day; at night the deep dark foliage of the banian-tree is illuminated by the tiny lamps of myriads of fire-flies (*lampyris*); while the broad branches of the tamarinds and other trees are sometimes converted into actual "pyramids of light." The true silkworm, *Bombyx mori*, does not appear to be a native of India, but has been introduced in comparatively modern times. Wasps and bees are ubiquitous,—the latter building their nests in caves and hollow trees, and producing an abundance of honey and wax, which were formerly articles of export. Insects of the mantis tribe, such as the species (*phasma*)

THE GIANT PHASMA.

that simulates a creeping leaf, are not uncommon. A silk of a useful quality is obtained from the cocoon of the *phalæna*, which inhabits the orange-tree; and among other insect-labourers may be named the *coccus larva*. Among the predatory tribes are spiders, scorpions, ants, and termites, which in every place arouse the hostility of man; while the destructive locust is an occasional visitor. But, by common consent, the most troublesome, though not the most formidable, of the insect-plagues of India is the mosquito, which not only inflicts a painful bite, but by its loud continuous buzzing "murders sleep" and makes night hideous. As some slight defence against their attacks, the beds are furnished with "mosquito curtains,"—a covering of gauze, which the occupant draws closely around him after he has made a hasty retreat to his pillow. Sometimes, however, a pertinacious insect will effect an entrance at the same time, and then there is no rest for the afflicted mortal until he has hunted out his persecutor and destroyed it. The natives smear their bodies with oil, as some slight precaution against the dreaded attack. But there is something so amazing in the restless pertinacity of this troublesome gnat, that an old Indian settler has declared to us his deliberate opinion, that it more than outweighs all the enjoyment which might otherwise be derived from India's wealth of tropical vegetation and plenitude of interesting forms of animated nature.

INDEX.

ACACIA TREES, species of, 245.
Adam's Peak, Ceylon, 250; footprint of Buddha on, 250.
'Adan, or Aden, 19.
Adinath, temple of, 172.
Administration of British India, 20, 21.
Agra, description of, 102; the Taj Mahal at, 105-110; the fort, 110; the palace, 110-112; tomb of Akbar, 112; Akbar's summer-palace near, 113; mausoleum at, 113; grand durbar at, 113-117; visit of Prince of Wales to, 117.
Ahmadabad described, 159, 160.
Ahmednuggur, 54.
Ajmir, 152; its bazaars, 152, 153; monuments and buildings at, 153.
Ajunta, caves of, 55.
Akbar, college erected by, 79; tribunal of, 110; tomb of, 112; summer-palace of, 113.
Alexandria, 18, 19.
Allahabad, situation of, 61; English character of, 61; its sacred plain, 62; its fort, 62; its native quarter, 63; indigo factory, 63; railway bridge, 64; mutiny at, 65; visit of Prince of Wales to, 65.
Amritsar described, 95; the Golden Temple of, 96.
Animal life in India, 250-267.
Ant-eater, the, 254.
Antelope-hunting at Baroda, 49.
Aravalli Mountains, the, 163.
Argali, or adjutant-bird, the, 222, 264.
Army, the Indian, 21.
Arrack-palm, the, 206.
Arrah, 233.
Attock, 30, 101.
Aûdh, annexation of, 125.
Aurungabad, 54, 56, 63.
Aurungzebe, Mosque of, at Benares, 138, 142.

BABOO, a house of, described, 219.
Bagur, or country of the Bheels, 160.
Bamboo, the, its utility, 211, 246.
Banana, the, 242.
Banian, or Indian fig-tree, the, 245.
Barker, Lady, quoted, 93.
Baroda, situation of, 46; procession at, 46-49; antelope-hunting at, 49; public buildings of, 49.
Barrackpur, 230.
Bathing-pilgrimages to the confluence of the Ganges and Jumna, 62.
Baya, the, nest of, 262; described by a Hindu naturalist, 263.
Begum, the, of Bhopal, 176.
Benares, a sacred city, 131; history of, 131; bathing ceremonies at, 132; life in, 132-136; famous temples of, 136, 137; festival of Ganesa, 138; the Ganges at, 141; visit of Prince of Wales to, 143.
Bheels, the, country of, 160; characteristics of, 160-163.
Bhopal, the Begum of, 176; town of, 179; Mosque of Pearls at, 179; festival at, 180; aspects of life at, 183.
Bhopal Tal, the, 180.
Bhurtpur, 154; sieges of, 154-158; Prince of Wales at, 158.
Birds of India, 257-264.
Birsing-Deo, palace of, at Duttiah, 147.
Bisheshwar, temple of, at Benares, 136.
Bison, the, range of, 188.
Boa constrictor, the, characteristics of, 264.
Bombax tree, the, 244.
Bombay, island of, 33; annals of, 33; distant view of, 34; fort of, 34; the Parsees' bazaar at, 35; strange sights of, 36, 37; population of, 38, 39; life at, 40.
Brahmaputra, the, origin of, 31; its course, 31; its delta, 31.
Browning, Robert, quoted, 15.
Buddha, 132; footprint of, 250.
Bullock-cart, a, described, 222.
Bundelcund, the, 144.
Bungalow, a, description of, 36.
Burdwan, 233.
Butter-tree, the, 249.
Buxar, 233.

CAIRO, 19.
Calcutta, impression produced by view of, 217; various aspects of, 218; temple of Kali at, 220; interesting features of, 222; trades and occupations of native population, 222-225; the Maidan, or Esplanade, at, 225, 226.
Camoens, quoted, 248.
Cape St. Vincent, 15; Cape Trafalgar, 15.
Cassia-trees, 244.
Caste in India, 204, 227.
Caves of Elephanta, 42, 43; Kenery, 44; Karli, 53; Ellora, 54; Ajunta, 55.
Cawnpur, a military station, 118; outbreak of the Mutiny at, 119; the English settlers besieged, 119, 120; massacre at, 121, 122; memorial church and well, 123.
Central India, 144-151.
Cereals, cultivation of, 241.
Ceylon, its boundaries, area, mountains, geology, 234; its vegetation, 235; its animal life, 236; its inhabitants, 236; its annals, 237; provinces and chief towns, 237-239; Prince of Wales in, 238.
Chandernagar, 230.
Chandnee Chowk, the, at Delhi, 66, 80.
Chandra, iron column of, 79; popular legend concerning, 79, 80.
Cheetah, the, 254.
Chenab, the, 101.
Chilka, Lake, 32.
Chini-ka-Rozah, mausoleum of, at Agra, 113.
Chinsurah, 230.
Chopaya-travelling, 184.
Chunar, ruins of a Hindu palace at, 64.
Churuk-Pooja, the, ceremony of, 220.
Chutter Bhoje, temple of, at Oorcha, 148.
Chutterpur, 148; festival at, 148-151.
Cingalese, the, characteristics of, 236.
Civil service, the, 21.
Cleopatra's Needle, 19.
Climate of India, 22.
Cobra di capella, the, bite of, 265; Indian jugglers and, 266.
Cockatoos, Indian, 260.
Cocoa-nut palm, the, 235.
Coffee-farm, a, description of, 238.
Colombo, 237.
Combermere, Lord, his capture of Bhurtpur, 157, 158.
Conjeveram, 205.
Cotton, production and manufacture of, in India, 240.
Cremation in India, 135, 138, 220, 225.
Cumming, Miss Gordon, quoted, 93, 141, 214.

DACOITS, the, 191.
Deccan, the, 22; villages of, 204.
Dehra, valley of, 95; tea plantations in, 95.
Delhi, position of, 66; the Chandnee Chowk, or "Street of Light," 66; the great mosque, 70; the palace, 73; ruins of ancient cities round about, 77; streets and trades of, 80;

historical sketch of, 81; outbreak of the Mutiny at, 82; massacre at, 83; besieged by the British, 83; assault and capture of, 84; Hodson captures the king of, 85; visit of the Prince of Wales to, 85, 86.
Deodar, the, 247, 248.
Dholepur, 144.
Doorga Khoond, the, at Benares, 137.
Doudou, 153.
Dowlatabad, 54.
Duff, Mr. Grant, quoted, 70, 105, 112, 113, 210.
Durbars, at Agra, 113-117; Oodeypur, 167.
Duttiah, 147.

EASTWICK, Mr., quoted, 203.
Elephant, the Indian, 250.
Elephanta, island of, 42; rock-caves of, 42, 43.
Ellenborough, Earl of, 111.
Ellora, caves of, 54.
Eucalyptus pendula, the, 244.
Euphorbias, or spurges, species of, 245.

FAKIR'S ROCK, the, 29.
Fergusson, Mr., quoted, 59, 110, 160, 187, 207.
Ferozebad, 80.
Forests in the neighbourhood of Sanchi, 191.
Forest trees of India, 244.
Fort, the, Bombay, 34.
Fruit trees of India, 242.
Fryer, Dr., quoted, 245.
Futteygurh, citadel of, 180.
Futteypur Sikri, 113.

GANESA, temple and festival of, 137, 138.
Ganges, the, source of, 25; sanctity of, 26; delta of, 26; valley of, 29; inundations of, 29, 30; at Allahabad, 61; at Benares, 141; at Hurdwar, 211.
Ganges Canal, the, 213.
Garry, a, descriptions of, 50, 88.
Gaur, or Indian bison, 188.
Ghât, the Burning, at Benares, 135, 138; at Calcutta, 220.
Ghazi-ood-deen Hyder, tomb of, at Lacknow, 130.
Ghazni, 111.
Gibraltar, description of, 16; its sieges, 16, 17.
Godavari, the, 31.
Golconda, fortress and necropolis of, 56.
Govindgurh, 192-196.
Grandidier, M., quoted, 208, 218, 220, 227, 228.
Grasses, the, of India, 246.
Great Chaitya, or Temple of Buddha, at Kenery, 44.
Great Imambara, the, at Lacknow, 129.
Grosbeak (or baya), the, habits of, 262.
Gum-ammoniac, 244.
Gwalior, 168; fortress of, 171; the King Pâl Palace, 171; temple of Adinath, 172.

HAVELOCK, Sir Henry, 122, 126.
Heber, Bishop, quoted, 110.
Himalaya, the, description of, 22; vegetation of, 23; view of, at Simla, 90; from Lallteeba, 95; from Sealkote, 98.
Hindu Kush, the, extent of, 24.
Hodson, Major, exploit of, at Delhi, 85.
Holi, the, festival of, 148-151.
Honore, Lake, 32.
Hopley, Mr., quoted, 19.
Hornbill, the, 262.
Hosseinabad Imambara, at Lacknow, 129.
Hugli, 217, 230.
Humayoon, mausoleum of, 77.
Hurdwar, scenery at, 211; character of, 213; great fair at, 214; pilgrims bathing at, 214.

IMPERIAL PALACE, the, at Agra, 110.
India, boundaries of, 20; divisions and administration, 20, 21; derivation of name, 21; physical contrasts, 22; climate, 22; mountains, 22; rivers, 25; lakes, 32; vegetable life, 240-249; animal life, 250-267.
Indigo manufacture, processes of the, 63.
Indus, the, source of, 30; its course, 30.
Insects of India, 266, 267.
Itmad-ood-Doulah, tomb of, 113.

JAINS, the, 175; architecture and religion of, 174, 175.
Jaipur, description of, 153; royal palace at, 153; Jey Sing's observatory, 153.
Jamboo, the, 242.
Jâts, the, account of, 154.
Jehanara, the princess, anecdote of, 112.
Jehangir, tomb and garden of, Lahore, 97; the Daulat Bâgh of, at Ajmir, 152.
Jey Sing, observatory of, 153, 154.
Jhansi, fortress of, 147.
Juggernath, temple to, at Dholepur, 144; at Puri, 228, 229.
Jugglers, at Bombay, 39.
Jummoo, 98.
Jumna, the, junction of the Ganges and, 62; bathing-pilgrimages to, 62; at Agra, 102.

KAILAS, temple of, 54.
Kaiser Bagh, the, Lacknow, 124.
Kala Masjid, Delhi, 77, 81.
Kali, temple and worship of, 220-222.
Kalighat, 220.
Kalka, 89.
Kandely, Lake of, 239.
Kandy, 238.
Kanha, hill of, excavations on, 44.
Karli, caves of, Khandala, 53.
Kashmir, scenery of, 98.
Kaveri, the, 32.
Kaye, Sir J., quoted, 83, 84, 126.
Kenery, caves of, 44.
Khariwara, 163.
King Pâl Palace, the, Gwalior, 171.
Kishengurh, 153.
Kolair, Lake, 32.
Kootub, the, at Delhi, 78.
Krishna, the, 31, 329.

LACKNOW, description of, 124; the Kaiser Bagh, 124, 125; the Residency, siege and heroic defence of, 126; memorable objects, 129; the Hosseinabad Imambara, 129; the Prince of Wales's visit to, 130.
Lahore, description of, 96; buildings and fort of, 96, 97; principal objects of interest, 97.
Lake, General, 154.
Lallteeba, or the Red Hill, 95.
Landoor, 95.
Lawrence, Sir John (afterwards Lord), grand durbars by, 113, 129; Sir Henry, 126; death of, 126, 127.
Lion, the, or leopard, 254.
Lions' Lât, the, 187.
Lotus, the, growth of, 241; its poetical associations, 241.

MACLEOD, Dr. Norman, quoted, 70, 112, 217, 221.
Madras, view of, from the sea, 200; landing at, 200; its English quarter, 203; Prince of Wales at, 203.
Madura, 210.
Mahabalipur, 206; temples at, 207.
Mahanadi, the, 31.
Maidan, the, at Calcutta, 223, 225.
Malabar Hill, Bombay, 36.
Malta, description of, 17, 18.
Man-ape, a, 192.
Mango-tree, the, 37, 242.
Marble Rocks, the, on the Narbada, 31.
Martin, Claude, the French adventurer, 124; palace of, 129.
Matheson, Mr., quoted, 217, 223.
Mazagon, 37.
Meeanmeer, 97.
Meerut, description of, 87; objects of interest at, 87, 88.
Memorial, the, at Cawnpur, 123.
Mhowa-tree, the, 249.
Midnapur, 227.
Milton, quoted, 245.
Mirzapur, 64.
Mitchell, Mrs. Murray, quoted, 250.
Mohurrum, the, festival of, 180-183.
Monkeys, the, habits of, 255; sacred character of, 255.
Montgomery Hall, Lahore, 97.
Moore, quoted, 96, 98, 111.
Mosque, the Great, at Delhi, 70-73; the Pearl, at Delhi, 74; at Agra, 110; Mosque of Aurungzebe, at Benares, 138.
Mosquito, the, 267.
Motibagh, the, at Baroda, 49.
Moti Masjid, the, at Delhi, 74; at Agra, 110, 112; at Bhopal, 179.
Mountains of India, 22.
Muchkoondo, Sacred Lake of, 144.
Muggra, 233.
Murshidabad, 233.
Mussoorie, 95.
Mutiny, the Sepoy, at Allahabad, 65; at Delhi, 82-85; at Agra, 117; at Cawnpur, 119-122; at Lacknow, 126; at Jhansi, 147.
Myhere, 191.

NAGA PAHAR, the, 153.
Nanak, founder of the Sikhs, 95.
Nana Sahib, the, at Cawnpur, 119-122.
Narbada, the, course of, 31.
Nautch party, a, description of, 39-41.
Nicholson, death of General, 84; monument to, 101.
Nowshera, 101.
Nursingurh, 184.

OODEYPUR, 163; palace at, 164; gardens and lake of, 167; country round about, 167.
Oorcha, 148; temples and palaces at, 148.
Opium, cultivation of, 240, 241.
Owls in India, 260.

PAHARIS, or hill-men, 89.
Palace of the Moguls, Delhi, 73.
Palanquin, a, described, 38.
Palar, the, 32.
Palms in India, 243.
Pandooah, memorial tower at, 233.
Paradise drongo, the, 260.
Parrots and paroquets in India, 260.
Parvati, temple of, 50.
Patna, 233.
Peacock, the, 258.
Pennair, the, 32.
Perfumes, Indian, 243.
Peshawar, 101.
Pheasants of India, the, 259.
Pigeons, 263.
Pinus, species of, 247.
Pompey's Pillar, 18, 19.
Pondicherry, described, 208.
Poshkur, Lake of, 153.
Prince of Wales, the, at Allahabad, 65; at Delhi, 85, 86; at Agra, 117; at Lucknow, 130; at Benares, 143; at Bhurtpur, 158; at Madras, 203; at Trichinopoli, 208, 209; in Ceylon, 238.
Procession, grand, at Baroda, 46–49; at Agra, 117.
Pulikat Lake, 32.
Puna, description of, 50.
Punna, 196; diamond mines at, 196–199.
Purana Kila, the, 80.
Puri, 227, 228.

RABIA DUARANI, tomb of, 59, 60.
Rajmahal Mountains, the, 233.
Rajputana, 160.
Râma, Pool of, 37.
Ramnuggur, 143.
Rawul Pindee, 101.
Reptiles of India, 264–266.
Rewah, 195.
Rhinoceros, the, 251.
Rivers of India, 25.
Rousselet, M., quoted, 46, 55, 61, 124, 141, 167, 217, 220.

SAHARANPUR, 88.
Salsette, island of, 33, 44.
Salvadora persica, the, 245.
Sanchi, 187; Great Tôpe at, 187.
Sandal-tree, 244.
Scindia's Ghât, 141.
Sealkote, 98.
Sehore, 183.
Seringham, island of, 209.
Seths, palace of the, at Ajmir, 153.
Shah Alum, mosque of, 159.
Shah Jehan, gardens of, Lahore, 97; builder of the Taj Mahal, 109, 112.
Shrikes, the, 261.
Sikandra, Akbar's tomb at, 112.
Sikhs, the, 95.
Simla, attractions of, 90; the Himalaya at, 90; monkeys at, 93; Himalayan forest, 93.
Somnauth, gates of, 111; capture of, 111.
Sonaghur, the "Golden Mountain," 147.
Strathnairn, Lord, 148.
Suez, 19.
Suliman Mountains, the, 24.
Sundarbans, the, 26; peculiarities of the district of, 230.
Suftur Jung, mausoleum of, 77.

TAJ MAHAL, the, at Agra, 105–110.
Tanjore, 210.
Tanna, 44.
Taragurh, fortress of, at Ajmir, 152.
Tavernier, quoted, 60, 73, 74, 245.
Tea-plantations at Dehra, 95.
Tennent, Sir Emerson, quoted, 236.
Throne of Peacocks, the, 74.
Tiger, the, 251; hunting, 252, 253; ravages committed by, 253; hunting at Govindgurh, 195.
Tintool, 163.
Toghlukabad, 80.
Tomb of the Queens, mausoleum of, Ahmadabad, 160.
Tôpe, a, described, 188.
Tower of Silence, Bombay, 37.
Trevelyan, Mr., quoted, 118.
Trichinopoli, 208; fort and Tamil temple at, 208, 209; Prince of Wales's visit to, 208, 209.
Trimeresmi, or viperine snakes, 266.
Trincomalee, 239.
Triveni, the, at Allahabad, 62.
Trogons, the, described, 260.

ULWUR, 154; mausoleum at, 154.
Umballa, 88.

VALERIA INDICA, the, 244.
Valetta, 17.
Veddas, the, of Ceylon, 236.
Vegetable life in India, 240–249.
Vindhya Mountains, the, 24.
Vishnu, temples to, 206, 209.

WALKESHWAR, 36.
Wazirabad, 101.
Well-worship at Benares, 137.
Wheeler, Mr., quoted, 61, 209, 238.
Wheeler, Sir Hugh, at Cawnpur, 119; murder of, 121.
Wilson, Mr., quoted, 94, 247, 257.

YAK, the, 256; riding upon, 257.

ZEBU, the, 256.